What readers are saying about
Technical Blogging

I'm in absolute awe at this amazing book, which goes above and beyond the best advice I've ever heard on the subject. I wish I had read this two years ago, as I had to learn this the hard way. This book has got me inspired to get back to writing more.

➤ **Derek Sivers**
  Founder, CD Baby

Antonio covers everything from the philosophy of what makes good blog content to the nitty-gritty of what software plugins to use and the best time of day to publish articles. Every few pages, I added another item to my to-do list to improve my blog.

➤ **Andy Lester**
  Author, *Land the Tech Job You Love*

Practical, to the point, and overflowing with handy advice and knowledge about blogging for technical folks—whether to make money, build a career, or just for fun.

➤ **Peter Cooper**
  Editor-in-Chief, *Ruby Inside*

Straightforward, informative, and practical, *Technical Blogging* does a great job of making sense of many of the key aspects of blogging in a fun, easy-to-digest manner. I highly recommend it!

➤ **Satish Talim**
  Founder, *RubyLearning*

Antonio's book concisely summarizes the lessons I wish I knew when starting out. If you value your time, read this book.

➤ **Kalid Azad**
Software developer and founder, BetterExplained.com

I felt as if Antonio were my own private consultant helping me every step of the way, updating and crafting my blogs for maximum value. I will be reading and rereading this book every few months to make sure I haven't missed anything. If you blog, read this book. If you're considering blogging, read this book. Do not let a day go by without reading this book.

➤ **Johanna Rothman**
Author, *Manage Your Project Portfolio: Increase Your Capacity and Finish More Projects*

I've been blogging for about six years now and have read much on the Internet, as well as one book about the subject. I really thought I knew just about everything I needed to know until I read Antonio's book! The guidance he provides in this book goes well beyond the standard advice. I truly appreciate the years of experience that he brings to this book and can see how using his advice will substantially increase the quality and interest in any blog by any blogger, regardless of experience.

➤ **Susan Visser**
Avid blogger and publishing program manager, IBM

Excellent book. Too bad competition from high-quality blogs will substantially increase as soon as this book hits the stores.

➤ **Ludovico Magnocavallo**
Co-founder, Blogo.it, the leading nanopublishing network

Technical Blogging

Turn Your Expertise into a Remarkable Online Presence

Antonio Cangiano

The Pragmatic Bookshelf

Dallas, Texas • Raleigh, North Carolina

Many of the designations used by manufacturers and sellers to distinguish their products are claimed as trademarks. Where those designations appear in this book, and The Pragmatic Programmers, LLC was aware of a trademark claim, the designations have been printed in initial capital letters or in all capitals. The Pragmatic Starter Kit, The Pragmatic Programmer, Pragmatic Programming, Pragmatic Bookshelf, PragProg and the linking *g* device are trademarks of The Pragmatic Programmers, LLC.

Every precaution was taken in the preparation of this book. However, the publisher assumes no responsibility for errors or omissions, or for damages that may result from the use of information (including program listings) contained herein.

Our Pragmatic courses, workshops, and other products can help you and your team create better software and have more fun. For more information, as well as the latest Pragmatic titles, please visit us at *http://pragprog.com*.

The team that produced this book includes:

Michael Swaine (editor)
Potomac Indexing, LLC (indexer)
Molly McBeath (copyeditor)
David J Kelly (typesetter)
Janet Furlow (producer)
Juliet Benda (rights)
Ellie Callahan (support)

Printed in the United States of America.
ISBN-13: 978-1-934356-88-3
Printed on acid-free paper.
Book version: P1.0—March 2012

To my wife, Jessica, for making everything possible. And to my parents-in-law, Lynn and Rick, for always being there.

Contents

Acknowledgments xi

Introduction xiii

Part I — Plan It

1. **What Kind of Blog Are You Going to Run?** 3
    1.1 Solo vs. Collective   3
    1.2 General vs. Niche   5
    1.3 Pundit vs. Instructional   8
    1.4 Business Blogs   9
    1.5 What's Next   10

2. **A Rock-Solid Plan for Your Blog** 11
    2.1 Define Your Blog's Main Topic   11
    2.2 Analyze the Size of Your Niche   13
    2.3 Give Readers a Compelling Reason to Stick Around   18
    2.4 Set Goals for Your Blog   20
    2.5 Choose and Register a Domain Name   22
    2.6 What's Next   28

Part II — Build It

3. **Setting Up Your Blog** 31
    3.1 Choose Your Blogging Software and Hosting   31
    3.2 Configure Your Domain Name   37
    3.3 Install WordPress   40
    3.4 Configure WordPress   42
    3.5 Enhance WordPress with Plugins   51
    3.6 What's Next   54

4. **Customizing and Fine-Tuning Your Blog** 55
    4.1   Pick a Professional Theme   55
    4.2   Enable Tracking of Your Site's Visitors   57
    4.3   Customize Your Sidebar   63
    4.4   Encourage Social Media Sharing   66
    4.5   Win Over Subscribers   69
    4.6   Don't Get in Trouble—Use Disclaimers   75
    4.7   Master On-page SEO with Platinum SEO   77
    4.8   Performance Considerations   80
    4.9   Enable Code Highlighting in Your Posts   82
    4.10 What's Next   82

5. **Creating Remarkable Content** 83
    5.1   Content Is King   83
    5.2   Write for the Web   84
    5.3   Can Linkbaiting Be Ethical?   86
    5.4   Write Catchy Headlines   87
    5.5   Develop Your Own Voice   89
    5.6   Where to Find Ideas for Your Posts   90
    5.7   Case Study: Math-Blog.com's Headlines   92
    5.8   Get Readers to Explore Your Content   95
    5.9   Copyright Matters   96
    5.10 Back Up Your Content   100
    5.11 What's Next   101

6. **Producing Content Regularly** 103
    6.1   What's the Post Frequency, Kenneth?   103
    6.2   Consistency Is Queen   105
    6.3   What Days Should You Post On?   105
    6.4   Schedule Time to Blog   106
    6.5   Manage Your Time with the Pomodoro Technique   107
    6.6   Survive Writer's Block   109
    6.7   Get Others to Write for You   111
    6.8   What's Next   115

Part III — Promote It

7. **Promoting Your Blog** 119
    7.1   Market It and They Will Come   119
    7.2   Correct a Self-Sabotaging Mindset   120

7.3	Perform On-page and Off-page SEO	121
7.4	Not All Links Are Created Equal	122
7.5	Guest Blog on Other Blogs	124
7.6	Other Forms of Article Marketing	128
7.7	Participate in the Community	130
7.8	Leverage Foreign Blogs	132
7.9	The Dark Side of Link Building	133
7.10	Promote Your Articles on Social Networks	134
7.11	Promote on Technical Social News Sites	137
7.12	Case Study: ProgrammingZen.com's Referral Traffic	142
7.13	What's Next	142

8. Understanding Traffic Statistics **145**
8.1	Baseline vs. Spike Traffic	145
8.2	Key Site Usage Metrics You Need to Consider	146
8.3	Interpret Visit Quantity and Quality	147
8.4	Where Do They All Come From?	149
8.5	Analyze Google Analytics and Clicky Statistics	150
8.6	Keep Track of Your Blog's Growth	155
8.7	What's Next	157

9. Building a Community Around Your Blog **159**
9.1	Engage Readers	159
9.2	Supplement Your Blog with Community Tools	163
9.3	Forms of Criticism	164
9.4	Your Mantras When Dealing with Criticism	169
9.5	What's Next	170

Part IV — Benefit from It

10. Making Money from Your Blog **173**
10.1	Common Monetization Strategies	173
10.2	Make Money with Ads	173
10.3	Make Money with Sponsors	180
10.4	Make Money with Affiliate Offers	183
10.5	Make Money with Other Monetization Strategies	194
10.6	Case Study: My Monthly Income	196
10.7	What's Next	198

11. **Promoting Your Own Business** **199**
    11.1 A Checklist for Company Blogs   199
    11.2 Identify and Understand Your Readers   202
    11.3 Craft Your Content for Your Prospective Customers   204
    11.4 Convert Readers into Customers   207
    11.5 What's Next   214

12. **Taking Full Advantage of Your Blog** **215**
    12.1 Improve Your Skills   215
    12.2 Advance Your Career   216
    12.3 Obtain Freebies   219
    12.4 Prepare for Success   221
    12.5 Other Benefits for Startups   223
    12.6 What's Next   224

Part V — Scale It

13. **Scaling Your Blogging Activities** **227**
    13.1 Scale Your Blog Vertically   227
    13.2 Hire a Team of Bloggers   228
    13.3 Build Your Blogging Empire   233
    13.4 What's Next   235

14. **Beyond Blogging: Your Strategy for Social Media** . . . **237**
    14.1 Define a Social Media Strategy   237
    14.2 Select the Social Networks You Intend to Target   238
    14.3 Create Your Social Media Profiles   239
    14.4 Cross Promote Your Site and Social Properties   243
    14.5 Post Frequently and Interact with Your Followers   245
    14.6 What's Next   252

15. **Final Words of Advice** **253**
    15.1 Try It Out   253
    15.2 Blogs to Follow   254
    15.3 Keep in Touch   254

A1. **Bibliography** **255**

    Index **257**

Acknowledgments

It is customary for authors to thank everyone who has even remotely touched their book and offer platitudes about the invaluable contribution these people have made.

In the case of this book, there is no false modesty. I genuinely have to thank a great many folk who have helped make it possible. The volume of feedback I received shaped the book and made it far more useful than it would have been otherwise.

I want to start by thanking my unofficial editor, my beautiful wife, Jessica. She put in countless hours helping me refine my message and provided me with endless support and patience as I worked on each chapter. Without her, this book would be a lot less clear.

I must thank the whole team at the Pragmatic Bookshelf, in particular my editor, Mike Swaine, for his insightful suggestions and for demanding nothing but the utmost quality from me throughout the writing of this book; my publishers, Andy Hunt and Dave Thomas, for believing in this project from the very beginning; my managing editor, Susannah Pfalzer, for providing important advice on the development of the book from its earliest stages onward; my production manager, Janet Furlow, for ensuring the book would end up in your hands as a polished product; and last but not least, David Kelly, for withstanding my incessant search for the perfect cover.

I was privileged to have a team of world class technical reviewers who cannot be thanked enough for their contributions. The impressive list includes Andy Lester, Brian Hogan, Dan Wohlbruck, Derek Sivers, Giles Bowkett, Gregg Pollack, Ian Dees, Ilya Grigorik, Jeff Langr, Johanna Rothman, John C. Dvorak, Kent Beck, Lukas Mathis, Patrick McKenzie, Peter Cooper, Satish Talim, Scott Mace, Sebastian Marshall, Steve Yegge, Susan Visser, and Thom Hogan.

My list of informal reviewers, a small group of friends and colleagues who read early drafts, must also be thanked for their feedback and support. In particular, I wish to thank Bradley Steinfeld, Davide Varvello, Henrique Zambon, Kalid Azad, Laurent Sansonetti, Leon Katsnelson, Ludovico Magnocavallo, Marco Beri, Marius Butuc, Ninh Bui, Piergiuliano Bossi, and Rav Ahuja.

Finally, I'd like to thank the customers who purchased the beta version of this book. Their detailed feedback, suggestions, encouraging words, and early success (having put the advice in this book into practice) motivated me to keep going until the book was ready for its official unveiling as a finished product.

For allowing me to create a relentlessly useful book I'm proud to put my name on, all these people have my sincere respect and gratitude.

*The reports of my death are greatly
exaggerated.*

➤ *Mark Twain*

Introduction

You may not know it yet, but blogging has the potential to change your life.

I didn't know it either when I first began writing online many years ago. I thought blogging would be a way to perform a brain dump of my thoughts from time to time. Perhaps I'd toss together some essays here and there; maybe something would come out of the whole blogging thing, but I wasn't holding my breath. Boy, was I wrong.

The positive impact that blogging has had on my career, income, and life in general is what persuaded me to share my knowledge with you through this book and to show you just what a meaningful impact blogging can have on your own life.

This book teaches you the art and science of technical blogging and shows you how to be a successful blogger. Whenever possible, I've tried to back up all assertions with past experiences, stats, and even case studies.

Nevertheless, this is an opinionated book. It's the distilled form of what I've learned from trial and error over the course of the past eight years through several blogs I started, both in English and Italian. As you read it, you may disagree with me, much like the readers of my blogs sometimes contest a point I've made in one of my posts.

That's OK.

My goal is to provide you with a road map to achieve success with your own blog. I'll supply you with step-by-step instructions, starting with the planning phase and going all the way to creating, promoting, benefitting from, and maintaining your blog. I won't shy away from expressing my opinion about what you should do and what is best avoided.

This is a team effort, so I also want to get you thinking in new ways, experimenting, and ultimately reaching your own conclusions about what does and doesn't work for your technical blog. I'll be your mentor, gently guiding you in the right direction while still allowing you to find your own way.

What Is Technical Blogging?

The most generic definition of *blog* (an amalgamation of the words *web* and *log*) is a site that contains a series of posts organized in reverse chronological order. This sterile definition doesn't quite convey what people really think when they hear the word *blog* though.

In the collective mind, *blog* often calls forth a picture of a writer in pajamas, talking about his or her daily life or (at the other end of the spectrum) breaking news stories before the media reaches them. Yet those two are by no means the only kinds of blogs on the block.

Many of the concepts we'll explore in this book will be beneficial to those who are interested in starting such a personal blog; however, our focus is specifically centered around technical blogging.

A technical blog is a nonfiction blog, the main subject matter of which is technical—rather than personal—in nature. Generally you won't delve into what you had for lunch or include pictures of your newborn nephew. Instead, you will use your blog as a way to share your expertise with others in your field. Examples of some of the most popular technical blogs you may already be familiar with include *TechCrunch*, *Gizmodo*, *VentureBeat*, *Smashing Magazine*, *Joel on Software*, *Signal vs. Noise*, and *Coding Horror*,[1] to name just a few.

As a developer and entrepreneur, I imagine my ideal readers to be developers and technically-minded entrepreneurs who are blogging about software development and business-related subjects, respectively.

Fitting into one camp or the other is not a requirement though. You may be launching a blog about biotechnology, dentistry, or photography, and the content of this book would still apply to you.

Blogging Isn't Dead

You may have heard that blogging is dead and thus are wary of investing your time and effort in an activity that's about to go the way of the dinosaur. Don't be. The blogging ecosystem has never been more vibrant and alive. What you are witnessing is just the evolution of the medium.

---

1. techcrunch.com, gizmodo.com, venturebeat.com, smashingmagazine.com, venturebeat.com, joelonsoftware.com, 37signals.com/svn, and codinghorror.com/blog

Figure 1—A sample technical blog

To adapt a famous quote by Mark Twain, rumors of blogging's death have been greatly exaggerated. If you follow sensationalist tech pundits, you may have been misled into believing that the emergence of microblogging services (like Tumblr and Twitter[2]) have marked the end of traditional blogging.

Among other reasons, microblogs are popular for the fact that they often take a minimal dose of effort on the author's part and are easy to follow from the reader's standpoint. With such sites you can share a link or a short thought with your readers in a matter of seconds. Conversely, a well-written article for a traditional blog could take hours to craft. Microblogs can be seen as one evolutionary branch of blogging, targeted toward an Internet audience that's stereotypically perceived as having a short attention span.

As a technical blogger you have nothing to fear from this family of microblogs. One hundred forty characters is sufficient to enable you to share what you're watching on TV, link to an article, quote a famous person, or share a quick thought, but it is ill-suited for essays or HOWTOs on technology. Instead,

---

2.   tumblr.com and twitter.com, respectively.

think of microblogging as a complementary way of blogging and broadcasting your messages. Later in the book we will explore how to take advantage of services such as Twitter in that capacity.

Blogging as a Megaphone

An established blog is like a megaphone: it amplifies your voice, allowing it to reach a wider audience. Creating such a following takes time and hard work, but the payoff is that the audience you've built up is going to be there for you when you need it.

This megaphone has also the wonderful advantage of coming with a built-in echo generator, as your audience may rebroadcast your message through social networks or their own blogs, helping you reach an even larger pool of interested readers.

It's up to you to decide how to use such a megaphone, but you'll be surprised by just how handy it is to have the same circulation as a local newspaper. Announcing a new project or product? Looking for a new hire? Having an issue with some cutting-edge open source project or perhaps with a company that is ignoring your valid complaint? Fear not; your audience can help.

Case in point: one time I had a problem with a computer store chain that wouldn't repair a brand-new but defective laptop that I'd just purchased for my wife's birthday. I wrote about the situation on my technical blog, and after a few days the story had been read by over a hundred thousand visitors. Among these readers were members of the traditional media, some of whom became interested in my story and wanted to interview me. After the whirlwind of attention that my story generated, the company had no choice but to cut their losses and reluctantly repair the laptop under warranty.

As with all situations in life, don't abuse your position of power. But whatever you use this megaphone for, know that thousands of tuned-in readers will be there for you. At times, it may feel as though you have an unfair advantage in this respect, and that's because you do.

Blogging as a Conversation

Blogging is not just about broadcasting a message to thousands of readers, it's also an ongoing conversation.

Most blogs have a comment section for this specific purpose, and that's definitely a positive thing, as your readers will want to interact with you by leaving

> **Joe asks:**
> ## How Many Blogs Are There?
>
> Exact blogging statistics are hard to come by, but at the time of this writing, blogpulse.com has over 170 million blogs indexed, with about 70,000 blogs and 1 million new posts indexed in the past twenty-four hours alone. As numbers like that clearly show, blogging is indeed alive and well.

comments (that you will often reply to as a means of further engaging your commenters). Some readers may even contact you directly by email or link back to your post from their blogs. Other discussions about your content may pop up on sites or communities such as Twitter, Facebook,[3] Reddit,[4] Hacker News,[5] or Slashdot.[6]

Thinking of blogging as a conversation can also be freeing because you don't need to have all the answers before approaching a subject you intend to write about. You are not expected to.

A blog post is a conversation starter that can lead to lengthy discussions that have the potential to spread far and wide across the Internet. It's important that you treat blogging as a conversation that will help you grow and learn, and not just as a megaphone.

As a blogger you are part of the blogosphere, a world with its own expectations, most of which are based around the idea of a community of bloggers and commenters interacting with one another.

Be part of this conversation by replying to comments wherever they're posted on your site and by linking to other blogs that are relevant to your articles. In doing so, your blog stands a very good chance of growing and quickly attracting a community of like-minded individuals. To boot, you may establish new professional relationships and make new friends in the process.

Bloggers with Benefits

As an author I'm aware of the fact that each reader has a different expectation of this book and different goals for his or her blogging activities.

---

3.   facebook.com,
4.   reddit.com
5.   news.ycombinator.com
6.   slashdot.org

Some readers may solely be interested in sharing their knowledge with the world. Writing and expressing thoughts for such readers is enough reward and motivation to blog on a regular basis.

At the other end of the spectrum, there are readers who are mostly interested in learning how to make a second income for themselves or how to better market their company's products via blogging. Regardless of where you stand on this line, I'm going to assume that you have something worthwhile to say and that you have a honest, noble intent to share your expertise with an audience.

Yet you'll see throughout the book a great deal of information on how to build a large audience and how to benefit to the fullest (including economically) from the success of your blog. One reason for covering such topics in detail is to satisfy those who may have different goals than you. Another good reason is that there is a natural audience for what you have to say, and it would be unfortunate and probably demoralizing for you to never reach it.

And consider this: any time you spend blogging is time you're not spending on paying pursuits or, more importantly, with your family. There will come a time when that weighs on you. Believe me; you will blog better, more consistently, and longer if your blogging pays for itself. So please don't think I'm being mercenary if I explain how you actually can get paid for doing what you want to do.

With that clarification out of the way, let's briefly list what some practical and tangible benefits of blogging are. Most such benefits, you'll notice, derive directly from your blog being the effective megaphone and conversation tool we discussed above.

- Blogging can advance your career. You could land a dream job or great consultancy gigs if you are a freelancer. If the latter applies to you, then blogging could help you be more in demand and therefore able to command a higher rate.

- Blogging can help you become notorious—in the best possible sense—in your field. You might receive invitations to speak at conferences, receive an offer to write a book on the subject you blog about, or have the awesome benefit of being able to quickly bring attention to your latest projects with a single post. As well, if you're into technical books, be prepared for the free review copies you'll be offered by publishers.

- Blogging can help you earn extra income. This can range from pizza money all the way up to thousands of dollars a month. Blogging is by no means a get-rich-quick scheme, but it has the potential to handsomely provide you with economic rewards, both directly and indirectly.

In addition to these benefits, if you are blogging to promote a business, you can also expect to achieve the following:

- Find new customers. Blogging is an extremely cost-effective marketing tool (often referred to as inbound marketing); it can definitely help you attract a large number of new customers to your own products.

- Build loyalty. Customers who regularly interact with companies tend to develop greater loyalty to those companies, their brands, and their products. A blog that allows for comments and an approachable social media presence are the ideal means by which to keep that communication channel open and operating smoothly.

- Find new employees, partners, and investors. When you put your business out there through a blog, you have the chance to meet an array of people online, including prospective hires. With a bit of luck, you may even catch the interest of potential business partners and investors. Blogging can enable you to network with the right type of people to help bolster the growth of your business.

Chapter 10, *Making Money from Your Blog*, on page 173, Chapter 11, *Promoting Your Own Business*, on page 199, and Chapter 12, *Taking Full Advantage of Your Blog*, on page 215, will show you how to obtain all of these benefits.

How to Get the Best Out of This Book

Before proceeding with this journey, I feel it's important to highlight how this book is intended to be read.

If you don't have a blog yet, it's worth reading this book from cover to cover, as you'll be provided with a complete set of steps that you can take to become a successful blogger. After reading each chapter, write down the steps you plan to take for your site. To take full advantage of the book, you must actively put some of the advice within it into action.

If you already have a blog, you'll still benefit from reading the book in its entirety, but doing so isn't as mandatory. You can focus on the chapters that interest you right now and come back to others whenever you need assistance with a specific topic.

Regardless of whether you are a new blogger or not, think of blogging as an experiment. You'll try suggestions from this book, and most of them will work

> ## So Many Links!
>
> This book contains a huge number of links. This was done in an effort to make the book as useful as possible.
>
> Depending on how you're reading this book, the act of typing in the URLs can get tedious pretty quickly. So I've created a list to help you easily access all of the links included in this book. You can find the list at technicalblogging.com/links.

for your blog, though a few may not. By using traffic statistics and user feedback, you'll be able to validate what works for you and what doesn't. Then iterate, constantly improving your blog with small enhancements. As you gain more experience, you'll be able to come up with your own hypotheses, experiments, and improvements.

Finally, remember that everything we do as bloggers is intended to showcase our content. Yet this book contains many chapters that focus on other aspects of blogging. These other chapters will help you maximize your ability to promote and benefit from your content. As you approach each chapter, however, you should remember the mantra "Content first." The underlying assumption throughout this book is that you are reading these pages with the intent of producing the best content you can.

Brilliant content that isn't promoted will likely be discovered and shared ...eventually, however suboptimal the approach. Conversely, mediocre content that is heavily promoted will still remain mediocre and unremarkable even if hundreds of thousands of people see it.

This book is written in the belief that each of us has something worth sharing. Each of us has a blogger within. I'm here to help you let your blogger out.

Part I

Plan It

*The Internet is really about highly specialized
information, highly specialized targeting.*

➤ *Eric Schmidt*

CHAPTER 1

What Kind of Blog Are You Going to Run?

The first step when beginning to plan your blog is to determine the type of blog you intend to run. We have already established that it's not going to be a blog about your personal life, but you still have some choices to make.

The decisions you make now will affect many aspects of how you develop your blog down the road, so you should try to answer these important questions before proceeding with the next chapters of this book.

1.1   Solo vs. Collective

You may already have decided that yours will be a single-author blog. This is the most common type of blog and certainly makes for a sensible default choice. It's possible, though, that a collective blog is a better option for what you want to do. To help you figure out which of the two is best suited for your situation, let's briefly consider the advantages and disadvantages of solo and collective blogs.

Solo blogs are relatively easy to start. They allow you to be the boss, and you don't need to collaborate with other people. Being the only blogger also has the advantage of lowering expectations in terms of how much content you produce (and perhaps even of the quality of the content). With a solo blog, you are just a person expressing your thoughts on the Web.

Start a Collective Blog

Collective blogs are a team effort. Not only do you have to worry about getting this whole blogging thing going, but you have to factor in the typical problems that can come with having multiple people working together on the same project.

You'll have to figure out who's going to cover what topics—and on what days—as well as the time commitment each blogger is willing to put in, the acceptable styles and conventions, who's going to handle the promotion, how the financial rewards are going to be split, and so on.

In my experience with such sites, the biggest challenge is to keep everyone motivated enough to continue writing while also ensuring that the deadlines are being respected. Sound familiar? Right, it's not that different from coordinating a team of developers who are working on a software project.

Just as with a software team, you'll probably want to have someone in charge (i.e., an editor-in-chief) who can oversee the project management and coordination side of things as well as ensure that the actual writing gets done well (particularly if your collective blog is portrayed as an online magazine that guarantees a certain standard of quality).

Tip 1

Collective blogs can benefit greatly from an editor-in-chief.

That's the hard part. On the plus side, you can crank out content very quickly thanks to the sheer number of authors, letting your collective blog grow rapidly. You'll also offer a greater variety of topics and viewpoints. On the extreme end of the spectrum are blogs with multiple paid authors that post as much as news sites. Such sites are commonly tech news ones that can hardly be seen as blogs anymore. Among this group you'll find well-known sites such as TechCrunch, Ars Technica,[1] and InfoQ.[2]

A few years ago I started a collective Italian blog called Stacktrace with more than a dozen unpaid authors.[3] We were able to quickly publish more than a hundred articles and grow our list of feed subscribers to over ten thousand members.

Our articles were very technical (e.g., Linux kernel hacking) and written in Italian, so these figures are far more respectable than they seem at first glance. In fact, in a matter of months this collective blog became, arguably, one of the most respected aperiodic technical publications in Italy.

---

1. arstechnica.com
2. infoq.com
3. stacktrace.it

It would have been impossible for me to achieve the same results if I'd launched Stacktrace solo. Unfortunately, as my interest in publishing in Italian waned, so too did the interest of the group of volunteers who had been contributing to it.

Due to the challenges associated with running a collective blog, I would discourage you from attempting this type of site if you're a novice blogger. This is particularly true when the group of bloggers you are trying to coordinate with is larger than two or three friends who are just writing for the fun of it.

The Team Blog

The one notable exception to this recommendation is this: if you've got a group of colleagues all working for the same company, it may make sense to set up a team blog. When writing for such a team blog is part of your work duties and you're held accountable to some extent for its success, you'll be far less likely to abandon the site (and so will your colleagues).

The perfect example of a collective blog that's run by a team from the same company is the previously mentioned *Signal vs. Noise* by 37signals. This is a company that literally owes its fame and fortune to the constant blogging activities of a handful of founders and employees (along with its remarkable products and open source contributions).

1.2 General vs. Niche

Now that you have thought about and hopefully decided to run a blog by yourself or with the help of a few people, it's time to consider another important question: Is your blog going to be general or cover a specific topic?

It's the old conundrum of choosing between being a generalist or a specialist, something that many developers have to deal with at some point in their careers—only this time it's applied to blogging.

This is an important question because your choice truly defines the type of content you'd typically include, as well as affects other vital aspects of running a blog, such as promotion and monetization.

The choice you make has a lot to do with your personality and interests. If programming in Python is your pride and joy, you may opt for a *niche* (i.e., a topic that is somewhat narrow in scope) blog on that subject. If you have a thousand interests within the grand scope of programming, as I do, you may find a general blog gives you more room to express your thoughts.

Abandoned Blogs

Sadly, the most common type of blog is the abandoned one. It's not unusual for new bloggers to start a blog and post for a while, only to discover they don't have the time or patience required to keep it alive. The incentives to continue blogging will also be relatively few at first. The average blog fails to attract a wide readership, and consequently the rewards will also be scarce.

If you follow the blueprint outlined in this book, you should have no problem avoiding most pitfalls and the common fate of abandoning your blog.

Remember that the distinction between general and niche blogs mostly has to do with the expectations your readers have. People who subscribe to your Python blog expect you to speak about Python-related subjects. That's their main interest and the reason why they subscribed in the first place. You risk disappointing your readers if you publish a rant about Apple or write a detailed HOWTO on developing apps for Android in Java.

Tip 2

Don't betray your readers' expectations.

If you feel that you're the kind of person who needs to express your thoughts on a multitude of subjects, then publishing a general blog is the safer choice. You can still post mostly about Python on *John's thoughts on programming*, for example, but you are not restricted to that niche.

I experienced the restriction of a niche blog myself when I started my current programming blog. It was originally called *Zen and the Art of Ruby Programming*. Despite its success as a Ruby blog, I simply couldn't stand not talking about other programming languages, frameworks, and even more generic tech topics. As a result I renamed it *Zen and the Art of Programming* with the very generic tagline "Meditations on programming, startups, and technology."[4]

It may be tempting to assume that a larger scope of subjects necessarily correlates to, or even implies, a larger readership that's easier to attract. After all, if you're posting about Ruby, Python, C#, Apple, and Arduino, you'll definitely attract the attention of multiple communities, right? Wrong. The truth

---

4. programmingzen.com

is that it's much harder to succeed with a general blog than it is with a niche one. Let's see why this counterintuitive notion applies.

Imagine that Bob, a passionate Clojure programmer, discovers a link to an interesting article on a blog called *Optimizing Clojure Code*. It may be very tempting for him to subscribe to that blog if he likes what he reads.

Now imagine the same article on *John's thoughts on programming*. Bob doesn't know John nor does he have any reason to trust him as an authority on the subject of Clojure. Why would he subscribe to John's personal blog? Sure, the article was good, but John also seems to talk about Ruby and Objective-C, which Bob is not interested in. In the end, Bob is far more likely to subscribe to and continue following the niche blog than he is the general one.

Tip 3

Do one thing, but do it well.

Niche blogs tend to make it more obvious why a visitor should subscribe more obvious, but there are other objective reasons why it's easier to succeed with a niche blog. For one, there is less competition. Performing SEO (search engine optimization) is easier when your blog's name, domain name, and most of its content already contain popular keywords you're targeting (we'll talk more about SEO throughout the book). Blog aggregators and other bloggers are more likely to link to you if you cover their specific niche (and establishing relationships with them is also more plausible).

Niche blogging makes you part of a community, and if you play your cards right, it can make you rather famous within such a community. It's not just easier to promote your blog and actually succeed when you opt to go this route, a niche blog can also simplify the process of reaping the benefits of your blogging efforts.

I can think of very few ways to better establish yourself as an expert on a given topic than by running an excellent, informative niche blog on that subject. It doesn't hurt either that such a targeted audience is gold to sponsors and advertisers, which translates to more dollars for you.

For all these reasons, start a niche blog rather than a general one that spans a whole industry—unless you really feel compelled to write about a large variety of topics that can't be contained in a well-defined niche.

If you do, don't worry. Less-focused blogs by polymaths can do well too. So don't feel like you have to put a limit on the scope of your professional interests for the sake of adhering to a single niche.

If you see yourself as that kind of person, opting for a general blog may be a worthwhile trade-off that will make you feel less restricted, more satisfied with your writing, and less likely to abandon your blog.

1.3 Pundit vs. Instructional

Look at many of the technical blogs out there, and you'll quickly get daunted by what looks like a bewildering range of approaches. But they really boil down to either providing commentary or giving actual technical instructions (or a mix of both).

A pundit blog showcases an author's insights into an industry or a particular niche. It is typically filled with essays on relevant topics or quotes from other interesting blogs and news stories to which an opinion is added. The perfect example of a pundit who mostly blogs about Apple is John Gruber and his popular blog, *Daring Fireball*.[5]

An instructional blog focuses on HOWTOs. The aim of this type of blog is to provide tutorials or reference material for readers. There may be an opinion here and there, but these are mostly a collection of factual posts. For an example, check out *igvita.com* (a screenshot of which is shown within the introduction to this book).[6]

Which one should you choose? In my experience, this is a false dichotomy and you should opt for both styles—at least in the beginning. Offer variety to your readers by including a mix of pundit-style commentary plus handy instructions on how to do certain tasks.

Depending on how your readership responds to either type of post, you'll be able to focus more on one or the other. Consider your readers' feedback before cornering yourself into a specific blogging style. You'll also quickly discover which of the two you enjoy writing the most, and that's just as important. You can always evolve and change your blog style at a later stage.

---

5.   daringfireball.net
6.   igvita.com

1.4 Business Blogs

Note: If you don't own, operate, or promote a company, you can safely skip this section.

Over the past few years it has become extremely common for companies to have an official blog. If you are trying to connect with existing customers, reach new ones, and sell more of your products or services, it definitely makes sense to have such a site in place.

The real issue is figuring what sort of style you intend to give to your company blog. During this initial planning phase, you may wonder if the writing should be technical or business-oriented; should it include product updates and announcements?

Although we'll cover the promotion of your own products and company in detail, particularly starting with Chapter 11, *Promoting Your Own Business*, on page 199, it's worth having a few preliminary thoughts on the matter in mind beforehand.

Who Is Your Audience?

Before you write a single word, it's important to decide who the audience of your company blog is.

Make your blog ultra-technical, with scores of behind-the-scene details regarding how you develop the software that you sell, and you'll attract the attention of fellow developers. If your ideal customer base is developers or if you're trying to hire some new talent, this could be a solid strategy. If that's not the case, however, the explanation of your fancy continuous deployment setup for your SaaS (software as a service) won't mean a thing to your customers.

Likewise, taking an all-business approach in which you either share the details of how you run your startup or go into business topics at great length will tend to attract fellow entrepreneurs. Again, if they are your potential customers (e.g., your product is B2B), this approach can pay off.

The aforementioned 37signals produces web applications that are aimed at helping companies better handle communication and collaboration. Their unique and opinionated take on the way a business should be run, broadcast through their blog and books, has attracted many of their customers.

In most other cases, you'll find that your customers won't be particularly interested in learning how your Facebook ad campaign generated a 300 percent ROI (return on investment).

More commonly and realistically, you'll find that your end users are interested in learning about offers and discounts, product updates and announcements, server issues that might affect them, and ways to use your products that will help them be more productive or solve certain problems.

You'll also want to throw testimonials and success stories into the mix, showcasing how other clients are using your products in unique or interesting ways, as well as including general topics of interest that are relevant to the industry your company operates in. The occasional behind-the-scenes post, either technical or business-oriented, is definitely OK too, but it shouldn't be the main point of your blog unless people who are really into such posts coincide with your target audience.

If you have the manpower to maintain them, you might even opt to have two blogs for your company. Your *product blog* will be dedicated to announcements, status updates, and product news. The other could be broader in scope and mostly aimed at prospective customers and peers.

The secret is understanding who your ideal customers are and then writing the sort of content they want, search for, can understand, and, ideally, relate to.

1.5 What's Next

With a clearer idea of the type of blog you plan to run, we can proceed to the next chapter, where we'll define the main topic of your site and a series of related choices. The next chapter also completes our plan before moving onto chapters that are dedicated to setting up your blog.

*The least of things with a meaning is worth
more in life than the greatest of things
without it.*

➤ *Carl Jung*

CHAPTER 2

A Rock-Solid Plan for Your Blog

The previous chapter should have helped you decide, broadly, the direction that you want to take your blog in. In this chapter we are going to finalize our plan by figuring out some more important details before you're ready to launch into actually setting your new site up.

In particular, we'll define the goals for your blog, determine if they're realistic, and adjust them if they're not, as well as plan how to meet them.

2.1 Define Your Blog's Main Topic

Whether you opted for a niche blog or for a more general one, your site is going to have a main theme. In the case of a niche, the scope will be well defined and easy to identify. For general blogs it can be much looser and less defined. Nevertheless, you need to have an initial idea of what topics you're going to cover in your blog.

Identify Your Niche

You should identify the main topic for your niche based on your interests and motivations. For example, an iPhone freelancer may want to start a blog about iOS development. That's a relatively large niche, but it provides the blog with a very well-defined scope. You'll know immediately what the boundaries for the blog are, as well as what does and doesn't belong on your site.

After picking the main topic, jot down a list of ten articles you could write for your blog. You don't need to write the actual articles yet, just the titles. When you are done with this task, ask yourself whether doing this exercise left you excited or frustrated. Was it hard to come up with ten titles, or could you have kept going for ages? The main point of this exercise is to understand if you have enough to say about the topic at hand.

In most cases you won't have to worry about this, but if you pick a tiny niche that's highly specific, you may quickly run out of ideas for articles and face other obvious problems, such as only being able to attract a minuscule audience. We'll discuss how to estimate the size of a niche in Section 2.2, *Analyze the Size of Your Niche*, on page 13.

Define the Main Theme for Your General Blog

If you intend to publish a blog on programming in general, web development, or a similarly broad topic in another industry, you don't have to worry about the possibility of running out of ideas or having too small of an audience to capture.

Your pre-setup exercise is a bit different from the niche one then. Instead of listing articles, come up with a main theme for your blog, then list ten relevant topics that you are passionate about and have some degree of expertise in. For example, if you're dealing with a blog about web development as your main theme, you might write down the following topics:

1. Ruby on Rails
2. HTML5/CSS3
3. JavaScript/CoffeeScript
4. Ajax
5. Deployment
6. Scaling web applications
7. Security issues
8. NoSQL databases
9. UI/UX/Usability
10. Using and creating RESTful APIs

As you can see, these are very broad topics, each of which would roughly correspond to different categories for your blog.

This task is not just meant to help you figure out what kind of topics you'll be covering in your blog. The real point of this exercise is to determine if you can cover enough topics to warrant creating a general blog on your main subject.

Was coming up with the list easy or did you struggle to complete it? If you find that your passion and expertise is limited to only a couple of categories, you may be better off running a niche blog that's solely focused on those subjects.

2.2 Analyze the Size of Your Niche

Before committing to your blog, you may want to assess the size of your potential audience. For most niches this is more of a curiosity than a requirement, but if you are trying to establish yourself in a very small niche and are uncertain about its size, this step can help you determine if it's worth pursuing or not.

We are after an estimate rather than exact numbers. More importantly, the process you'll go through in order to estimate the size of your niche will also turn out to be invaluable when researching keywords and topics for your articles later on.

Use the Google Keyword Tool

As you probably know, Google makes the bulk of its profits from selling ads. And ads are annoying, right? Well, in this case Google's keen eye on advertisers actually works in our favor. Google has released a series of tools that are meant to help users of its AdWords program find new keywords to advertise with, as well as help users estimate search volumes for those keywords.

Of course we have no intention of buying ads from Google through its AdWords program now, but we're going to use Google's free Keyword Tool to estimate the search volume for a few keywords in your niche.

Visit the Keyword Tool page and enter the primary keyword for your blog (e.g., CoffeeScript) in the "Word or phrase" text area.[1] Leave the Website box empty, given that we are not interested in looking up keyword recommendations for an existing site. (Entering the URL of a competitor in Keyword Yool would be an easy way to get ideas for target keywords.)

Click the check box next to "Only show ideas closely related to my search terms." This will ensure that all the similar keywords suggested by Google (i.e., *keyword ideas*) will include your main keyword. If your blog isn't in English or your primary market isn't the United States, you will need to change the language and regional settings; otherwise you can leave the defaults on. Fill in the CAPTCHA that may appear to verify that your request isn't an automated one.

At some point you may be requested to register with Google AdWords to continue using the tool. It's a good idea, because a greater number of results and details (e.g., search trends) are provided to users who are logged in.

---

1. adwords.google.com/select/KeywordToolExternal

Going Pro with Market Samurai

A handy tool for performing this type of market analysis is Market Samurai. It's an all-in-one program that includes modules for keyword research, SEO competition analysis, rank tracking for your target keywords and sites, and much more, as shown in Figure 3, *Market Samurai*, on page 16.

Market Samurai isn't free or even that cheap (coming in at about $100), but it's a major time saver if you perform these types of operations frequently. In fact, its use is very common among Internet marketers and SEO experts, especially affiliate marketers who routinely launch new blogs each month (we'll talk more about affiliate marketing in Chapter 10, *Making Money from Your Blog*, on page 173).

Click the Search button, and you should see your keyword, a series of related keywords, and their respective search volumes, as shown in Figure 2, *Google Keyword Tool*, on page 15.

The Competition column indicates the number of advertisers who are bidding for the particular keyword you looked up. Global Monthly Searches refers to the worldwide number of searches containing that keyword, while Local Monthly Searches is limited to the country you specified (i.e., USA, by default). In the example of CoffeeScript, a web scripting language that compiles down to JavaScript, the number of global searches is estimated to be approximately 22,200 (at the time of this writing, of course).

Is that number big enough? It's definitely a small audience if you compare it to established mainstream languages like JavaScript or Perl, which have over 24- and 7-million global searches, respectively, per month. However small of a niche, generally speaking, we know that our potential audience will be comprised of at least a few thousand people, which can be encouraging.

Just as important as the current search volume is the search trend. Is your keyword becoming increasingly popular over time, or are you setting yourself up to create a blog about a technology that is about to slowly regress? In the case of an emerging niche language like CoffeeScript, for example, you can't help but have a gut feeling that it will become ever more popular as time goes on.

Use Google Trends

Thankfully we don't have to rely on intuition. We can verify our theory by using another Google tool called Google Trends.[2] By searching in Google

---

2. google.com/trends

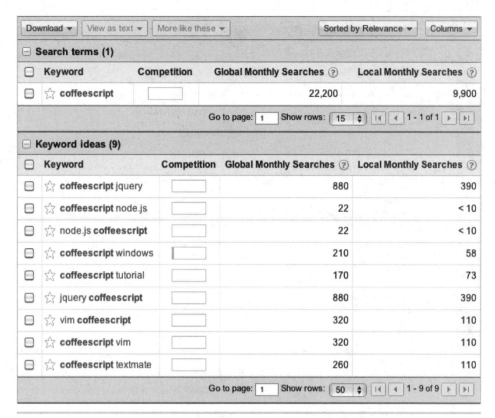

Figure 2—Google Keyword Tool

Trends for our language, technology, or main keyword, we can easily assess its search volume over time. The specific example of CoffeeScript (Figure 4, *Google Trends*, on page 17) clearly shows strong growth over the past few months. Past performance is never a guarantee of future results, but we can assume that the increased adoption is unlikely to have reached its peak already for such a new language. (Google Insights for Search is another valuable tool for this kind of analysis.[3])

Google Trends offers details about the regions and cities in which a given keyword is popular. CoffeeScript seems to be searched for primarily in San Francisco, New York, Sydney, Tokyo, and London. This isn't too surprising, given that such cities are hotbeds of startup activity and that, in turn, startups are most likely to adopt cutting-edge technologies like CoffeeScript.

---

3. google.com/insights/search

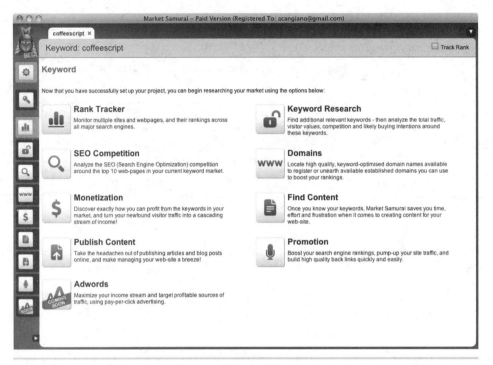

Figure 3—Market Samurai

This kind of information is particularly useful to you if you live in one of the cities in which your niche is going strong. Along with starting a blog on the subject, you could decide to become active in your local tech community (and perhaps even launch a relevant Meetup group). A local environment that is favorable to your technology of choice would also be beneficial if you are looking for a job, intend to offer your freelance services to local companies, or are hiring talent for your own business.

Despite being a relatively small niche, the CoffeeScript blog idea is looking up. In fact, if we were to use Google Search, Google Blog Search,[4] or Technorati Search,[5] we'd quickly discover that the blogosphere is buzzing about Coffee-Script, but there are (at the time of this writing) very few blogs dedicated to this topic.

With competition levels so low and the popularity of the language rapidly increasing, we can conclude that now would be a great time to establish a blog about CoffeeScript.

---

4.   blogsearch.google.com
5.   technorati.com/search

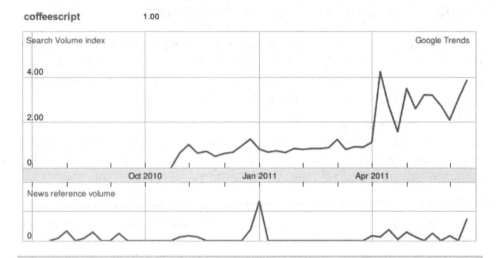

Figure 4—Google Trends

Make an Executive Decision

Perform similar searches for your own niche. Personally, if money was one of my main goals, I wouldn't likely consider starting a niche blog whose main target keyword had fewer than 20,000 searches per month, as the audience would be too small to likely generate significant income.

Some Internet marketers make a very comfortable living through a series of microniche blogs (usually affiliate or ad-ridden sites) that have a much smaller target audience than that. However, their business model and approach to blogging are quite different from the ones recommended in this book. Here we favor quality over quantity.

If smaller search volumes were the case for a candidate niche, I would definitely need to see really promising trends or have a lot of passion for a topic before taking the plunge when it comes to such a tiny niche.

The exception to this is a brand-new technology that has just been announced by a well-established company like Apple or Microsoft. While such technologies may show zero search results initially, they are virtually guaranteed to become popular—at least to a certain extent—in the future. Also, keep in mind that, as a rule of thumb, the larger the niche, the bigger the competition.

2.3 Give Readers a Compelling Reason to Stick Around

At this point, you've determined the style and topic of your blog, as well as validated the existence of a sizable audience. Now you should start thinking about answering a question that many of your visitors will ask themselves, Why should I subscribe to this blog?

I phrased that question so as to intentionally imply a subscription to your upcoming posts via feed or email, which is something that's common among a technical readership. For less technical readers who don't use subscription tools, the question may become, Why should I come back to this blog?

Whatever the exact question, you need a convincing answer. What's the reason your blog exists? Why did you start it in the first place? What's your compelling story? Answer these questions and you'll have a much clearer picture of what your blog is really about and why visitors will want to return.

The Elevator Pitch

In the business world there is a concept called the *elevator pitch*. Its name derives from the hypothetical scenario of finding yourself in an elevator with a potential investor. In such a context, all you have is between thirty and ninety seconds or so to summarize what your product or company is all about. While you don't need to raise money for your blog, this is still a worthwhile exercise.

Tip 4

Focus your elevator pitch on the why, not the how.

Your elevator pitch should quickly summarize the essence of your product or company. Why does it exist? What problem does it solve? What's its value proposition?

We are dealing with a blog here, but the same principle applies. Characterize your blog in one or two sentences at most and give a reason why people should come back and visit again.

Case Study: Popular Tech Blogs

To help you with this task, let's briefly take a look at a few blogs (listed by URL) and analyze the compelling reasons behind their existence.

- rubyinside.com: The most important news, events, and releases in the Ruby community. Reason to read it: To stay up-to-date and keep a pulse on the Ruby ecosystem.

- daringfireball.net: News and opinions about Apple by an unrepentant advocate of Apple products. Reason to read it: It provides fresh insight, interesting controversy, and news about Apple and its competitors delivered by an established community pundit.

- thedailywtf.com: Daily examples of bad programming. Reason to read it: To learn more about anti-patterns in programming, and for the amusement.

- igvita.com: HOWTO articles on cutting-edge open source technologies. Reason to read it: To learn how to use some of the coolest technologies around and apply them to real-world problems.

- sethgodin.typepad.com: Marketing ideas and opinions. Reason to read it: To improve your marketing skills with the aid of a leader in the marketing world via thought-provoking ideas and insight.

- techcrunch.com: News about startups, technology, and VC investments. Reason to read it: To stay up-to-date with the world of technology and startups.

- engadget.com: News about gadgets. Reason to read it: To stay abreast of exciting news pertaining to technological gadgets.

- flowingdata.com: The visualization and statistics blog of a PhD statistics student. Reason to read it: To learn, in the blog's words, "how designers, programmers, and statisticians are putting data to good use." It's a must for those who are interested in data visualization and statistics.

In each and every example above, the reason why it makes sense to follow these blogs is pretty obvious and can be stated in a single sentence.

Come Up with Your Blog's Reason for Being

Your goal is to make it just as obvious, to yourself first and then to readers, why your blog is worth following. Remember the elevator pitch we discussed earlier. You only have from a few seconds to a few minutes (at the very most) to effectively win your readers over. You want to state your blog's intent through your title, tagline/motto, About blurb in the sidebar, and the About section, in as direct a manner as possible (rather than being subtle about it).

In the example of the CoffeeScript niche, we could set our sights on becoming the *Ruby Inside* of CoffeeScript, thus becoming that one-stop resource for folks who are interested in CoffeeScript news. Alternatively, we could make the blog about tutorials on how to accomplish various tasks in CoffeeScript or, again, create a blog that's dedicated solely to converting from JavaScript to CoffeeScript programming. What about one that is devoted to documenting your journey as you try to become proficient in CoffeeScript?

Pick the idea that suits you best for your own subject; pretty much any will do as long as you give it an angle and clearly communicate the point of your blog to your visitors.

Over time you'll find that many other elements corroborate with your effort to make your blog compelling for your readers. These include the design of your site, having catchy headlines, the quality and usefulness of your articles, your professional credentials, the type of comments and commenters your blog manages to attract, and so on. We'll examine each of these in detail in the coming chapters.

2.4 Set Goals for Your Blog

With such a clear picture of your blog's theme/topic and the reason for its existence, it's time to start thinking big and coming up with some goals for the months ahead. Don't worry if this looks like more planning than you bargained for. This is a practical book, and we'll take off in the next chapter. But as with many situations in life, it's important to develop a clear flight plan first.

Write down goals for your blog. What do you want to get out of the blog you are starting? What do you expect from it in one month, three months, a year, three years?

Clarify your initial expectations now so that you can revisit and compare them to the results you actually achieve from your blog later on. If you're on track, well done. If not, you'll be able to make adjustments to your blogging efforts or even readjust your goals if your initial ones have proven to be unrealistic.

Don't write down vague goals. Try to be as specific as you can. One of your first-year goals shouldn't be phrased as "Make some extra money from my blog." It should be more along the lines of "Earn an extra $500 USD per month from my blog." Or if you're a startup blogger, you could have a goal such as "Use the blog to increase sales by 30 percent over the next twelve months."

Tip 5

Always set verifiable goals.

If you are not interested in supplementing your income or increasing your product sales via blogging, then focus on different points while still aiming for goals that are verifiable.

As you set your short-term goals, please understand that most of the benefits you'll get from blogging are likely to kick in after a few months or a year. So don't jot down goals that are too ambitious for your one-month milestone.

Good first-month goals can include ensuring you've determined your blogging strategy with the help of this book. You may also want to throw in a goal about respecting the schedule you set throughout the month (more on this in Chapter 6, *Producing Content Regularly*, on page 103).

Readership Expectations

As you work on this goal-setting exercise, you may be tempted to define a specific numerical readership goal. Don't. It's seriously hard to predict the readership of your own blog before you launch it because you're dealing with so many variables that can affect the outcome.

For this reason I wouldn't define an arbitrary number of readers by a certain date as a goal; instead, let's just consider what your traffic expectations should realistically be for the first year of blogging.

Readership can be evaluated by using a number of key metrics. I like to look at subscribers, visitors, and pageviews. The following numbers refer to subscribers—either via feed or email—that you can expect to attract in your first year of blogging. Those are your regular readers, so this figure tends to be a less transient metric of the popularity of your blog.

- *0–100 subscribers*: Your blog is still struggling to attract an audience. Unless you are in a very tiny niche, you may need to improve your strategy, content quality and quantity, promotion, etc. to help bolster your readership.

- *100–500 subscribers:* Not a bad number for a technical blog. You are off to a decent start.

- *500–1,000 subscribers:* Above average readership. I expect many of my readers to be able to pull these kinds of numbers off.

- *1,000–5,000 subscribers:* Very successful blog. Few bloggers can boast such figures in their first year.

- *5,000–10,000 subscribers:* An extremely successful site that has quickly established itself as an authority blog in its field.

- *Over 10,000 subscribers:* Statistical outlier. Huge potential for the blog to become one of the most popular sites in its field, as well as a major source of income.

If you want a realistic single number to shoot for as your traffic milestone, try to reach the thousand-subscriber mark as fast as you can. In my experience, the magic of blogging and its many benefits start to manifest themselves visibly after you reach the general ballpark of a thousand subscribers.

With such a large fan base, your other metrics will no doubt be equally impressive. It's not uncommon to get an order of magnitude more monthly visitors than feed subscribers.

2.5 Choose and Register a Domain Name

The last step of this initial planning process is to choose a name and register a domain name for your new blog.

Keep Your Blog on the Same Domain as Your Company

If the blog you are creating is for your company, the domain name choice is very straightforward. Assuming you've already gotten a site for your company, you don't need to register a new domain name for your blog; simply define a subdomain or subfolder such as blog.yourcompany.com or yourcompany.com/blog.

The reason for going this route isn't limited to URL consistency and the need to make obvious the connection between your blog and the company to your customers. When you use the same domain for your main site and blog, any SEO efforts you make on the part of either will end up benefitting (to a lesser extent) the other as well. This is because they both reside on the same domain. Your blog will also have better positioning from day one, thanks to the existing authority—in the eyes of search engines—of the main domain name. The subdomain blog.yourcompany.com looks arguably better and is easier to host separately; however, it's also less effective from an SEO standpoint.[6]

Name or Domain Name?

Before delving into the topic of picking a good name for your blog, let me state one important distinction that is often overlooked. The name of your blog and your domain name are two different entities. Though the two names are often one and the same (because this approach helps cut down on confusion and ensure that your visitors easily remember your domain name), taking this approach is not strictly required.

For example, TechCrunch uses techcrunch.com as its domain name, whereas my blog *Zen and the Art of Programming* uses programmingzen.com. I opted for a different domain name because I felt that zenandtheartofprogramming.com would have been far too long. Other times, you may opt for different names because the exact domain name that matches your desired blog name is simply not available.

I strongly suggest you strive to find a domain name that matches your desired blog name. However, if a perfect match isn't possible, do not turn your back on a good domain name.

Naming the Baby

Bestowing names on things looks easy from the outside, but the process can all too quickly become a time-consuming endeavor. You might think that it would take only a few minutes to find the perfect name, but once you start searching for a name, your brainstorming sessions can sometimes end up lasting for hours and spanning the course of several days.

To help you decide on a good domain name for your blog (and its corresponding name) much more quickly, I've listed a series of guidelines below that I tend to use when I find myself in this situation. Most of them should be common sense if you have a good degree of web awareness, but there might be a few novel ideas that will make the process of coming up with a good name easier and quicker for you.

Which TLDs?

Try as hard as you can to acquire a .com domain. Failing that, you can consider a .net or .org domain name. These three TLDs (top-level domains) are the most SEO-friendly and are what most people expect to type in.

---

6.   www.mattcutts.com/blog/subdomains-and-subdirectories

Accept that registering a .net or .org domain name when .com is being used by a *domainer* (a domain name speculator who mainly buys domain names with the intent of reselling them for a large profit margin) implies that you'll inevitably end up sending some of your traffic to the .com version of your site, as users may assume that your site is located on the .com version.

Conversely, if the .com is actually being used by someone with a real site, it's common courtesy not to register the exact (or very similar) .net or .org version of the domain name, even if it's available. I'm pointing this out because you'll inevitably create confusion for readers of both sites if you decide to do this.

A litigious individual or business may also decide to pursue legal action, which is annoying to deal with, whether there is a legitimate case or not (this is even worse in the case of registered trademarks, where the owner is often required by law to protect it by going after violators).

If you are trying to break into a local market with your blog, it may make sense to register a country-specific domain name. For example, a Canadian freelancer who's interested in promoting his or her web design services locally may opt for a ccTLD (country code top-level domain) .ca domain name. Doing so also makes sense from an SEO standpoint, as search engines like Google absolutely love country-specific domain names when showing local search results.

Tip 6

If your target audience is local to a country other than the US, favor ccTLDs.

In the example of the Canadian site, all things being equal, the .ca will beat out the .com SERP (search engine results page) positioning on Google.ca. (Hosting your blog through a Canadian host would also help the cause, eh?)

Keyword- or Brand-Based?

Search engines love keyword-based domain names and generally give them an unfair advantage in the result pages. Having the one or two main keywords you are targeting placed within your domain name will boost your blog ranks on Google and Bing (as well as on other search engines that, quite frankly, very few people use).

The reason for this is that search engines take the keywords within your domain name as an indication of your site's relevance to a given user's query. If I'm looking for "old-fashioned programmer keywords," all things being equal, Google will assume that oldfashionprogrammerkeywords.com is more relevant than undermyfingertips.com (note that these are entirely fictional names, even if these sites were to exist).

An SEO-friendly domain name is not the only aspect to consider, though. The human perception of your domain name is incredibly important in the case of a reputable technical blog. Most programmers I know would probably guess that oldfashionprogrammerkeywords.com is a commercial or spammy site of some sort. undermyfingertips.com on the other hand, would be seen as a clever name that could easily host a blog that reviews all kinds of keyboards.

In short, humans tend to remember and love good brand names, while search engines favor domain names with keywords. The trouble with brand names is that they take time to establish, even when we're just dealing with blogs and not company names.

My suggestion is to find the right balance. If your keyword-based domain name makes for a decent, catchy brand, definitely go for it. If not, see if mixing it up with other words (e.g., blog) can help. The textbook example of this is engadget.com, which managed to include the word *gadget* and the pun on *engage* in such a short brand domain name.

As a less clever example, I went with programmingzen.com myself because it's easy to remember and is fairly "brand-ish" sounding, whereas at the same time it also contains the keyword *programming*. At the time of this writing, searching for "programming blog" shows my blog on the first page of results returned by Google, despite the existence of hundreds of thousands of other programming blogs. My domain name choice alone didn't achieve these results, but it certainly didn't hurt either.

Other Suggestions for Picking the Right Domain Name

So far we've covered the essentials of picking a domain name, but what about using hyphens in your name, choosing your domain length, and other things like that? Let's briefly look at a few other criteria that are important when picking out good domain names.

- Keep your domain name as short as possible. A short domain name is easier to type and is more memorable. (It also fits better on printed materials such as T-shirts and business cards.) As a general rule of thumb, I try to keep domain names under twenty characters at most (TLD extension excluded). The average number of characters, which only stands to grow as time rolls on, appears to be around thirteen characters.

- Choose a domain name that is easy to pronounce and communicate. Any ambiguity in the way the domain name could be spelled should be eliminated. In light of this, I would also avoid using numbers, if at all possible, because of the general ambiguity of spelling them in full vs. typing numerals (e.g., *ten* vs. *10*). Of course, between search engines, social media, bookmarking, and feeds, many of your visitors won't actually type your URL into their browsers.

- Avoid hyphens if possible, and if not, limit them to one at most (like I did with math-blog.com). Multiple hyphens have a tendency to cheapen your brand and make your site look less trustworthy. In fact, many Internet marketers have abused them over the years in an effort to register keyword-rich domain names.

- Use your own name as the domain name (provided that it's not particularly complicated to spell and that you're mostly aiming at promoting yourself through your blog). If such is the case, securing namelastname.com is a good idea. Just keep in mind that blogs of this kind tend to be perceived as more general and personal than your typical niche blog.

- Be careful with unintentional double meanings. Amusingly, this lesson was quickly learned by expertsexchange.com, which was intended to represent "Experts Exchange" but can all too easily be read as "Expert Sex Change." This site's owner had to register experts-exchange.com, a hyphenated version of the existing domain name, just to clarify the way the domain name is supposed to be read.

- Use tools to quickly check results for your name ideas. As you try to come up with your unique domain name, you'll quickly discover something very frustrating. A lot of the time it seems like all the good domain names have already been taken. If you are struggling with this issue and want to speed up the process, use an Ajax-based tool that provides instant availability results for your selected name. I like to use instantdomainsearch.com and domainsbot.com for this task. I also recommend bustaname.com to generate and check many variations from a few keywords.

Register Your Domain

Countless ICANN (Internet Corporation for Assigned Names and Numbers) accredited registrars exist, and the only real distinction between the lot comes down to TLD availability, price, ease of use, and the handling of disputes.

Aftermarket Domains

Aftermarket domains are domains that have been registered and are available for sale by their owners or which have expired and will soon become available for sale after a grace and redemption period.

It is possible to purchase a domain from a domainer either directly or via marketplaces like sedo.com. Whether you should take this approach, however, is an entirely different matter. Good domain names tend to be very expensive, so I wouldn't recommend that you start your blogging career by making a large investment. (If you find that your ideal domain name is for sale for $200 USD, however, then by all means consider purchasing it).

When it comes to expired domains, you may be able to snap up some great deals if you wait for the domains to become available. This process tends to give the existing owners ample time to change their minds and renew the domain, if desired. If they don't do so after about ninety days, however, you can theoretically register the expired domain just as you would with a regular domain name.

In practice, valuable expired domain names are watched carefully by domainers, so you may have to use specialized bidding services such as snapnames.com to snap them up and in turn end up spending several times more than you would for a regular unregistered domain name.

To read a dated but insightful account of this process, head over to www.mikeindustries.com/blog/archive/2005/03/how-to-snatch-an-expiring-domain, where you can check out the story behind the domain registration that took place for newsvine.com, a popular news site.

Based on these criteria, for .com domains I've found namecheap.com and dynadot.com to be reasonable choices. Opt for one of them, unless you already register your domains with someone else you've found to be reliable. In that case, having all of your domains under one registrar is preferable.

Once you have decided on an available name, the next step is to register your domain name (this should cost about $10 USD per year for a .com domain).

Albeit not universally accepted, empirical evidence suggests that search engines prefer—all things being equal—domain names that are not expiring soon. The reason for this is that spammers rarely commit to domains for multiple years. Registering the domain for multiple years may offer SEO advantages and even savings.

When you register a domain name, your name, mailing address, and other personal information will be made available in a public WHOIS database.[7]

---

7.   www.internic.net/whois.html

If you wish to protect your privacy, many registrars offer WHOIS protection services in which their own mailing address and business details are listed on your behalf (this service is sometimes offered for free for the first year by Namecheap and is inexpensive to keep using after your blog's initial year of life).

2.6 What's Next

OK, you've planned it. Now it's time to jump right in and start implementing your blog.

In the next two chapters you'll learn everything you need to know to create the perfect initial setup, whether you opt for the recommended WordPress self-hosted solution or an alternative arrangement.

Even if you own a blog already, don't skip these two chapters. They'll teach you tips and tricks to help fine-tune your existing setup.

Let's build it!

Part II

Build It

They say Rome wasn't built in a day, but I
wasn't on that particular job.

➤ *Brian Clough*

CHAPTER 3

Setting Up Your Blog

You've now decided what kind of blog you'll create. You've identified your topic and your niche, and you've done a sanity check on these decisions in terms of markets, trends, and competition. You've also set some reasonable goals and expectations for your blogging.

Now it's time to get your hands dirty. In this and the next chapter you'll install, configure, style, and fine-tune your blog. You'll start by making a few crucial decisions about blogging software and hosting before moving on to actually setting up your blog.

3.1   Choose Your Blogging Software and Hosting

One positive effect of the popularity of blogging is the wealth of blogging solutions you can choose from. There are so many options available these days that it can be overwhelming for newcomers when they first venture out into the blogging arena.

Unsurprisingly, according to Google Keyword Tool, there are hundreds of thousands of searches each month regarding blogging software. Let's shed a beam of light on this subject by shortlisting some of the most sensible options.

Your Three Main Options

As a technical blogger, consider the following three options:

- *WordPress(.org)*[1]: The absolute leader in blogging software. This open source application currently powers an impressive 14.7 percent of the top million sites (not just blogs) on the Web.

---

1.   wordpress.org

- *Static site generators*: Increasingly popular among developers, site generators such as Jekyll or the more user-friendly Octopress framework (which is built on top of Jekyll),[2] typically generate your blog from template text files that you can edit in a markup language like Markdown or Textile without the need for a database or a complex server setup. The compiled output will be a static site with HTML and CSS files that you can upload to any web server (even Amazon S3 and GitHub Pages[3]).

- *Blogging services*: A variety of providers offer the ability to host a blog using their web platform without having you install anything. Common services of this nature include WordPress.com (not .org, which was described in the first bullet point), TypePad, Blogger,[4] LiveJournal, Posterous, and Tumblr (however, blogs hosted on the last two services tend to be shorter and considerably more akin to micro- or nanopublishing).

Let's quickly review the pros and cons of each of these solutions.

WordPress: the Smart Choice

As the most popular blogging software, self-hosted WordPress is able to boast thousands of plugins and themes that let you customize your blog however you like. It has one of the richest online ecosystems, even when compared to other software outside the blogging world.

Should you ever need help with WordPress or wish to have custom features created, there are plenty of developers who are familiar with the system and ready to help for a fee. Likewise, countless designers have worked with WordPress themes before, so finding a good one should be fairly easy.

As a self-hosted solution, WordPress has the disadvantage of requiring a server to host it on (unless you opt for the commercial hosted solution provided by WordPress.com). Your server will need a web server such as Apache or nginx and MySQL for storing and retrieving data, plus support for a recent version of PHP. You'll also need to update WordPress itself pretty frequently so as to avoid security vulnerabilities that crop up from time to time.

According to some critics, WordPress is also bloated and slow (particularly when filled with numerous plugins of varying quality). Thankfully, there are excellent caching plugins that make WordPress very fast. We'll cover these plugins in the next chapter, which is dedicated to fine-tuning your blog.

---

2. github.com/mojombo/jekyll and octopress.org, respectively.

3. pages.github.com

4. blogger.com

Static Site Generators: The Hacker Way

Static site generators are still very much a niche, but their increasing popularity with (the good kind of) hackers may be justified. Such generators offer you the ability to directly edit your posts, blog structure, and design by using a text editor such as Emacs, Vim, or TextMate.

Many of these generators are simple, small, and written in scripting languages such as Python, Perl, and Ruby; so if you are familiar with these languages, you'll be able to easily extend them to customize their behavior. This process is arguably much simpler than learning how to customize a large system such as WordPress.

Other points in favor of Jekyll and similar static generators are the ability to store your blog under revision control through tools like Git or Subversion and the simplicity of being able to deploying the output site pretty much anywhere, as well as its positive performance implications. In fact, since your blog ends up being a static site, its performance should be very good—even on commodity hardware.

The major disadvantage is that you are on your own. There are very few pre-made add-ons that aid you in accomplishing even a small percentage of what you can do with software like WordPress. For example, if a new social network is announced, you can expect free widgets for it from some WordPress plugin developer in a matter of days. Using a static generator, you'd most likely have to write the code yourself. Depending on the type of blog you envision and your coding abilities, this may or may not be a deal breaker for you.

Blogging Services: The Easy Way

Blogging services come with the major advantage that you don't have to worry about servers and their configuration. The company behind the service is responsible for the blog software and server upkeep.

Even some large organizations use hosted services for their official blogs. For instance, Amazon uses TypePad for many of their blogs, while Netflix uses Blogger. This choice allowed both companies to immediately inject themselves into an existing community of bloggers and commenters. In doing so they also guaranteed for themselves open communication with their customers should their main sites become unavailable.

Status updates become crucial to placate irate customers during outages. So if you're blogging for a company, consider hosting your blog on a different hosting solution from the one you use for your company site.

The main problems with blogging services are a relative lack of flexibility and customization, the possibility of being kicked out at the discretion of the service owners, vendor lock-in, and other arbitrary restrictions imposed by the vendor.

For example, WordPress.com will not allow you to upload your own themes and plugins, and your choices are limited to what they provide. Likewise, you won't be able to insert arbitrary JavaScript code or Flash files into your pages, which in turn limits your ability to use third-party tools that are based on JavaScript (e.g., web traffic tracking) or Flash. Their policy is also less than friendly to bloggers who use affiliate links as a way of earning extra income.

While some blogging services are better than others, they all share certain kinds of restrictions when compared to a self-hosted solution. With some platforms you'll also have to pay a monthly or yearly fee. WordPress.com is free; however, it does require that you pay for every little customization, including associating your own domain name to the blog. (I definitely don't recommend that you use one of their subdomains, such as yourusername.word-press.com, for blogging as this may cause a URL-based lock-in).

Should you decide to go this route, carefully evaluate features, customization options, policies, and export facilities before committing.

Which Blogging Platform Is Right for You?

So which one should you go with? Opt for a self-hosted WordPress installation if you are the kind of person who doesn't mind dealing with a remote Linux box. The chief reason for this is that you'll be working with what is a de facto standard in blogging that offers you maximum flexibility and independence. If you don't have an IT background or would like to test the waters before committing to something that requires you to rent hosting, then by all means go for a hosted blogging solution. Doing so will be a much easier and friendlier choice that will get you up and blogging in very little time.

In such a case, I recommend Blogger (from Google) due to their somewhat lax policies and because they allow you to associate your own domain name with your Blogger blog for free, as explained in *Using Your Own Domain Name with Blogger*, on page 39. Plus, you'll tap into the existing community around this well-established blogging platform.

Given the technical audience of this book and my recommendation that most committed bloggers opt for a self-hosted WordPress platform, I will provide a lot of guidance for those who have chosen WordPress, both within this and the next chapter.

If you went with an alternative solution like Blogger, however, do *not* skip these two WordPress-heavy chapters. You'll find plenty of useful information about DNS, SEO considerations, sidebar configuration, subscribers, and much more that still fully applies to you!

I've provided hints for Blogger users throughout these two chapters, but it would have been impractical for me to provide detailed instructions for each major blogging platform that exists. If you didn't opt for WordPress (or Blogger), you may have to figure out on your own or look online how—and if—a given feature discussed is available to you. While references to WordPress (and Blogger) may still appear here and there throughout the book, all other chapters will be blog-engine agnostic.

Select a Hosting Service

Unless you opt for a service like Blogger, you need a web hosting provider to run your blog. Hosting offerings exist for all budgets. Favor the bottom rung of the price range ladder while still aiming for quality providers. Spending as little as you can on hosting in the beginning is the key to keep your blogging expenses to a minimum before your blog has proven itself. Various kinds of hybrid and complex hosting arrangements are available from hosting providers, but the spectrum can be roughly divided into the following four types of hosting plans.

- *Shared hosting*: Up to hundreds of sites from many different customers are hosted on the same web server. The hosting provider takes care of managing and maintaining the server, while the customer tends to have limited access to system administration tools and little flexibility in terms of what can be installed on the machine. Often running you only a few dollars a month, shared web hosting is the most inexpensive option.

- *VPS (virtual private server)*: The resources of a powerful server are divided between a handful of customers through virtualization software. Each customer gets their own virtual server running in a virtual machine that uses a proportional share of the physical resources that are available on the host machine. This option is more expensive than shared hosting, but it also provides you with much better and more predictable performance. It can be provided as an *unmanaged* service, in which the customer needs to take care of installing and maintaining the server's software, or as a *managed* service, wherein the staff handles the system administration for you.

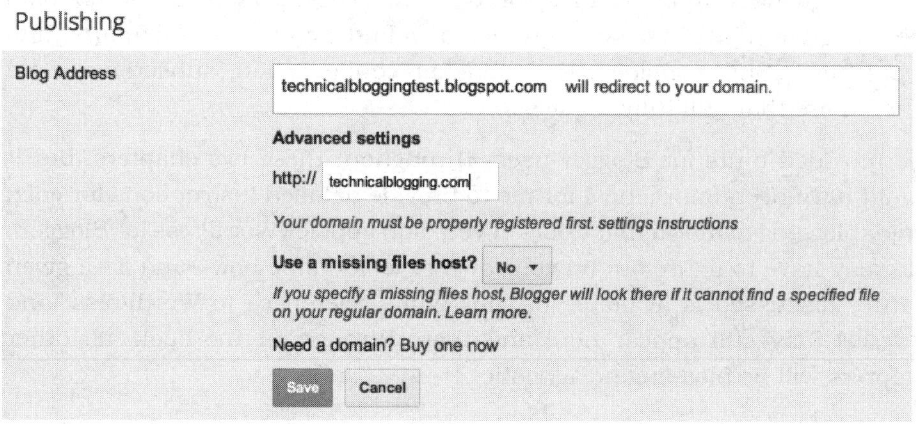

Publishing

Blog Address	technicalbloggingtest.blogspot.com will redirect to your domain.

Advanced settings

http:// technicalblogging.com

Your domain must be properly registered first. settings instructions

Use a missing files host? No ▾

If you specify a missing files host, Blogger will look there if it cannot find a specified file on your regular domain. Learn more.

Need a domain? Buy one now

Save   Cancel

Figure 5—Using a custom domain with Blogger

- *Dedicated servers*: A server is entirely dedicated to you. Just like VPS hosting, dedicated servers come in managed and unmanaged forms, depending on the provider. Some people even go so far as to provide their own machines that are hosted in a local data center as part of a so-called *colocation* arrangement.

- *Cloud computing*: Computing resources are provided and billed based on usage. You could rent three instances (think the equivalent resources of three dedicated servers) an hour and switch back to a single instance an hour later when the traffic spike is gone. The value of cloud computing mainly resides in the ability to easily scale your computing needs without requiring a datacenter investment upfront. The cost scales accordingly with the resources you need.

Unless you already rent web servers and have experience working with them, start with shared hosting. Without a doubt, it's both the most inexpensive and the easiest way to get started with self-hosted blogging. Keep in mind, though, that shared hosting is not as reliable or as fast as the other options, and that you may eventually get kicked out (I was several years ago) if your blog starts experiencing heavy traffic on a daily basis. For the time being, which may be many months, this option should do the trick.

Do your homework when it comes to these kinds of services, and be aware of the many fake reviews posted by some unscrupulous affiliate marketers who are after the hefty commissions hosting companies provide for referrals.

Companies that I have personally used and feel confident in recommending are described in the following paragraphs.

For shared hosting I recommend HostGator or Bluehost.[5] They're inexpensive and generally reliable (even though virtually all shared hosting companies tend to oversell and overcrowd their servers). It's also worth noting the official list of recommended WordPress hosting companies at wordpress.org/hosting.

For unmanaged VPS, Linode is hard to beat.[6] For managed VPS, both ServInt and LiquidWeb are decent choices (albeit fairly expensive ones).[7]

How about dedicated servers? You don't really need to look at these options quite yet; nevertheless, SoftLayer (unmanaged) and again ServInt (managed) are both excellent choices.[8]

Finally, the king of cloud computing is Amazon AWS,[9] with other providers such as Rackspace and SoftLayer also offering popular cloud-based solutions.[10]

An honorable mention goes to companies that specialize in WordPress hosting and provide you with WordPress.com-like simplicity and convenience despite allowing virtually the same degree of flexibility you'll find with self-hosted WordPress.

WP Engine, ZippyKid, and Page.ly are reputable choices,[11] but they offer a premium service that is priced accordingly. If your blog were to become extremely popular, you may also consider the expensive WordPress.com VIP option at vip.wordpress.com.

3.2 Configure Your Domain Name

Regardless of your blogging platform, you need to ensure that the domain name you registered is properly configured. If you are using a hosted service like WordPress.com or Tumblr,[12] simply follow the instructions provided by your vendor. If you are self-hosting WordPress, Jekyll, or different software, pay close attention to the following instructions.

---

5.   hostgator.com and bluehost.com, respectively.

6.   linode.com

7.   servint.net and liquidweb.com, respectively.

8.   softlayer.com

9.   aws.amazon.com

10.   rackspace.com/cloud/

11.   wpengine.com, zippykid.com, and page.ly, respectively.

12.   en.support.wordpress.com/domain-mapping or www.tumblr.com/docs/en/custom_domains, respectively.

Blogging About Controversial Topics

If the subject of your blog is truly controversial in nature, you may need to take extra steps to prevent an overzealous registrar or host from kicking you out. Such companies can't take away your right to freedom of speech, but they are usually able to get rid of you as a customer for violating their own terms of service. I wholeheartedly recommend nearlyfreespeech.net as both your registrar and hosting provider if you feel that a regular provider may take issue with your content.

The majority of tech bloggers don't have to worry about all this, of course, but it's something to keep in mind if you were to engage in legal yet highly controversial topics, such as discussions about security exploits, file sharing, etc.

For a self-hosted blog to be associated with a domain name, you'll need to take two steps: set the DNS (domain name system) servers for the domain, and then add your domain to the appropriate DNS zone.

The first step usually requires you to use the domain registrar's interface to set the nameservers to those of your hosting company (e.g., "ns1.softlayer.com" and "ns2.softlayer.com").

Next, you'll need to use the interface provided by your hosting company (e.g., cPanel, Linode DNS Manager, etc.) to add your domain name or subdomain to their DNS zone. If you declared your domain name during the registration of your hosting account, this step should have already been taken care of for you.

If you're not sure how to go about these two tasks, any reputable domain or hosting company will have instructions on how to accomplish them. If you are truly stuck, feel free to contact the company's customer support folks; they should definitely be able to help you out with the process.

If you prefer, you can also use a hosting-agnostic DNS management service such as DNS Made Easy or DNS Simple.[13] You can set your domain's nameservers to those provided by one of these services and then configure through their interface where the domain should be pointed at any time. These services can simplify, speed up, and centralize your DNS management, particularly if you own multiple sites.

You can always verify if your domain has been properly set up by running the command dig yoursitename.com, which should show you the nameservers as well as the IP your domain points to. The nameservers should be the ones that you just set. Dig is usually available by default on *nix systems. Windows

---

13. dnsmadeeasy.com or dnsimple.com, respectively.

Using Your Own Domain Name with Blogger

Blogger users should opt for a custom domain name instead of the default address they selected at registration (e.g., yourname.blogspot.com).

To do so, head over to Settings > Basic and use the Blog Address section of the page to specify the domain name you intend to use for your blog, as shown in Figure 5, *Using a custom domain with Blogger*, on page 36.

Next, in the DNS section of your domain's registrar control panel, you'll need to set a CNAME record pointing your domain or chosen subdomain (e.g., blog.yourcompany.com) to ghs.google.com.

More detailed setting instructions are provided by Blogger in the Blog Address section, should you encounter any difficulties.

users can either install a version that runs on Windows or use a web version of the tool (search for "web-based dig" to find some).

Note that DNS propagation can take several hours, so if you want to work with your domain name right away, you can edit your local hosts file to have the domain name point to the right IP locally. This change enables you to use your domain name instead of the IP as you configure your self-hosted blog even before the DNS records have become visible to the world. On *nix systems this is usually located at /etc/hosts. For Windows, consult the Wikipedia page at en.wikipedia.org/wiki/Hosts_(file).

In your hosts file, you should include a line that looks like this:

```
174.122.8.30  yoursitename.com
```

Replace the fictitious IP and domain name with your real ones. If you don't know the IP of your server, you should check the emails your hosting company sent you when you registered with them, because it's usually located there. Logging into your hosting account will also typically provide you with this information. If all else fails, just ask your hosting company.

As mentioned earlier, the rest of this chapter will show you how to install and perform a basic configuration of your blog using self-hosted WordPress as the main tool. Tips to guide Blogger users will be provided as well. If you opted for Jekyll, Octopress, TypePad, or any other different blogging platform, the information will still be useful to you. Read on.

3.3   Install WordPress

Blogger and other non-WordPress users: Skip this section.

WordPress can be installed in several ways. I recommend that you install it from scratch because doing so is a quick, straightforward process. Taking this step will allow you to have the newest version from the get-go and then upgrade whenever an update is released.

This isn't the case, however, if you install WordPress through a popular script library installer such as Fantastico, which is common among shared hosting companies. Fantastico simplifies the installation process further, reducing it to a few clicks and the collection of some credentials from you. Unfortunately, Fantastico's version of WordPress tends to be several revisions behind the current version, and this could expose you to security vulnerabilities. So as tempting as it may be, don't install and maintain your WordPress instance via Fantastico.

Requirements

Let's get started by considering what we need in order for the from-scratch installation to work.

LAMP Stack Required

The overwhelming majority of shared hosting companies already provide a compatible LAMP (Linux, Apache, MySQL, PHP) stack (or some variation of it) for you. If you opted for a VPS, dedicated server, or cloud solution, you'll need to ensure that all these components are installed, configured, and working properly.

WordPress requires a recent version of PHP, MySQL, and the mod_rewrite module if you're using Apache as your web server. Requirements rarely change, but you can always find an updated list of them at wordpress.org/about/requirements. Apache and nginx are the recommended web servers, with nginx being significantly faster and less memory hungry than Apache.

Installation

Follow the instructions provided at codex.wordpress.org/Installing_WordPress to install WordPress on your server.

During the installation process you should see a straightforward wizard similar to the one shown in Figure 6, *WordPress's setup wizard*, on page 41.

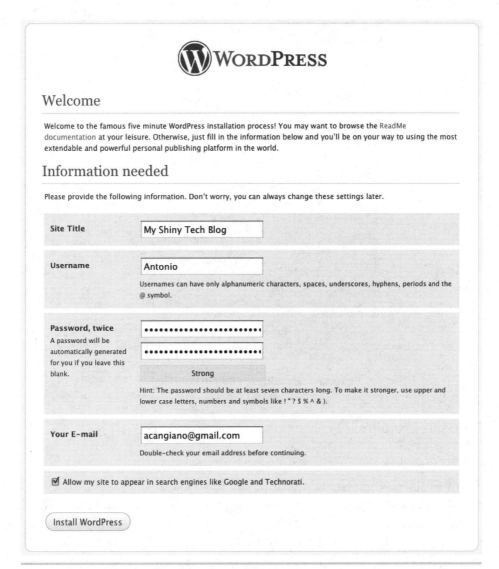

Figure 6—WordPress's setup wizard

Once the setup is complete, do a quick sanity check by logging in at /wp-admin and taking a look around.

Visit the home page as well to see the default look of your newly installed blog. If you don't spot any errors or issues, congratulations on having successfully installed WordPress.

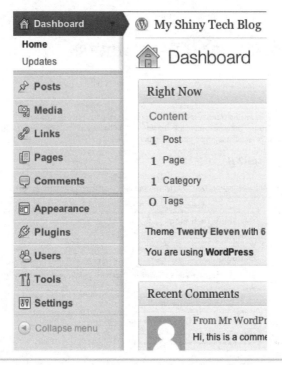

Figure 7—WordPress's admin interface

3.4 Configure WordPress

Blogger and other non-WordPress users: Read this step.

With WordPress correctly installed, it's time for us to start configuring the default installation. Log into your admin section again by appending /wp-admin to the URL of your blog and submitting the credentials for the WordPress account you created during the setup stage.

Once logged in, you should see a series of menu entries in the left sidebar, as shown in Figure 7, *WordPress's admin interface*, on page 42. We'll start from the top and work our way down to the bottom to perform an initial configuration.

Posts Menu

Blogger and other non-WordPress users: Skip this step.

Click the Posts menu in the sidebar. In the main area of the screen you should see a sample "Hello, World!" post that's been created for you. Feel free to play with and edit it, then ultimately delete this sample post from your blog by clicking the Trash link that will appear when you hover over the post title. We want to start with a clean slate. (Note that deleting the sample post will also delete the associated sample comment).

Links Menu

Blogger and other non-WordPress users: Resume reading here (pay particular attention to sidebars).

We can skip the Media menu and click Links instead. As you can see, there's a series of default links grouped in the Blogroll category. Delete the existing links and replace them with your own set if you'd like to link to other relevant sites of yours or of your friends. If you're running a company blog, definitely place your key company links in the blogroll, too. Conversely, if you don't have other sites or friends who blog, feel free to leave the blogroll empty.

In theory, blogrolls are meant to link to other blogs in your niche. The problem with this nice gesture is that your blogroll will typically end up in your sidebar, which in turn is then generally displayed on every single page of your blog. This has SEO consequences that negatively affect your blog while, at the same time, not providing much of a useful service to your readers.

Your home page has a certain authority score that's determined by a Google algorithm known as PageRank (sometimes shortened to PR, not to be confused with the other PR, meaning "press release"). The more people that link to you and the greater their respective PageRank scores, the higher your own score will be. Likewise, every time you link to an external site, you're implicitly telling Google to increase the PageRank of that site because you trust it. As well, albeit to a smaller extent, every time you link to internal pages, you are also increasing the PageRank of those specific pages on your site. You are telling Google that those internal pages are important.

If a given page on your blog links to 10 external sites and 2 internal pages, the PageRank you pass to the internal pages will be greatly reduced due to the presence of the external links. You can think of it as 1/12 each, instead of the half each you'd have if you weren't linking to external sites—even if the real math is actually more complex than that.

There are good reasons to link to other sites in your posts—as we'll see in future chapters—including showing Google that your site is natural and not artificially built in order to score high in the SERP (again, search engine result pages). Nevertheless, think twice before deciding if you want to have a site-wide blogroll. The alternatives of not having one or placing a list of links on a single Links page of your site are both better options in most cases.

Pages Menu

When you click Pages, you'll see a sample page. Delete it. Pages are different from posts. They don't appear in your RSS feed, don't have categories, and can have specific templates applied to them to make them look and behave differently from other pages. They also tend to be linked to from the navigation menu. As such, they should be used for *sticky* information you want people to see (much like forums have sticky posts at the top).

While you're in the Pages tab, go ahead and create an About page. This should contain information about who you are and what your blog is about, and it should definitely include some of the results of the mental exercise we did in the past chapter in regard to why readers should stick around.

If you can, include a photograph of yourself, your office, or your whole team if you're running a team blog (use the icons above the editing area to upload and insert multimedia content). Remember that a picture truly is worth a thousand words, and that it can give a very human and relatable element to your blog.

When putting this page together, your tone should reflect how you want to come across on your site. In general, being friendly, approachable, and thankful with readers for their time and interest in your blog is definitely a safe bet in even the most professional context. Avoid boring, official biographies that are written in the third person (unless for comedic effect).

Don't forget to include information on how you can be reached: include your full name (or pseudonym) and email address. As a successful blogger, you will be approached and pitched to by a variety of people. Among the emails you'll receive from such folks, you will find concrete opportunities, so you don't want to make the task of tracking down your contact information difficult. (Some people have a dedicated Contact page for this purpose).

Users Menu

On this menu, skip Comments, and for the time being let's also bypass Appearance and Plugins (we'll come back to those two later). Click Users (you should see the user account you used to log in), then click the Edit link that appears when you hover on your username. Here you'll be able to fill in more details about yourself. Depending on the blog theme you're using, some of this info may be shown publicly as well, so you may want to pay attention to what you share here. The only option you should really be careful with is Visual Editor. Checking "Disable the visual editor when writing" will remove the WYSIWYG editor when editing posts and leave you with only the HTML

> ### Pages and Blogrolls in Blogger
>
> With Blogger you can create pages from the Pages menu. You can also define a blogroll by adding a Blog List or Link List gadget to the sidebar from within the Layout menu. If you don't see the Layout menu/tab, you may have to switch to the most recent interface that Google offers. The same applies for all other Blogger-related instructions and hints provided within this book.

code editor. (A basic understanding of HTML is expected here.) I like to disable the visual editor because I prefer the control I get from writing HTML code directly.

Switching from Visual to Code view in the editor also has a habit of changing and rearranging your posts' HTML code. This can break the post's code at times. If you wish, start with the visual editor and disable it only if you find its behavior to be problematic.

Finally, ensure that your full name is shown via the "Display name publicly as" option. Even if you are using a pen name for your blog, it's worth including a full name as opposed to "admin" or a nickname. This is a matter of giving the right perception to your readers of standing behind your writing and your blog.

Edit Your Blog's Settings

Skip everything else in the sidebar and jump to Settings. When you click it, you should see General Settings in the main area and a series of submenu items in the sidebar. This is where most of your configuration lives. Let's take a moment to dissect it.

General Settings

In General Settings, you should ensure that the title of the blog is set exactly as you want it to appear. Eliminate the default tagline (i.e., "Just another WordPress site") and define your own in its place. Once again, refer to the exercise you did when we discussed finding the purpose of your blog to help create a good tagline. Your tagline is your motto and should reflect what your blog is all about. Or if nothing else, it should at least be witty or funny.

Change the time zone if necessary, and pick the date and time formats that your target audience is most accustomed to (the default will work for most people).

Blogger Settings

Many of the WordPress settings described within this chapter exist for Blogger as well and are located under the various menus within Settings.

For example, you can define blog authors in Settings > Basic. The author name that appears in your posts will be obtained from the Google account that is associated with your blog.

Look within Settings > Basic and Settings > "Language and formatting" to set your blog title, tagline, and time zone settings.

Settings > "Mobile and email" enables you to define options for posting by email or through a mobile phone, as well as define the email address that should receive a notification when a new comment is posted. Settings > "Posts and comments" allows you define your comment policy as well as the number of posts that should be shown on your home page.

Your feed options are available in Settings > Other. There you'll be able to specify your FeedBurner URL (more on FeedBurner in Chapter 4, *Customizing and Fine-Tuning Your Blog*, on page 55). Also, you can, and should, enable a mobile version of your blog within the Template page.

Finally, your blog's privacy should be set to "Listed on Blogger" in Settings > Basic. This will make it visible to search engines.

Writing Settings

Click the Writing submenu under Settings. Here you can customize a few details that relate to posting. The only sections that are really worth your attention are "Post via e-mail," Remote Publishing, and Update Services.

The first two are useful if you want to publish posts directly by email (I don't generally recommend that you do this, though) or through a client (for example a desktop client like Windows Live Writer for Windows or MarsEdit for Mac). The third one, Update Services, is crucial if you wish to notify a series of so-called *ping services* of your blog's updates. These services will in turn inform search engines of your updates so that your new posts will be indexed quickly. You should see the default rpc.pingomatic.com, which is more than good enough. If you don't see it, you absolutely need to add it for the aforementioned SEO reasons.

Reading Settings

Reading Settings is where you define how many posts you'd like to see featured on your home page and how many of your entries should appear in a new subscriber's feed reader. It's up to you to decide what numbers you'd like to input here. Ten is a healthy compromise that pushes your content without overwhelming new visitors and subscribers. Start with the defaults and remember not to sweat the small stuff.

A much bigger and insidious issue is the debate of full vs. partial feed. An overwhelming majority of people will want a full feed in order to read your articles in Google Reader or in other feed readers of their choice. However, there is also a minority who might be annoyed by the wealth of content you share with them if you opt for full feed. You can't win this one or make everyone happy, so there's no sense in trying. In short, leave every setting in this section as it appears in the defaults.

Discussion Settings

In the Discussion Settings tab, you can customize your commenting policy and notifications entirely. Personally, I like to leave everything set to the defaults, with the following exceptions:

- Uncheck "Anyone posts a comment" and "Comment author must have a previously approved comment" and instead go with "An administrator must always approve the comment." This enables comment moderation, with a single notification given by email when a new comment has been posted and is being held for approval.

- Switch the default avatar to one of the generated choices (Identicon is the most professional-looking, in my opinion). Doing so will help make it more obvious if someone is using sock puppets (i.e., commenting multiple times while pretending to be different people) to amplify a viewpoint with multiple comments in the same thread. It's not foolproof—changing IP via a proxy will change the generated avatar image—but it makes the job a bit harder and it may discourage a few overzealous commenters in the process.

No doubt the most controversial statement in this chapter is my recommendation that you moderate comments. Moderation may slightly lower the overall number of comments you receive and the level of engagement seen in the comments your posts bring in, but doing so has several advantages when dealing with trolls, spammers, and flame wars that can arise from time to time in the comment section of your blog.

If you are ideologically opposed to the idea, simply uncheck the "An administrator must always approve the comment" option and instead check off that you want to be notified when "Anyone posts a comment." This way you'll at least know about new comments that are being posted and can then reply or remove them (if they're not appropriate) afterward.

Enable Akismet Antispam

Akismet is a must-have plugin for dealing with spam unless you are using a third-party commenting system that already includes some form of spam control. The current settings that we have in place now should guarantee that no spam is going to end up on your blog. The problem is that you'll still receive numerous email messages for spam comments that you need to manually reject.

Akimset, which ships with WordPress but is inactive by default, can take care of this for us. Click the Plugins menu item and activate Akismet. Once activated, this plugin will ask you for an API key that can be obtained by signing up at akismet.com.

You may be unsure about which plan is right for you. If your blog is for a small company, you should go for the pro plan. Otherwise, you (large corporations excluded) can safely opt for the free plan and upgrade later if you start making some serious cash from your blog.

This plugin, in conjunction with the actual Akismet service, tends to do a pretty good job. You won't have to sort through thousands of spam comments and trackbacks.

Trackbacks or *pingbacks* are link notifications from other blogs that have mentioned your post. In most themes they appear just above the comment section. They are so widely abused by spammers looking for free links to their sites that many people prefer to disable trackbacks in Discussion Settings. The occasional false positive (genuine comments that are initially seen as spam) or false negative (spam comments that reach your inbox for approval) will still crop up with Akismet, but using this service will make your life so much easier.

Alternatively, some bloggers have shown a preference for Defensio over Akismet due to the presence of more advanced features such as a profanity filter.[14]

Alternative Commenting Systems

Over the past few years, a new breed of alternative commenting system has been emerging. The basic idea behind it is that you can embed a new comment system in place of the standard one. These commenting systems tend to have some bells and whistles that make them attractive, such as the ability for your readers to log in via Twitter or Facebook before leaving a comment as well as good built-in spam control. Their popularity also implies that many

---

14. defensio.com

users, particularly technical ones, will already have an account with the major players in this field. If they don't, they can register at one blog that uses them and reuse that account on any other blog that uses the same system.

Three popular options are Disqus, IntenseDebate, and more recently, Facebook Comments.[15] Facebook, in particular, is ubiquitous with users, be they technical or not, and would in theory make for an excellent choice. In fact, it even won over the popular blog TechCrunch, despite the less-than-enthusiastic reaction from some commenters (Facebook isn't exactly loved by everyone).

Facebook Comments are automatically arranged by popularity (i.e., the number of "Likes") and also enable you to see the real names of most of your commenters. If they're logged into Facebook when commenting on your blog, users' comments will be automatically associated with their Facebook profiles.

When people comment with their real name, they tend to be a lot more civil and careful in what they say. Unless commenters uncheck the option to do so, their comments on your post will also appear on their friends' News Feeds, along with a link back to your article, further spreading your post via the popular social network.

However, three negative aspects need to be considered before uploading and activating a plugin for an alternative commenting system such as Facebook's:

- Dynamically loading the content from a third-party site tends to significantly slow down your pages' loading time. This has a negative impact from both a UX and an SEO standpoint.

- Third-party commenting systems are usually not "crawlable" by search engines. Their content will not be indexed, so you may miss out on showing up in the SERP for quite a few keywords that were organically included in the comment section by your commenters. (Some new plugins are emerging, such as Crawlable Facebook Comments, that try to counteract this problem).

- A third party will own your comments. Should this party change its policies or go out of business, you may or may not be able to revert back to the regular built-in WordPress comment system without data loss. As usual when dealing with third parties, there is a risk for vendor lock-in, so ensure that you carefully read the conditions and export options before committing.

---

15. disqus.com, intensedebate.com, and developers.facebook.com/docs/reference/plugins/comments, respectively.

If you want to switch to Facebook Comments, I recommend Facebook Comments for WordPress. You'll find it, along with other alternative plugins, by searching for Facebook Comments in the Plugin directory located at word-press.org/extend/plugins or by clicking the "Add new" button after entering the Plugins area of your admin section.

Privacy Settings

Skip or customize Media as you wish (its defaults are generally fine), and click Privacy instead.

You unequivocally want to keep the "I would like my site to be visible to everyone, including search engines (such as Google, Bing, Technorati) and archivers" option selected. Without it, your blog will miss out on search engine traffic. This option is selected by default, so unless you unchecked it during the WordPress setup process, you should be safe.

Permalinks Settings

Click Permalinks and you'll be presented with Permalinks Settings. What we'll change in this section is going to be absolutely crucial from an SEO standpoint, so do not skip this important step.

The term *permalink* is used to indicate the permanent URL of your posts. By default, WordPress will generate permalinks that have the following structure: http://yoursitename.com/?p=ID, where ID is the numeric identifier of your post. The problem with this URL structure is that search engines give a great deal of weight to the content of your URL.

For example, if a user is searching for "CoffeeScript tips" in Google, a post with a permalink including /ten-coffeescript-tips will appear highly relevant to the user's query. In fact, it contains the target keywords and little else. If the post was to be located at /?p=42, Google would determine your post's relevance based solely on other factors, such as content and incoming links.

Regardless of your permalink structure, search engines will use plenty of other indicators to figure out the relevance and authority of your pages. It just so happens that the keyword density of your URLs is very important, so leaving this out would be foolish. (The portion of the permalink that comes after the domain name is also known as the *slug*.)

Plenty of blogs, even commercial ones, make this mistake. Since it's such low-hanging fruit, change the permalink structure right away. To do so, you can select "Day and name" or "Month and name" or opt for a custom structure such as /%postname%/. These will create permalinks that include the title of your post in the URL.

Most SEO experts would opt for the last choice. Doing so has the advantage of increasing the density of the keywords (by removing unnecessary date-related characters). It also makes the URL shorter and can positively impact the perception of your content by sneakily hiding the date of your old content.

Go for the /%postname%/ slug, which is nice-looking and SEO-friendly. Just ensure that your theme takes care of showing the date and time of your posts and therefore doesn't trick your users into thinking that obsolete content is actually more recent material.

When you click Save Changes, WordPress will update your .htaccess file if the web server has write permissions on the file to do so and you're using Apache. If WordPress is unable to write to the file, you'll be advised to manually copy a snippet of code for mod_rewrite into your .htaccess file yourself. Keep in mind that .htaccess is a hidden file on *nix systems such as Linux and Mac OS X, so it may not show up in your FTP program unless you show hidden files. (Cyberduck and FileZilla are good FTP clients you can use for free.)

Finally, .htaccess is not required if you're using nginx.

3.5 Enhance WordPress with Plugins

Blogger users: Skip this section.

There are a myriad of plugins available for self-hosted WordPress blogs that can be found at wordpress.org/extend/plugins or by searching through the Plugins menu.

Install Plugins

To install plugins, you can download, unzip, and upload them to your wp-content/plugins folder on the server, then activate them in the Plugins section of your WordPress administrative interface.

Alternatively, if your web server has write access to the wp-content/plugins folder, you can install them by following these simple steps:

1. Click the Plugins menu, then the "Add new" button or submenu link. There you can search for plugins by term, as shown in Figure 8, *Adding plugins via WordPress*, on page 53.

Steps Not Needed for Blogger

As you read through the WordPress instructions, you'll find plenty of information that's universally valid, regardless of your blogging platform of choice. However, there are a few suggestions that do not apply to Blogger users.

- You can ignore update/ping services because such features are built into Blogger.

- Blogger comes with a built-in spam filtering system. You don't need any external service such as Akismet.

- You can't use a third-party commenting system. Thankfully the built-in commenting system is excellent and integrates with visitors' Google, LiveJournal, WordPress.com, TypePad, Open ID, and other accounts.

- Permalinks are SEO-friendly in Blogger by default.

- You are not able to, nor do you need to, install any of the other WordPress plugins listed in this and the next chapter. This includes SEO, caching, and security plugins mentioned later on. If you want to see how extensible your platform is, you can check out the list of gadgets in the Layout menu area.

2. Click Install Now under the name of the desired plugin to install it. Once the installation is complete, you'll be offered an Activate Plugin link that will enable you to actually activate the plugin.

Most plugins add their own menu entry in the admin section so that you can configure their specific options, if applicable.

Tip 7

Only install plugins that you strictly need.

Recommended Plugins

The following is a list of plugins I commonly use for my blogs. You should consider installing most of them, but feel free to skip those that are not of interest to you. You can find each one by simply searching for it in the aforementioned Plugin directory.

- *Jetpack*: A collection of features extracted from WordPress.com with the intent of providing the same functionality to self-hosted WordPress blogs. It includes in an ever-expanding list statistics, Twitter widgets, the WP.me

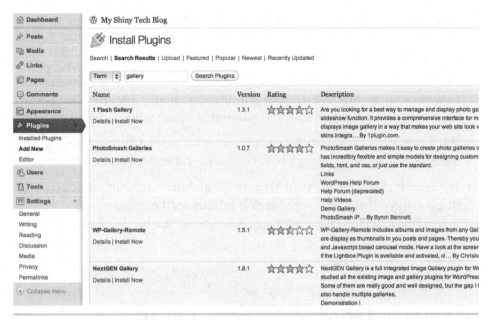

Figure 8—Adding plugins via WordPress

URL shortener for social media sharing, LaTeX support to embed mathe-matical formulas,[16] an excellent spell checker known as "After the Dead-line," and more. You'll be asked to register a WordPress.com account to enable all these features (doing so doesn't imply that you have to blog at WordPress.com though).

- *Platinum SEO pack*: An essential plugin for onpage SEO optimization. Install it now, and we'll configure it in Chapter 4, *Customizing and Fine-Tuning Your Blog*, on page 55. (Note, however, that you won't need this plugin if you installed a premium theme with built-in SEO options.)

- *Google XML sitemaps*: Creates and keeps an updated XML sitemap that aids Google in discovering and indexing every nook and cranny of your blog.

- *PuSHPress*: This plugin is used to enable PuSH notifications for your post updates. In my experience, it has the advantage of helping to get your content indexed quickly by search engines. You can read more about PuSH on the home page of the protocol at code.google.com/p/pubsubhubbub, if you are curious.

---

16. en.support.wordpress.com/latex

- *WPtouch*: Presents your content in a mobile-friendly way for your visitors who use smartphone devices (it's not just for iPhone and iPod Touch users, as the name may imply).

- *Contact Form 7*: Easily create contact forms within pages without having to write a single line of PHP yourself. If you install it, include the associated CAPTCHA plugin to limit the amount of spam you receive from bots.

- *WP Authors*: Creates a widget containing a list of blog authors, which can then be displayed in the sidebar. Useful for collective blogs.

- *WP Security Scan*: Scans your WordPress installation for possible security threats. (If your site gets popular and profitable, it may be worth investing in a premium malware monitoring and removal service, such as Sucuri.[17])

> **Tip 8**
>
> ## Promptly update WordPress and outdated plugins.

Please note that this is not a complete list of all the plugins you may need. It's a starting point, upon which we'll build as the need arises. For example, in the next chapter we'll discuss other plugins, including W3 Total Cache, an excellent caching suite that will speed up your WordPress blog immensely.

3.6 What's Next

We covered a lot of ground in this chapter, from platform and hosting choices all the way to a basic configuration of your blog.

In the next chapter we'll take things a step further by fine-tuning the blog to optimize its behavior and speed.

After the next chapter, we'll promptly head towards discussing content, which is, after all, the real reason your readers would want to visit your blog.

---

17. sucuri.net

Visualize this thing that you want. See it, feel it, believe in it. Make your mental blueprint, and begin to build.

> ➤ *Robert Collier*

CHAPTER 4

Customizing and Fine-Tuning Your Blog

By following the instructions in the previous chapters, you should have a well-configured, basic installation of WordPress or a roughly equivalent setup for the platform of your choice.

In this chapter, you'll step it up to the next level by fine-tuning and customizing your new blog so that it's less bare-boned. You'll take your basic blog and turn it into a full-fledged publication platform that's carefully tailored to your needs and goals.

4.1 Pick a Professional Theme

The default WordPress look is clean and minimalist. Depending on your aesthetic preferences, you may like that look a lot. But it would be a mistake to settle for this default theme for three reasons:

1. Most new blogs use the default theme. Sticking with it won't help your blog stand out from the crowd.

2. Visitors value eye candy. Beautiful design will greatly help your blog succeed.

3. The default theme has very limited features and customization options.

Spend some time evaluating other themes until you find one that fits your style and the type of blog you intend to run. If you're running a team blog that will be updated on a daily basis, for example, a magazine- or even newspaper-style theme may be a good idea.

Free themes can be found at wordpress.org/extend/themes and on other sites around the Web. I generally don't recommend that you opt for a free theme unless your budget is extremely tight. Premium themes that you purchase offer the following advantages:

- There is an economic incentive for the developers to keep the themes up-to-date for the latest version of WordPress. Such themes are also generally updated and improved over time.

- Purchased themes tend to offer all sorts of options and features that are not available with the average free theme, given that premium themes have to justify their price tag. Some include a full-fledged framework built on top of WordPress, which greatly extends its capabilities.

- They don't require you to advertise that you're using a free theme and credit the designer in the footer (which then appears on every single page of your blog) or include affiliate links to dubious sponsors. Now, not all free themes are like that, but you'll find not having to worry about such conditions quite refreshing.

Buying a feature-rich, well-designed theme is a wise investment that won't cost you much (generally less than $100). Common premium themes are available from WooThemes, StudioPress (whose themes are built on top of its Genesis framework), and Elegant Themes.[1] Other good providers can be found at wordpress.org/extend/themes/commercial.

Tip 9

Ensure your font size is large enough to be read comfortably.

Take the time to get to know your theme and read its documentation, if available. Common perks of premium themes include the ability to feature posts, display the home page as a newspaper with clickable summaries and icons rather than as the full posts, and many other appealing features. If you can't afford to or don't want to commit funds to the project quite yet, you will certainly find a free theme that you'll like and be able to customize yourself, though.

If you are creating this blog for a company, you don't have to mimic the look of your main site and integrate your blog with the company site 100 percent. If you wish, you can make the blog a visually separate entity with a slightly different look and a greater degree of editorial freedom. An example of this approach can be seen at spittoon.23andme.com.

---

1.   woothemes.com, studiopress.com/themes, and elegantthemes.com, respectively.

Tip 10

Prominently link to your company site from your blog.

Given that company budgets (even startup ones) are usually larger than what your typical solo bloggers have at their disposal, you may even consider having a designer create a custom theme and logo for your company blog. Another appealing option for those on a tighter budget is to heavily personalize one of the premium themes. They generally offer a great degree of control over their look and feel. And a relatively inexpensive logo can be commissioned on sites such as 99designs.[2]

4.2 Enable Tracking of Your Site's Visitors

Being able to understand who your visitors are and what they do when they arrive on your site is a fundamental part of running a successful blog. To accomplish this goal, we'll need to set up a traffic analytics suite. In Chapter 8, *Understanding Traffic Statistics*, on page 145, we'll discuss how to analyze the data you collect in greater detail, but for now let's start by choosing and installing one traffic analysis tool.

A multitude of traffic analysis tools have been created over the years. Some work by analyzing your web server logs, while others avail themselves of a JavaScript tracker that you must embed in each page of your site. I strongly recommend that you opt for the latter.

Third-party web-based analytics will in fact keep track of your traffic stats for years to come and will not be impacted by or require further maintenance if you were to move your blog to a different server. More importantly, the most prominent hosted analytics suites tend to be very sophisticated and can provide you with highly customized reports.

In particular, you should consider the following three analytics services, all of which are widely used.

---

2.   99designs.com

Customizing Blogger's Look and Feel

If you are using Blogger, you can select a variety of themes from the Template menu. This page also allows you to visually customize the template of your choice through a template designer.

If you require further flexibility, you can use HTML and CSS to edit the template directly. For example, the navigation bar at the top can be hidden via CSS. This doesn't violate Google's terms of service (contrary to popular belief).

You can even embed JavaScript into your template, which means that you can then add third-party tracking. (Essential traffic statistics are included by default within the Stats menu.)

Finally, you can edit your sidebar from the Layout page by adding and removing gadgets. Using the Follow by Email gadget, you can easily embed the FeedBurner newsletter signup form in your sidebar.

Google Analytics

Regardless of what other traffic suites you decide to install, you really should use Google Analytics,[3] which has become the de facto standard. It's free and extremely rich in features (entire books have been written about it). It also integrates well with Google's other services, such as Google AdWords, which is great for keeping track of your return on investment if you ever need to run ads for any of your products.

Google Analytics makes it easy to share statistics with colleagues or prospective buyers as well. This is particularly useful for team sites or as proof of your traffic claims if you ever decide to sell your blog.

Once you've signed up for the service, you'll be provided with a snippet of JavaScript that needs to be embedded in your pages. That's the individual tracking code that identifies the collected data and associates it with your personal Analytics account. The quick and easy way to accomplish this is to install a specific plugin that adds Google Analytics for you (e.g., Analytics360).

If you'd prefer not to install yet another plugin for such a small task, you'll need to edit the footer of your blog. Some WordPress themes, particularly premium ones, offer the ability to enter footer or analytics code that will be dynamically added at the bottom of each page. If that's the case for your theme, definitely add your tracking code there.

---

3.   www.google.com/analytics

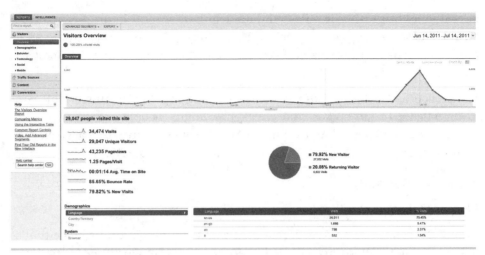

Figure 9—Key metrics in Google Analytics

Finally, you have the option of editing your theme directly through a text editor. The file that you need to modify is wp-content/themes/yourtheme/footer.php (replace yourtheme with the actual folder for your theme). Place the code Google provided just above the closing body tag.

```
<!-- Google Analytics -->
<script type="text/javascript">

var _gaq = _gaq || [];
_gaq.push(['_setAccount', 'UA-XXXXXX-1']);
_gaq.push(['_trackPageview']);

... more code ...

</script>

</body>
</html>
```

(Of course, this is only an example. Use the tracking code that Google Analytics provided you with.)

Once the tracking code is installed, load your blog's home page once, then double-check its status in Google Analytics. If it's been properly installed, you should receive a message along the lines of "Waiting for data," or a "tracking code not installed" error if it hasn't been.

Google Analytics is an amazing tool for Internet marketers and bloggers. Historically, the only down side has been that your statistics didn't appear in real time, but rather it reflected data acquired several hours before. This meant that very often you weren't able to study a spike in blog traffic as it was actually happening. Instead you had to settle for a postmortem analysis a few hours later.

More recently, Google introduced some real-time capabilities that enable you to investigate traffic spikes and check how many people are on your site during a given moment.[4] An example of the Google Analytics interface can be seen in Figure 9, *Key metrics in Google Analytics*, on page 59.

WordPress.com Stats

Blogger and other non-WordPress users: Skip this section.

Unlike Google Analytics, WordPress.com Stats is a plugin and service that's only available for WordPress blogs (it can be hosted by WordPress.com itself or be self-hosted). It's a free service; however, it requires an API key, which can be obtained by registering at WordPress.com.

If you've installed and activated the JetPack plugin in the previous chapter, you should already have this feature ready and available to you as Site Stats in the admin menu (after having configured your API key, of course). Alternatively, you can still install the plugin on its own and forgo the rest of JetPack. This applies at the time of writing; in the future, though, you might not be able to do so anymore.

WordPress statistics give you a nice snapshot of where your traffic is coming from, what search engine keywords lead people to find to your site, and which of your articles and pages are popular at the moment. Unfortunately, the simple interface offers little else. It's also limited in practice, showing these metrics for only the past few days.

I've found the interface (shown in Figure 10, *WordPress Stats*, on page 61) to be somewhat slow as well, at least when you start receiving many hundreds or thousands of pageviews per day.

Despite its evident shortcomings, you may still want to install it when you wish to quickly glance at incoming traffic in a way that's faster than logging in and checking Google Analytics.

---

4.   analytics.blogspot.com/2011/09/whats-happening-on-your-site-right-now.html

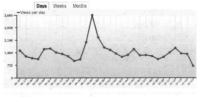

Figure 10—WordPress Stats

Clicky

Blogger and other non-WordPress users: Resume reading here.

Clicky is an excellent real-time web analytics suite.[5] It offers many of the same features as Google Analytics while having the advantage of being able to show you data for visitors who arrived on your site mere seconds ago. (At this stage, its real-time capabilities are far more advanced than those offered by Google.)

Clicky also includes many unique features that are not available with Google Analytics, as shown in their comparison page at getclicky.com/#theotherguys. One of my favorite premium features is called Spy. It allows you to see details of who is currently on your site, as shown in Figure 11, *Clicky Spy*, on page 62. I find Clicky to be invaluable for determining what's causing a current traffic spike.

As a user of the Chrome browser, I also enjoy using its Clicky Monitor extension,[6] which allows me to quickly check on my sites' stats without typing anything. The number on the Clicky icon acts as an in-browser traffic notifier,

---

5.　getclicky.com
6.　bit.ly/clicky-extension

Figure 11—Clicky Spy

showing the concurrent number of visitors on the currently selected site (if you have more than one configured). From time to time, I glance at it, and if I see a particularly large number, I investigate the spike.

Support for more platforms, including apps for iOS and Android can be found in the Apps & Plugins page at getclicky.com/user/#/help/apps-plugins.

Clicky is inexpensive, but it is a premium service. Its free plan lacks a number of premium features and is currently limited to recording just the first three thousand pageviews per day. Still, the real-time nature of the stats that are available for free subscribers may make it worth signing up for, even if you don't want to pay for the premium plans. (Expenses can add up. Opt for free subscription plans and only upgrade to paid versions when strictly needed.)

Installing Clicky on your blog is very similar to the procedure for including Google Analytics. After you've signed up and set up your site at getclicky.com, either obtain and install a dedicated plugin (e.g., Clicky by Yoast) or edit your footer to include the tracking code.

If you want to use both Google Analytics and Clicky, like I do, simply place Clicky's tracking code above that of Google Analytics.

As with Google Analytics, we'll explore how to get the best from Clicky in Chapter 8, *Understanding Traffic Statistics*, on page 145. For the time being, feel free to explore the suite on your own.

So which of the three should you install? You really need to have Google Analytics, so the choice of a second option is between WordPress.com Stats and Clicky. Installing both isn't a problem, but if I had to pick just one, I'd go with Clicky. Its insight into your visitors' browsing behavior and large list of unique features make it a perfect real-time complement to Google Analytics.

4.3 Customize Your Sidebar

Your main sidebar is a crucial component of your blog. In fact it will be shown prominently on virtually every page of your blog. Its position, usually on the right of your article's content, makes it prime blog real estate that should be allocated wisely.

As you learn more from this book and gather real-world experience as a blogger, you can revisit your sidebar to customize its contents however you like.

What Should You Include in Your Sidebar?

Your sidebar, particularly the area above the fold at common screen resolutions, should include your "calls to action." Think about the most important goals you have and what you want your visitors to do, and then adapt the sidebar accordingly. For example, if your priority is to increase your pageviews and engage your readers more, you could add a list of recent posts and mention the top commenter toward the top of your sidebar.

In the beginning you shouldn't be overly concerned with making money from your blog; your main challenge is attracting readers. But let's just say that at some point your primary goal will shift to or focus more on "monetizing" (i.e., making money via) your blog. In that case, your sidebar should become a spot where you also advertise whatever you're selling, be it your own product, someone else's product through an affiliate link, sponsorship, ads, or anything else you're comfortable with being paid to promote on your blog.

As an example, take a look at the annotated sidebar of my programming blog, as shown in Figure 12, *ProgrammingZen.com's sidebar*, on page 64. Many people might argue that it's way too commercial. They may be right, I admit, but like most things in life, it's a trade-off. At the risk of putting some readers off, my blog is able to generate a lot of revenue relative to its traffic. Just don't try this at home with a relatively new blog that isn't well established.

Feed

Sponsors

Social

Affiliate Links

Ad Unit

Figure 12—ProgrammingZen.com's sidebar

Regardless of your main goals, you want to give the utmost priority to your subscription options, such as your RSS/Atom feed and newsletter (more on newsletters in a moment). You should also include a one-paragraph blurb about you and your blog that links to your main About page. Include a small-sized, nice portrait of you (unless you're running a team or company blog).

Further down on the sidebar, you should also include your categories, tags (called *labels* on Blogger), recent posts, social media widgets that invite people to like or follow you, and so on. Keep in mind that the further down the sidebar an element is, the less visibility it will generally attract.

If your theme doesn't include a search box at the top, make sure you add one toward the top of your sidebar. Likewise, if your pages, categories, or other important elements are not available elsewhere in the theme, ensure that you add them to the sidebar.

Sidebars and Heatmaps

Heatmaps are a tool that's used to understand where users focus their attention on a given page. A service such as crazyegg.com makes it easy to experiment and adjust elements on a theme or specific page so as to ensure that users are focusing on the things you want them to. When you try it on your own blog, you'll quickly see how the top of your page and the sidebar tend to be attention grabbers.

As discussed, the sidebar is certainly a tool for getting users to subscribe, explore your site more, and take the kinds of actions that you'd like them to. Let's not forget, however, that the sidebar is mainly a useful tool for your visitors. Below the commercial stuff in my sidebar, for example, I include a disclaimer, recent posts, recent comments, categories, and so on. Don't get so caught up in creating a self-serving sidebar that you forget to list purely useful stuff, too.

While you begin to think about which widgets you'd like to display in such a prominent spot, let's take a look at how to actually add them to your sidebar.

How to Edit Your Sidebar

To edit your sidebar, head over to the Widgets link under the Appearance menu inside your WordPress administrative section. You should see a scene similar to the one shown in Figure 13, *WordPress widgets*, on page 66.

All you have to do is drag and drop widgets that are available or inactive onto the main sidebar on the right side. Each widget may have configuration options that will be presented to you. For example, the Categories widget will ask you to name the resulting div section in your sidebar (typically Categories or Topics), as well as other options, such as whether you wish to display the post count for each category.

The most flexible widget is Text. This widget enables you to enter arbitrary HTML in the sidebar without having to edit the sidebar.php file from within your theme folder. Depending on what your chosen theme already includes, a sample starter configuration for your sidebar, using only default widgets, may resemble the stack shown in Figure 14, *A sample sidebar layout*, on page 67. The Text widget toward the top would typically include HTML code that invites visitors to subscribe to your blog.

If the sidebar is for a company blog, remember to include a link (or linked logo) to your main site or product.

Figure 13—WordPress widgets

4.4 Encourage Social Media Sharing

One of the quickest ways to market your content is to have your readers do the marketing for you. If all the readers who find your content useful were to share your site with their friends online, you'd quickly have more traffic than you could handle.

In practice, very few readers bother sharing your articles even if they found them to be exceptional. Depending on how explicit you are with your request and how much you solicit social media sharing, you'll likely only receive a few mentions from other people.

For example, my article "The need for good vocational schools for programmers" that I published on ProgrammingZen.com has received 10,933 visits to date. According to Topsy,[7] it received 47 retweets. Facebook reports 85 likes. If you do the math, you'll quickly realize that only 1.20 percent of my visitors actually bothered sharing the article either on Twitter or on Facebook.

That's OK. It's still worth it, as these mentions are essentially free publicity that help get your signal out there further, where it may be picked up by popular social media users, fellow bloggers, or perhaps even journalists.

---

7. topsy.com

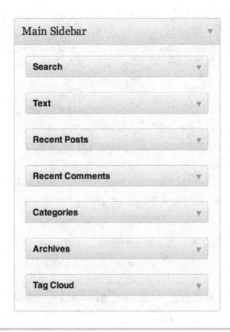

Figure 14—A sample sidebar layout

Facebook, Twitter, and Google +1 Counters

If you read many blogs, you may have seen people showcasing more than a dozen social media icons at the bottom of their posts. Don't bother doing this. In my experience, these icon buttons are a waste of time, as almost no one actually clicks them. It's the paradox of choice at work. If you ask me to take one, two, or a maximum of three actions, I may do so. If you offer me fifteen options, I might not know which one to take and I'll feel less obliged to do anything at all.

If you want to provide these buttons as a service to your readers, you can use compact widgets from sites such as AddThis or ShareThis.[8]

I would suggest that you start by including Facebook Like, Twitter, and Google +1 buttons in your articles via AddThis. These buttons have the advantage of providing social proof,[9] because they show a counter of how many people have already shared your post with their friends.

---

8.   addthis.com or sharethis.com, respectively.

9.   en.wikipedia.org/wiki/Social_proof

Social Toolbars in Blogger

By default, Blogger already provides you with a social toolbar that includes Facebook, Twitter, and Google +1 among others. You also have the Addthis Sharing gadget at your disposal.

On the flip side, if you are struggling to attract traffic, they may unintentionally end up providing negative social proof (of how few fans you have) and in turn tell new visitors that nobody is reading and sharing your content. That said, you need to start somewhere, and if you don't include these buttons (perhaps without a counter at first), you certainly stand to have fewer people sharing your work around the Web.

Contrary to common belief, you'll receive relatively little traffic from social networking sites like Facebook, Twitter, and Google+. In the example about my article, less than two hundred people came from Facebook, Twitter, and Google+ combined. We'll delve further into the reasons for this in Chapter 7, *Promoting Your Blog*, on page 119.

To make matters worse, in the past I've had Twitter superusers who have more than 150,000 followers retweet my articles to their followers, only to see just a few hundred visitors head over to my site as a result of this nice mention.

Why bother then? Aside from the argument that every little bit adds up, there is increasing evidence that search engines are going to consider more and more social indicators in their strategy to evaluate the importance and relevance of content (e.g., a link liked by a friend of yours is more likely to interest you than one that isn't).

To install these buttons, you can embed the code provided by their respective sites or simply install AddThis (also available as a plugin for several platforms, including WordPress). For WordPress, you can also enable the sharing feature that's available in the JetPack plugin.

Reddit and Hacker News

For technical blogs, there are two large communities for which it may be worth having sharing buttons. They are Reddit, with its extensive list of subcommunities known as subreddits, and Hacker News.

In the previous section I mentioned how less than two hundred visits to one of my recent articles came from Facebook, Twitter, and Google+ combined. What I didn't tell you though, was that more than seven thousand people showed up from Reddit, specifically the Programming subreddit. Likewise, Hacker News brought close to one thousand visitors to the article, despite the fact that my post didn't get particularly popular on that site or make it to the home page as a popular story.

If your site is about programming, you should consider both Reddit and Hacker News buttons. If it's more business or startup oriented, then Hacker News alone may be more appropriate.

Just find a fine line (between too few and too many icons), and focus on the buttons that you care the most about. Don't try to include too many, or their CTR (click-through rate) will quickly approach zero.

4.5 Win Over Subscribers

When your blog is starting out, your sole goal should be to attract new subscribers. Translating these regular readers into dollars or into the other benefits you may be after is something that you can concern yourself with once your site is already established and has been running for a few months.

In the beginning, your goal is to increase your subscriber count. Sure, other metrics such as visitors, pageviews, time on the site, and bounce rate are all interesting and important in their own way, but nothing beats subscribers as an indicator of growth (and that you are doing this whole blogging thing right). If your subscriber count isn't growing, your blog is not living up to its full potential.

By subscribers, I mean readers that follow your blog via feed or receive your posts via email. Before discussing how to win over new subscribers, we'll need a system that allows us to measure how many readers you have. That system is FeedBurner by Google.

Set Up FeedBurner

Note: At the time of this writing, FeedBurner has a new beta version. Unfortunately, it does not currently allow you to do much. You can't, for example, create a new feed. For this reason, I provide instructions in this section that are specific to the current, non-beta version. If the interface is different by the time you read this section, you may have to adapt the instructions and find the described features within the new user interface.

FeedBurner is a service that allows you to specify a feed and then provides you with a different feed URL that has analytics capabilities baked right in. Head over to feedburner.google.com and log in with your Google account. You'll be asked to burn a feed by providing the URL of your site or its feed (by default http://yoursitename.com/feed for WordPress blogs).

If you receive an error such as "Received HTTP error: 'Not Found' while fetching source feed," it's because you've either provided the wrong feed URL or do not have any posts yet. Creating a Welcome post in which you highlight what your blog is going to be about, as well as a little blurb about yourself, will take care of this issue.

Once your feed has been added successfully, FeedBurner will ask you to choose a feed title and address. You should use the name of your blog for the title and define a related address. For example, the feed title may be "Coffee-Script Tips" and the address "coffeescripttips." Your FeedBurner feed will then be available at feeds.feedburner.com/coffeescripttips.

This is the feed URL you must share from now on, not the old default one (i.e. "/feed"), to ensure that all your subscribers are accounted for in Feed-Burner's statistics. In the next screen of the setup, select all the options except for enclosure downloads (unless you are creating a podcast).

Once you are done with the setup, you will be redirected to a page where you'll be congratulated on your new feed and presented with a series of options for blogging engines. For WordPress, you'll be instructed to download a FeedBurner FeedSmith plugin. Follow the instructions that are provided for WordPress so that traffic to your preexisting feed will be redirected to your new FeedBurner one.

Keep in mind that some WordPress themes, such as the ones based on the Genesis framework by StudioPress, don't require FeedBurner FeedSmith because they allow you to specify your FeedBurner ID within the settings for the theme.

You'll also want to customize your feed further by making the following changes from within the FeedBurner interface.

- In the Optimize tab, enable SmartFeed to maximize compatibility.

- Within the same tab, also enable FeedFlare to include options such as "Email this," "Save to del.icio.us," "Share on Facebook," and so on. These will appear at the bottom of your articles in your subscribers' feeds (or at the bottom of emails for email subscribers).

- Under Publicize, consider clicking Headline Animator to obtain a snippet of code that you can insert in your personal email signature to promote your latest posts in rotation.

- Activate PingShot, FeedCount, and Awareness API.

- Leave Email Subscriptions and Chicklet Chooser alone for the time being, as we'll be discussing them further in the coming sections.

You Need a Newsletter

Now that you have your feed taken care of (thanks to FeedBurner), it's time to discuss newsletters. A portion of your readers will want to follow your blog via email rather than a feed reader like Google Reader. It's imperative that you provide a post-to-email service for those who wish to subscribe via email.

Before you think, as most web savvy people tend to, that this is a legacy service you just offer for old-fashioned people, allow me to let you in on a secret: newsletters are the most powerful tool an Internet marketer can have. Nothing else even comes close. The most valuable visitor you can have is the one who subscribes to your site via email.

The reason for this is that the relationship you have with email readers, unlike feed readers, is an intimate one. There is an unwritten contract that people will read most—or all—of the messages that they receive in their inbox. The implicit contract is weaker when it comes to newsletters, but you are still in their inboxes every time you publish a new post, and that's a very powerful advantage.

In my experience, the number of people who will open your newsletter will only be a small percentage of the total subscribers—about 5–50 percent (more if you have an exceptional following). However small that number may sound, it still tends to be higher, percentage-wise, than the actual reach of your feed.

You have two main options when it comes to setting up an RSS-to-email newsletter. You can handle the newsletter yourself through a third-party newsletter management service such as MailChimp or Aweber,[10] or you can let FeedBurner take care of it for you.

The advantage of FeedBurner is that it handles everything automatically for you. Once enabled through the Email Subscriptions link in the Publicize tab, all you really have to do is embed the Subscription Form Code provided by FeedBurner somewhere in your blog. Google will take care of everything, including forwarding your posts automatically and providing a physical address in order to be compliant with current bulk email regulations (i.e., the CAN-SPAM act).

---

10. mailchimp.com or aweber.com, respectively.

The main disadvantage is that the interactions with your list are limited to what you post in your blog. You can't really send messages out just for those on your list, contact subscribers with *autoresponders* (messages sent at set intervals after a user signs up), customize emails with users' names, or add all sorts of other nice touches that are often used by email marketers. In other words, it's extremely easy to set up and does what it's supposed to do, but it does little else.

If you choose to go with a service like MailChimp or Aweber, you'll generally have to pay for it, but you'll have full control. (Technically MailChimp is currently free up to two thousand subscribers.)

The main steps to emulate what you get with FeedBurner via email would be to create a list and then an RSS feed-to-email campaign with these email providers. You'll need to customize the look of your messages and your signup forms and then embed one on your site. You'll also have to provide your own address or rent a PO box to respect the CAN-SPAM act. (Funny name for antispam legislation, isn't it?)

It's worth noting that you could technically export email addresses from FeedBurner and then import them via MailChimp at some point, but doing so is a delicate operation that must be handled very carefully due to the high probability of spam reports and complaints by users who may see your new newsletter as something they didn't technically sign up for. (And some email providers won't allow the procedure at all because of this).

Which of the two is right for you? If you don't mind spending some time setting it all up and the primary intent of your blog is commercial, go with a service like MailChimp. You'll get your money's worth from it. If, on the other hand, you are mostly in it for other, non-monetary reasons, using a newsletter as a marketing tool becomes less critical, and FeedBurner's email service is the easy way to go.

Invite People to Subscribe

When it comes to attracting subscribers, there are two variables at play: the number of visitors and your conversion rate. All things being equal, the larger the number of visitors, the higher the number of subscribers. The problem is that if your conversion rate (from visitor to subscriber) is low, most of your effort to attract new visitors will be wasted. These visitors will reach your blog and then leave. Most are unlikely to ever come back.

The real issue then becomes increasing your subscriber conversion rate. Excellent content definitely helps, but that's not enough in and of itself. You

Single vs. Double Opt-In

If you choose to operate your own newsletter and currently reside in Canada, you are legally required to make your signup double opt-in. This means that your users will have to enter their email addresses and then confirm their request to join by clicking an activation link that gets sent to them by email.

Even if you are not legally requested to do so where you live (e.g., in the United States), it's a good idea to implement double, not single, opt-in. Your list will only contain addresses from people who really signed up for your newsletter (i.e., they proved ownership of the email address). As a result, your subscriber list will be much more valuable than a list of unconfirmed emails. As well, you'll get less fake emails, mis-spelled emails, bounce responses, spam reports, and abuse complaints. You may lose a few subscribers who never received your activation email or didn't bother reading it, but that's a small negative you can easily live with as one of the costs of doing business via email.

need to remind people that the subscription is available. Solicit them to take the kind of action you want.

Give Away a Freebie

If you want an even greater conversion rate, you may have to take things a step further. Don't just invite people to join your newsletter: bribe them. The easiest way to attract new subscribers is to offer them something for free when they sign up for your newsletter. For example, you could offer a short collection of CoffeeScript tips in PDF format, if your niche is CoffeeScript.

There are three caveats to this approach.

1. You can't verify feed subscriptions, so you'll have to tie this to email signups only.

2. You can't automate this process with email subscription via FeedBurner. You will need your own newsletter, and you will have to create an autoresponder, which will include a link to the download for those who sign up. (In MailChimp, you could even include it in the confirmation email without setting up an autoresponder for the download).

3. Technical people tend to dislike the idea of having to sign up just to download a file, so you may get a few people complaining about it. Remember, however, that you are not doing anything wrong—you are the one who sets the conditions for your own content. Users can always subscribe, download, and then unsubscribe if they wish.

Even if you want to ignore this freebie technique, which converts extremely well, you still need to prominently advertise your feed and email subscription options regardless.

Do so in two spots. The first and most obvious spot is somewhere at the top of your theme or in the sidebar. The second is at the bottom of your posts.

For the header of your theme or top of the sidebar, you can use the code provided by FeedBurner in the Publicize, Chicklet Counter section. There you can opt for a standard RSS icon or for a chicklet counter, which shows the current number of subscribers.

In the beginning, when you have less than five hundred subscribers, it's probably better not to include a counter. Later on, including one will act as proof of your site's popularity and can help convince more people that your blog is well worth following.

You'll also want to grab and embed in your sidebar the code from Email Subscriptions in FeedBurner (or the equivalent signup form from your newsletter management provider). Requesting a first name along with an email address can be a powerful tool in your future email campaigns to make your messages come across as more personable.

The file that you need to edit to add custom code at the bottom of your posts is single.php, which you can find in your WordPress theme folder. (Assuming your theme doesn't have an option for this too).

At the bottom of each post on my own programming blog, I have a little message that says the following:

> If you enjoyed this post, then make sure you subscribe to my Newsletter and/or Feed.

Both the words *Newsletter* and *Feed* are linked to their respective signup pages.

Alternatively, you can use a plugin such as WP Greet Box or WP BTBuckets, which will greet your visitors with a custom message based on where they are coming from and invite them to subscribe at the top of your posts.

Within your posts, you'll also want to refer to your subscription options when it's fitting to do so. For example, if you are writing the first article in a series, you can suggest within the body of your article that your readers subscribe so as not to miss future installments.

Are Pop-Ups Evil?

Most people would agree that pop-ups are annoying. Some may consider them downright evil. Yet, pop-up newsletter signup forms are also extremely effective at converting traffic into subscribers.

In different niches they can be more acceptable, but think twice before placing them on your technical or business blog. Pop-up forms will end up annoying the majority of your technical audience, and you won't hear the end of it from your readers.

Instead, if you really want to include a pop-up, consider less annoying forms, such as plugins that show an overlay at the top or bottom of your page or that only show after a visitor has scrolled to the end of the article.

4.6 Don't Get in Trouble—Use Disclaimers

Honesty and integrity when dealing with your readers are fundamental principles that will serve you well as a blogger. Your visitors will no doubt appreciate them, too.

More importantly, being honest and transparent will also help you stay out of trouble with your employer (if you have one) or even with the authorities.

Include an Employer Disclaimer

If you work for a large corporation, it's likely that your employer has employee guidelines for blogging and social media engagement. You should respect these rules so as to avoid being the nth blogger to lose your job because of what you wrote online.

These guidelines vary from company to company, but they usually boil down to not revealing company secrets or unannounced products, not being a jerk with other people online, not engaging in slandering your competitors, and similar common-sense advice.

What some may not be aware of is that most large corporations also require you to disclose your work affiliation. In other words, you're required to include a disclaimer on your blog that identifies what you write as your own opinions and not those of the company you work for.

As an example, the About section of my programming blog includes the following disclaimer:

> I'll start with a disclaimer that is required by both my employer and the type of job I have. It's my personal blog, which is entirely independent from IBM. My

articles and comments are my own and don't necessarily represent my employer's positions, strategies, or opinions.

For your own blog you could use or adapt the following standard disclaimer:

Disclaimer: The posts on this site are my own and don't necessarily represent [COMPANY]'s positions, strategies, or opinions.

Disclaimers such as these may appear silly to technical people, but they can help get you out of trouble with your employer should a complaint be filed against you.

Include a disclaimer like this in your sidebar and/or About section if you are employed by a company that requires you do so.

Include an FTC Disclaimer

If you think being fired for blogging is bad, how about being investigated by the feds?

In short, the FTC (Federal Trade Commission) expects bloggers to clearly disclose any commercial affiliations with third-party products they're reviewing or promoting. If your post or review includes a link to an affiliate product, including Amazon affiliate links, you need to disclose that fact to your readers. If the book, game, software, or any other product or service you are reviewing was obtained for free, you need to let your readers know that, as this may affect your judgment of the product. You are also not allowed to make any false, misleading, or deceptive claims.

If you are a US-based blogger, it's worth checking out the latest guidelines on the ftc.gov website to ensure that you are operating within the borders of the law. Non-US-based bloggers may or may not have similar rules in place, depending on their country, but it's worth adopting the same standard of transparency that's asked of our peers in the States. Despite being based in Canada, which doesn't have such strict regulations, my programming blog includes the following disclaimer in the middle of the sidebar:

Some of the links contained within this site have my referral ID (e.g., Amazon), which provides me with a small commission for each sale. Thank you for your support.

Also include a disclaimer at the bottom of each relevant post that you manually include to explain your connection to the product being promoted. This also helps you to be covered from a legal standpoint when it comes to readers who subscribe to your posts and may not see your sidebar disclaimer.

If you post a review of a book you received for free from a publisher and are including affiliate links to Amazon, you may want to include the following disclaimer (or a very similar one) at the bottom of your post:

> Disclaimer: I received this book for free from the publisher for reviewing purposes. Furthermore, the links in this post contain my Amazon Associates ID, and I will receive compensation if you make a purchase through them. Thank you for your support.

Feel free to copy or adapt this disclaimer accordingly, depending on your specific circumstances and blog post.

You might assume that this kind of disclaimer will kill your sales, but it can actually help bolster them because you'll come across as being more trustworthy in the eyes of your readers.

4.7   Master On-page SEO with Platinum SEO

It's important to ensure that your blog is properly indexed and evaluated by search engines. In the previous chapter we saw a new permalink structure that will greatly aid your blog in being able to rank better. We also briefly mentioned a couple of SEO plugins. In this section, we'll quickly configure those plugins, as well as get acquainted with Google Webmaster Tools.

Configure Platinum SEO Pack

Install and activate the Platinum SEO plugin for WordPress if you haven't already done so. More advanced plugins have been created, but Platinum SEO will ensure that all of your essentials are covered.[11] As usual, we don't want to sweat the small stuff.

In the admin section of your WordPress installation you should see a new Platinum SEO menu where you can set a series of SEO-related options. Leave all the default values, but make the following changes:

- Enter your home title, which should coincide with the name of your blog. Limit it to 70 characters or less so that it can appear in full as the title of your blog in the SERP.

- Enter a natural sounding yet keyword-rich description of your blog that is actually relevant to your content in the Home Description text area.

---

11. All-in-One SEO Pack, WordPress SEO by Yoast, and SEO Ultimate are all good alternatives.

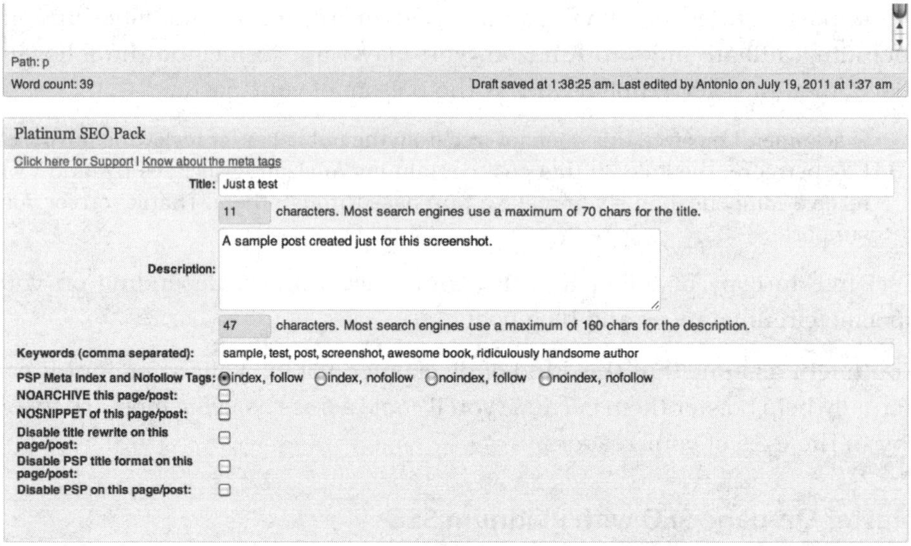

Figure 15—Meta tag options for new posts

This meta tag is used by search engines to display a description in the SERP, so limit it to 160 characters or less.

- List a series of comma-separated keywords or key phrases in the Home Keywords text area. Include less than twenty keywords. Not all search engines value these keywords (e.g., Google doesn't), but they're still worth specifying.

- Change both Post Title Format and Page Title Format to remove | %blog_title%. The reason for this is that we want our posts and pages to rank based on keywords that are relevant to their titles. Excluding the blog name from a post or page title will increase the density of the target keywords.

- Select "Use no index for Categories" so that you end up providing less duplicate content to search engines. Google's official stance is that it doesn't penalize duplicate content, but they are not fond of it either. Regardless of Google's views, there is no point in having the same post indexed under different URLs (the permalink and the Category page, for example).

When you are done, click Update Options to save these changes.

Thanks to Platinum SEO, whenever you create a new post or page, you'll be able to specify meta tags for search engines on a singular post or page level, as shown in Figure 15, *Meta tag options for new posts*, on page 78. (Though this hasn't been widely adopted yet, it looks like search engines are going to allow further customization of the way your site appears in the SERP. You can learn more about this interesting topic at schema.org.)

At times you may wish to provide search engines with a title tag that is slightly different from the one you used for your post. For example, your post title could be "Ten CoffeeScript Tips That Will Wow You," which may be attractive for social media traffic but is not particularly SEO-friendly. Thanks to Platinum SEO you can indicate a different title via meta tags that you can specify at the bottom of each post—perhaps something like "Ten CoffeeScript Tips." After all, virtually nobody will search in Google for the "That Will Wow You" part of your title.

When you change the page title meta tag via Platinum SEO, you should also consider giving the post a matching slug (e.g., /ten-coffeescript-tips). This way, search engines will see an optimized page title and URL.

Configure Your Google XML Sitemap

Continuing on our quest to get search engines to notice and index all of our valuable content, we need to install and activate the Google XML Sitemap plugin for WordPress.

You'll find the configuration options under Settings as XML-Sitemap. In truth, there are countless options available, but the default selections work just fine.

All you have to do now is generate the initial map by clicking the link provided (i.e., "Click here to build it the first time").

Set Up Google Webmaster Tools

Before putting our on-page SEO configuration to rest, I encourage you to sign up with Google Webmaster Tools at google.com/webmasters/tools.

This is a set of invaluable tools that helps you better understand how Google sees your site. Among this site's many features, you'll be able to diagnose if your site is being properly crawled, which keywords Google thinks are relevant to your blog, what sites link to you, the impact of Google +1 on your blog, whether Google has any suggestions for you, and much more.

If you were to ever rename your blog's domain, Webmaster Tools will also enable you to inform Google of your change of address (but you'll need to set up the HTTP 301 redirects yourself). Keep in mind that changing your domain name is generally a terrible idea and should be considered only as a last resort.

4.8   Performance Considerations

Many good things can be said about WordPress, but speed isn't one them. A default installation connects to the database and dynamically generates content with each request, thus becoming extremely demanding on your server's resources.

When you first start blogging, your main challenge is to attract eyeballs, so a slow CMS may not be a huge deal initially. However, by following the roadmap that I outline in this book, you may manage to attract several thousand visitors in the span of a few hours upon publishing and subsequently promoting a new post—even in your early days as a blogger.

A vanilla WordPress installation will most likely die under the weight of so many requests, and you certainly don't want to see your site become unresponsive when so many people are eager to read what you've written—what an ugly, if not uncommon, first impression that would be. So let's see what we can do to help prevent this situation.

Cache Everything

Server side, if you have control over your server, feel free to optimize the optimizable. Use nginx instead of Apache, and configure both PHP and MySQL to make them speedier than their default configurations. More importantly, however, you must install a caching plugin.

Two leading WordPress caching plugins are W3 Total Cache and WP Super Cache. I personally tend to prefer W3 Total Cache because it's currently a more complete caching solution, with multiple options that are not available in WP Super Cache. Nevertheless, both are excellent and will speed up your blog immensely.

Even on shared hosting, a properly cached WordPress installation can easily handle thousands of visitors. The magic of caching lies in its ability to serve static versions of dynamically generated pages. Once a cached version of a page has been generated, the performance levels are not far off from those of a static HTML page.

Don't forget to monitor your blog's uptime with a service such as UptimeRobot or Pingdom.[12]

Configure W3 Total Cache

Once you've installed W3 Total Cache, you'll want to configure it in the Performance menu that will be added to your admin section. Enable the page cache, object cache, and browser cache. Those should get you properly covered. If you are a server pro and have fancy caching servers such as Varnish installed on your server, you can specify its IP address through the plugin as well.

Likewise, CDN (content delivery networks) can greatly improve performance when serving static content such as images, JavaScript, and CSS files. W3 Total Cache supports the ability to specify a CDN for your files, even though this usually means that you'll have to pay extra for such content delivery services.

Please note that you may receive error messages if W3 Total Cache is unable to write over your web server's configuration file or create a cache folder. Thankfully, for each error of this kind, the plugin provides a good explanation of what you need to do to fix it. The plugin allows you to test your settings in preview mode to ensure that everything looks good before committing to these changes.

To conclude this section, two excellent browser extensions for learning more about what could be improved performance-wise are Google Page Speed and YSlow.[13] Page Speed is also provided as a service and not just as a browser extension.[14]

W3 Total Cache integrates with Google Page Speed, provided you register for an API key. When you do so, your performance advice will be presented to you in your WordPress dashboard upon logging into the admin section of your blog.

Finally, you can also test the speed of your blog online with WebpageTest.[15]

---

12. uptimerobot.com or pingdom.com, respectively.
13. code.google.com/speed/page-speed and developer.yahoo.com/yslow, respectively.
14. developers.google.com/pagespeed
15. webpagetest.org

4.9 Enable Code Highlighting in Your Posts

Before wrapping up this chapter, let's discuss how to embed highlighted code, a task that most technical bloggers need to do.

By default, you can embed small pieces of code in your paragraphs by using the <code> HTML tag. For snippets of code that span several lines, you can use <pre> instead. Your code will appear in the right monospaced font but won't be colored or highlighted, so that it's more readable and easier on the eyes.

I invite you to consider the following solutions.

- Use a WordPress plugin. If you are using WordPress, there are many options to choose from, including Prettify GC Syntax Highlighter, Google Syntax Highlighter for WordPress, and Syntax Highlighter MT.

- Use a JavaScript library. As long as your blogging platform supports JavaScript, you can use a syntax highlighting library. Recommended choices are Prettify and SyntaxHighlighter.[16] (Yes, these are the libraries used by the plugins above.)

- Use a snippet-sharing service. gist.github.com is probably one of the best services of its kind, and this too has the advantage of working even if your blog engine isn't WordPress.

- Use a command-line tool. If you live and breathe the shell, you may want to consider a syntax highlighter tool such as Pygments.[17] Once you've uploaded and linked the CSS theme of your choice, you'll be able to copy the HTML output from the tool directly into your posts. Of course, this method will work regardless of your blog engine.

4.10 What's Next

This was admittedly a large chapter, in which we worked through a wealth of topics related to the customization of your blog. At this point you should have all the tools you need to get started and crank out some content.

The next two chapters will be dedicated solely to maximizing your ability to produce great content that attracts readers. After that, we'll move into the promotional and marketing phase—an area that can easily make or break you as a blogger.

---

16. code.google.com/p/google-code-prettify and alexgorbatchev.com/SyntaxHighlighter, respectively.
17. pygments.org

Great minds discuss ideas; average minds discuss events; small minds discuss people.

> ➤ *Eleanor Roosevelt*

CHAPTER 5

Creating Remarkable Content

You've worked hard, choosing software and setting up and customizing your blog. Now here's where all that hard work comes to fruition as you focus on what it's all about: your blog's content.

5.1 Content Is King

In the world of Internet marketing, the saying is Content is King. The idea is that anything else you do to attract visitors or sell more products only counts if you have compelling, original content.

From an SEO perspective, content is certainly king. Your site will only show up in the result pages if your content matches the queries entered by search engine users. The more original content you have, the more people will find you via search queries.

It's not just about search engine traffic, though. Real people will read the words you write. Bland, poorly written content may trick search engines in delivering traffic your way, but it won't satisfy intelligent beings once they're on your site. And they won't come back.

Blogging's many benefits all derive from well-written, interesting content. Great articles will be linked to more often, be shared a greater number of times on social networks, receive more positive comments, attract an increasing number of regular readers, and convince more potential employers, customers, or employees that what you're saying or selling is worth their attention. The quality and quantity of, as well as how you promote, your posts is what determines the success of your blog.

This chapter delves into the quality side of the equation. Quantity will be dealt with in the next chapter. Finally, in Chapter 7, *Promoting Your Blog*, on page 119, you'll learn how to let the world know about your great articles.

> ### Tip 11
>
> ## Write epic content you'd love to read yourself.

5.2 Write for the Web

Writing for the Web is different from writing a book or a letter. You only have a few seconds to captivate a visitor, who often has the attention span of a chipmunk on crack.

How do we capture the reader's attention then? Let's consider a few do's and don'ts when writing for the Web to make your text more readable and more likely to be read.

Do:

- Write a catchy headline and first paragraph. Most visitors follow an F-shaped pattern with their eyes when scanning a web page.[1] Your headline and top paragraph (or two at most) is what the majority of your visitors will read. You need to grab their attention and lead them to the rest of your post.

- Divide your text into short paragraphs. Nothing bounces visitors away like a huge wall of text.

- Make lists using numbers or bullet points. They tend to make your content quick to scroll through for the many readers who aren't going to read every word of your post.

- Divide your long posts into sections through the use of headers such as <h2> or <h3> tags. This approach is good from an SEO standpoint as well. In fact, your theme should surround your post titles in <h1> tags for SEO purposes.

---

1. www.useit.com/alertbox/reading_pattern.html

- Be concise. Although long articles are a sensible style of blogging, understand that their length will greatly reduce the percentage of readers that actually follow through and read your post until the last line. Keep to the point. The expression TL;DR ("too long; didn't read") is quite popular online for a reason.

- Reference, link, and quote other blog posts. Generously link to other people's posts, and other bloggers may return the favor and do the same with you.

- Include one or more pictures. If applicable at all, strive for at least one image in each post.

- Try to kick off each paragraph with useful information. When users scan your article on the left side of your site (at the bottom of the aforementioned F-shaped pattern), they'll find keywords that are of interest and they will be more likely to actually read your post.

- Be as clear, direct, concise, and unceremonious as possible. For example, don't use words like *unceremonious*. Always assume that some of your readers will misunderstand what you're saying; clarify ambiguous parts to ensure the concepts are clear to your audience.

- Be informal. Your posts initiate conversations.

- Acknowledge corrections. If you make corrections to your text after a post has been published and the problems aren't just typos, use the <del> HTML tag to strike through the erroneous content. Doing so conveys an important sense of honesty to your readers.

- Add updates. If you publish small updates to existing articles, disclose that you did so at the bottom of your post (with a date stating when the changes occurred). In particular, credit the updates if they are the results of corrections or comments left by your readers.

- Proofread. Web readers are often quite forgiving of typos and mistakes, but to be taken seriously you must try to be grammatically correct and make sure to proofread your content before sending it live. From time to time, you may run into a so-called "grammar Nazi," who will point out every typo you make. Most readers however, understand that your blog is not *The New Yorker* and will rarely, if ever, point out small typos.

- "Natify" your content. If you are not a native English speaker and plan to write your content in English, disclosing this point in your About section will cut you some slack with your readers. If possible, you could also get some help from a native English reviewer, either through friends or colleagues or by paying a native speaker to be your virtual assistant.

Don't:

- Don't abuse bold or italic text. Use font emphasis parsimoniously. They can increase readability, but they also tend to annoy readers if they're employed too frequently. One exception to this statement would be to set off headings.

- Don't use underlined text for anything but links. Ever. Your readers will assume your underlined text is a link and click it.

- Don't engage in *blogspam*. Blogspam is the act of republishing someone else's original content without adding much (or any) of your own in terms of commentary or value. Quoting and crediting others as you add your own ideas is OK and encouraged. Scraping, republishing, or even rephrasing without adding much is not. As a rule of thumb, your posts should primarily contain your own original writing.

5.3 Can Linkbaiting Be Ethical?

The two most important off-page SEO factors are the quantity and quality of your inbound links. It's not surprising that people go to great lengths to attract links.

The most ethical bloggers work hard on the quality of their content and at diligently promoting it, whereas the so-called "black hats" will pretty much do anything to get links, including buying them in bulk.

Tip 12

Never buy links.

Somewhere in the middle of the link-building ethics spectrum lies *linkbaiting*. In principle, the concept is innocent enough. Linkbaiting (or link baiting) is the art of creating content that attracts a lot of links and generates buzz. In practice, however, linkbaiting often has a negative connotation. Even the inclusion of the word *bait* in the name echoes the idea of tricking people into linking to you.

When commenters say, "This is just linkbait," what they are really saying is that they feel that the sole purpose of a particular post was to attract links rather than to provide readers with valuable or interesting information.

In the wild, linkbaiting can be good "white-hat" marketing, or it can be a questionable "gray-hat" practice. It all depends on how you do it.

(*White, gray,* and *black hat* are terms borrowed from the security world. White hats operate within the rules and take a strong ethical approach to their work. Black hats do not and will do everything necessary, including illegal activities, to obtain what they are after. Gray hats are, as their name implies, in a gray zone between the two.)

At heart, all forms of linkbait, good or bad, share two common traits: a catchy headline and some form of content that will instigate readers into linking to a particular post.

Bad linkbaiting is characterized by the following traits:

- Overly sensational headlines that don't match the content.
- Needless controversy for the sake of controversy.
- Content that has no real value to the end user but that people may at first think is cool (e.g., shiny infographics with no real insight).

Here's what you should do instead:

- Write catchy but not overly sensationalistic headlines.
- Create unique content that people genuinely want to read and will find value in.

5.4   Write Catchy Headlines

You should stay away from writing sensationalistic titles for your posts, but don't write boring ones either. Through enticing but factual headlines, you can attract inbound links without misleading your readers with content that doesn't match the headline of your post.

As you write your post titles, keep in mind that you are not simply doing so for the sake of linkbaiting reasons (of the good kind). Your title is what needs to convince a passerby to read the rest of your article and not just the headline. Lastly, your titles should also try to organically include relevant keywords for SEO purposes. As usual, finding the right balance is key.

Let's see this at work with a practical example. Assume that you're writing a review of a relatively new search engine called DuckDuckGo that you compare to Google. What should the headline be? The second and third ones below would work.

1. "Review of DuckDuckGo": It's boring, and it doesn't tell people what DuckDuckGo is.

2. "Google and DuckDuckGo: A Tale of Two Search Engines": Definitely honest and interesting. It also contains the keywords *search engines*.

3. "DuckDuckGo—A Google Alternative You'll Love": Catchy, and it will definitely grab the reader's eye and pique curiosity. You're being bold by telling your readers that they'll love the alternative search engine, but you are not being overly sensationalistic.

4. "The Search Engine That Will Put Google Out of Business": Unnecessarily sensationalistic. It would certainly attract links, but you stand to quickly lose the respect of many of your readers. The content would in fact have to be extremely outrageous to try and justify an indefensible position (controversy for the sake of controversy) like this or, alternatively, not address the point made in the title at all (thus being a misleading headline).

Capitalize your titles to make them stand out better. Other elements commonly used to create catchy headlines are providing numbered lists (e.g., "Ten Ways to Improve Your Code"), using attention-grabbing words like *free* (e.g., "Free NoSQL Course Available for Download"), and asking questions (e.g., "What Minimum Specs Should Your Development Machine Have?").

Remember to be useful to your readers. Your headline should sell your audience on the benefits of what you're conveying instead of the features within your article. Why should they bother reading it? Why read it now? Consider introducing an element of urgency, if one is applicable. For example, "Free CoffeeScript Webinar. Sign Up Before the Deadline!" In this particular case, a strong call to action (i.e., needing to sign up) has also been put out to the reader.

The degree of catchiness you can get away with also depends on the type of audience you have and the kind of communities you promote your articles in. For example, if I thought I could derive most of my traffic for a given article from Hacker News, I would choose headline 2 over headline 3 because that particular community has little tolerance for sensationalism.

Hacker News also frowns upon numbers in lists and the use of exclamation marks, so much so that they are often removed from submissions when a story you submit becomes popular.

> ### Write Your Headline First
>
> Write your headline before your post. This will give focus to your writing. In fact, you should adopt the so-called Inverted Pyramid approach to writing that journalists use. Put the most important information first, starting with the headline, then in the first paragraphs. Proceed to providing other important details and background information as the article carries on.
>
> It's tempting to provide a lot of background info and slowly work your way up to the essence of your post; however, try not to do so or you'll bury the point of your article, and many readers may give up on it before they get to the marrow of your post.

5.5 Develop Your Own Voice

If you do a good job with the headline, people will click and check out the actual content of your article. When they do so, what they expect to read is useful, interesting, unique content. Above all else though, your regular readers expect to find your familiar voice.

Your style and approach to writing, your selection of topics, your personality, and your way of interacting with your audience is what makes your blog truly unique. These elements work together to create your voice and are what you need to hone and develop as you start blogging.

You could be caring, friendly, witty, funny, clever, enlightening, bold, controversial, pretentious, off-putting, vulgar, or a downright bully. It's up to you and your character, but in my experience it pays to be humble and admit that you don't know everything while at the same time being bold with what you truly believe without the fear of coming across as controversial.

Tip 13

Don't ever belittle or mock others in your posts.

Nothing you do or write will ever please everyone, so don't try to impress or please the whole world. Write what you really think and on topics you're genuinely passionate about. Controversy works extremely well not when it's done purely for the sake of stirring the pot, but when it stems from real conviction. Convey passion in your writing and you're bound to garner a following.

Adjust your tone and content to match the blogging goals you defined and the audience you hope to attract. If you have a business blog or are a free-lancer, you don't want to come across as pretentious; try being approachable instead.

Whatever voice you develop, become a bit of a storyteller. People love stories that go with useful information. So rather than putting just the bare facts out there, try to give your writing a more human element by expressing why you were facing a certain problem, how you felt, what you learned in the process, what could have been done differently, what you are still unsure about, and similar points. Provide some background and context for what you're writing about. Derek Sivers attracted a huge following to his blog at sivers.org thanks to this technique. Read a few of his posts to see how powerful storytelling can be.

5.6 Where to Find Ideas for Your Posts

Before writing a post, you should ask yourself if your idea for an article satis-fies any of the following criteria.

- Do I care about this topic?
- Will readers find it useful?
- Does it tell a compelling story?
- Is the post in line with the goals of my blog?
- Does it add any value to my field?
- Does it start a conversation with the community that's worth having?
- Is it newsworthy in the context of my niche?

If the answer is no to most of these points, you shouldn't write that post. Instead, search for a topic that qualifies with a resounding *yes* to one or more of the rhetorical questions above.

Finding ideas for your posts is not too difficult when you expose your brain to other people's writing in your own field and in other niches. I highly recom-mend you use a feed reader such as Google Reader to subscribe to blogs that you find useful, inspiring, and entertaining. Spending as little as thirty min-utes a day reading other blogs will fill your mind with new ideas.

Personally I use an iPad for my casual blog reading at night. It's given me a workflow that's very useful to me because it clearly separates work and play, leaving me feeling more focused when producing content or doing other work on my main laptop. Now, you don't need an iPad just for this, of course, but if you own a similar device, you may consider taking the same approach.

Ask Your Readers What They Want

The easiest way to figure out what your readers really want is to ask them. Don't be shy in your posts, and feel free to ask your readers how you are doing and what they'd like to see next.

You can also run a survey once in a while to learn more about how regular readers see your blog and what they think can be improved upon. Don't take everything at face value; instead, consider the overall feedback you receive.

To run surveys for free, you can use Form on Google Docs. Alternatively, you can avail yourself of more sophisticated premium solutions such as SurveyGizmo, SurveyMonkey, or Wufoo.

I also like to keep an idea.txt file in a Dropbox folder that is synchronized in the cloud. This file contains a list of ideas for my posts, which I add to whenever something new comes to mind. You can use Google Docs for this purpose if you want to have your list available anywhere there's an Internet connection and you don't use Dropbox. Either way, this file usually contains at least ten prospective headlines for each of my currently maintained blogs.

You can use tools such as Keyword Tool and Insights for Search (or Market Samurai) to find ideas for highly sought-after content and keywords (it's useful for coming up with good headlines, too). With this system in place, the real bottleneck is not finding ideas but rather finding the time to sit down and actually write out the content that's in your head.

To help you look for ideas as you get inspired by other bloggers and compile your idea file, here are some types of posts to consider.

- Write about what you've been working on lately (just be sure it's not confidential).

- Write hands-on guides or tutorials for subjects that you are an expert on. Spread these guides across multiple posts to create an engaging series.

- Tell a story about your past failures or successes.

- Quote and link to an interesting idea found elsewhere on the Web, but be sure to add your own commentary. Disagree and stir controversy if that's truly how you feel about the issue.

- Write an essay or even a rant about a subject you care about. It could be something that grinds your gears or simply a topic you believe more readers should know about.

- Interview popular people in your field (more on this in the next chapter).

- Review books, services, gadgets, or products that are relevant to your niche.

- Collect, organize, and present links to relevant resources all in a single post (e.g., "White Papers on the Scalability of Web Applications").

- Create cheatsheets (e.g., HTML5 Cheatsheet). If possible, include both an HTML version and a PDF version for printing.

- Collect interesting data about your industry and compile it into a useful infographic. If you are not a designer, you can usually commission it to designers who specialize in creating infographics that go viral online. Check out Visual.ly for inspiration and to find good designers who specialize in infographics.[2]

- If you run a business, consider writing about your social media campaigns, A/B testing experiments, and sales and earnings figures. Traditionally this would be considered bad advice, but being open and frank in posts on such topics has allowed several companies to become the center of attention.

5.7 Case Study: Math-Blog.com's Headlines

Now that you have a solid understanding of the importance of well-worded headlines and at a least a general idea of the type of content that people value, let's take a peek at our first case study. When discussing domain name choices in Chapter 2, *A Rock-Solid Plan for Your Blog*, on page 11, I mentioned my math-related authority blog, math-blog.com. I'm going to show you some statistics for both the most and least popular articles from that site.

My intent is to show you how I applied most of the principles discussed in this chapter and the results that you stand to achieve by following them.

Your mileage will certainly vary, and there are other factors that determine how well a piece does visitor-wise. Nevertheless, I'd like to offer this unique glimpse into the stats of a relatively popular niche blog.

The Web Pageviews column doesn't include feed readers, email subscribers, and other readers who didn't actually visit the post on my site. It also excludes search engine bots and other crawlers (rightfully so), because the stats are pulled directly from Google Analytics, which filters such hits out.

Let's start with the top ten performers. (Of course, older articles have an edge).

---

2. visual.ly

Rank	Post Title	Web Pageviews
1	13 Useful Math Cheat Sheets	269,908
2	3 Awesome Math Programs	246,522
3	A 10 Minute Tutorial for Solving Math Problems with Maxima	166,034
4	Ten Must Read Books About Mathematics	109,118
5	The Most Enlightening Calculus Books	99,231
6	Refresh Your High-School Math Skills	57,676
7	The Nicest Math Book I Own	44,002
8	10 Remarkable Female Mathematicians	35,528
9	On the Importance of Mathematics	31,223
10	Forget Pi, Here Comes Tau	22,415

Now, let's look at the worst five performers, ordered by the least popular.

Worst Rank	Post Title	Web Pageviews
1	Help Us With Your Feedback by Taking Our Survey	178
2	Switching From FeedBurner Email to Aweber for My Newsletter	238
3	An Apology to My Feed Readers	306
4	Eberhardt Rechtin and the Barrier Course...	311
5	Protecting Valuable Intellectual Property in Octave	382

Can you see how what we've discussed relates directly to both the best and worst performers? Notice how the top articles were both attractive to social media users (the immediate traffic) and to search engine traffic, which keeps coming for several months or even years after the articles were published.

Now consider the five worst performers for a moment. The worst one has no appeal to either social media or search engine traffic. It also doesn't offer anything that's useful to the reader. In practice, a few thousand people actually read that article via feed and more than a hundred people bothered to provide me with excellent feedback. It's worth having, but it's the kind of post that has virtually no appeal to nonregular readers.

The second and third worst articles, in terms of circulation, are both service updates. Again, nobody outside of affected regular readers really cared about them. They were necessary announcements, but no value is really being offered to the majority of visitors stopping by the site.

The fourth and fifth were good articles with plenty of value. In the case of the fourth-worst performer however, very few people really know who Eberhardt Rechtin is. The headline comes across as obscure and catchy only to the narrowest of audiences.

Objectively, the fifth should have performed better. Certainly, Octave (an open source alternative to Matlab) is still pretty much a niche and the article is relatively new, but a post on protecting intellectual property should have fared better. I would have expected at least a couple thousand new visitors above and beyond the few thousand regular subscribers who read it (again, such additional feed/email viewers are not reflected in the numbers shown in the table).

This brings us to another important point. There is a certain unpredictability to blogging, no matter how careful you are with your headlines, content, and promotion. Depending on a multitude of variables that are not under your control, articles that you think will be a home run end up flopping entirely. Conversely, posts you put together in ten minutes are sometimes received with great enthusiasm by tens of thousands of readers.

Ask many famous musicians and they'll tell you how their most popular hits were almost cut because they didn't meet the artist's own standards. Yet audiences absolutely loved them. Don't censor your creative output. Let the public be the judge of your writing.

Where Traffic Is Coming From

To complete this case study, I want to share with you where over a million visitors came from.

- 48.55% was *referral traffic*. Almost half of my visitors came from other sites that link to mine.

- 36.29% was *search traffic*. More than a third of these visitors came from search engines (primarily Google).

- 14.04% was *direct traffic*. These are people who entered the URL of my domain or of one of my articles directly into the address bar of their browsers. Typically these are regular readers who visit the site from time to time.

- 1.12% was *campaign traffic*. In my case, this number mostly represents the newsletter subscribers who clicked on my messages and ended up on the blog. This number can generally include paid ad campaigns as well, if you run any.

The referral traffic came from the following sites.

Rank	Referral Site	Visits
1	StumbleUpon.com	197,893
2	Reddit.com	71,168
3	Digg.com	65,611
4	Maxima.SourceForge.net	44,728
5	News.YCombinator.com	38,004
6	Delicious.com	17,030
7	En.Wikipedia.org	7,459
8	JustMathTutoring.com	5,746
9	Popurls.com	5,163
10	Facebook.com	3,323

As you can see, most of these are social media sites (in part because that's where I tend to promote my articles). Note also how, as I mentioned in the previous chapter, Facebook is far from the top referral, and Twitter doesn't even appear in the top ten. (Please note that Digg performed very well years ago, but now it's pretty much dead.)

5.8 Get Readers to Explore Your Content

In the previous chapter I briefly addressed the issue of getting your visitors to explore more of your content. In particular, we covered how certain sidebar widgets can encourage your readers to visit additional popular or recent posts on your site.

You can turbocharge your efforts to guide your readers to more of your content by taking the following five steps.

1. Install a plugin such as Yet Another Related Posts Plugin. It will allow you to automatically display a few related posts at the bottom of each new post. In my experience, the CTR (click-through rate) of related posts is high when people liked the one they just read.

2. Create a sticky Getting Started page that guides newcomers through your blog. Organize a collection of introductory posts you've already written as well as information about how to subscribe, join the newsletter, participate in the comments, share your content, and other similar topics. Make this page a useful guide to getting started with your blog, then promote it within your own blog as much as you can.

> ### Blogging Clients
>
> Many advanced bloggers tend to prefer desktop blogging clients over the default web interface that's available for WordPress, Blogger, or equivalent blogging engines.
>
> Hacker types may enjoy blogging directly from TextMate, Vim, or Emacs, given that these text editors can be configured to post directly to your blog either through a blog generator, such as Jekyll/Octopress, or via the remote API that's available from WordPress, Blogger, and others.
>
> These three programs excel at editing text, but there are more user-friendly solutions out there that were designed specifically for bloggers who want some help with their workflow to maintain multiple blogs, create drafts, take notes, and so on.
>
> For Mac, I recommend MarsEdit. For Windows, it's hard to beat Windows Live Writer by Microsoft.
>
> Mobile devices and tablets have blogging clients too, particularly for WordPress. Explore some of these options before committing to one client.

3. Do the same with a "Best of" page. Unlike the Getting Started page, this should just link to your best posts, perhaps organized by category or some other logical criteria. This too should be promoted within your blog as much as you can (definitely link to it from your home and About pages, for example).

4. Create a Table of Contents page. WordPress already has archives, but these are not as nice as having a list of posts that have been organized by month all included on the same page. For my blogs, I use the WordPress plugin called Clean Archives Reloaded, which allows me to achieve the look shown in Figure 16, *A table of contents*, on page 97. Blogger doesn't offer this capability, so you may have to settle for its Blog Archive gadget in the sidebar or come up with some clever piece of code to showcase such a list within a page.

5. Assign tags to your posts. Through them, users will be able to quickly access similar posts. This is also beneficial from an SEO standpoint, as it increases your blog's level of interlinking.

5.9 Copyright Matters

Online content of any kind, much like its printed counterpart, is protected by default by copyright (in most countries, at least). The moment you write something, you own the copyright on it, even if you haven't registered it with a copyright office in the country you reside in.

Please find below my 289 posts, ordered by month. This "Table of Contents" is automatically updated.

- July 2011 (2)
    - 19: <u>Speeding up queries by a factor of 100 or more with DB2 Text Search</u> (3)
    - 09: <u>The need for good vocational schools for programmers</u> (27)
- June 2011 (4)
    - 23: <u>Programming in Objective-C, 3rd Edition is out</u> (0)
    - 13: <u>jQuery Air: An outstanding introduction to jQuery</u> (5)
    - 08: <u>IBM is Looking for a University Student with PHP skills in Toronto</u> (2)
    - 02: <u>10 Ruby One Liners to Impress Your Friends</u> (24)
- May 2011 (6)
    - 31: <u>Interview with the Compilr.com team</u> (2)
    - 16: <u>The Great Web-Reality Divide</u> (1)
    - 12: <u>Installing Python, Django, and DB2 on Ubuntu 11.04</u> (0)
    - 11: <u>Installing Ruby on Rails and DB2 on Ubuntu 11.04</u> (2)
    - 09: <u>Download DB2 Express-C 9.7.4</u> (1)
    - 01: <u>Google I/O developer event in Waterloo, Canada</u> (0)
- April 2011 (4)
    - 26: <u>Results of the Technical Blogging survey</u> (1)
    - 20: <u>Review of Rails Best Practices</u> (4)
    - 11: <u>I'm thinking of writing an ebook and would love your feedback</u> (2)
    - 04: <u>Running Radiant CMS on DB2 in the Cloud</u> (0)
- March 2011 (6)
    - 28: <u>FAQ: What programming language should I learn first?</u> (4)
    - 21: <u>Programming is a Super Power</u> (34)
    - 14: <u>Getting Stuff Done With the Pomodoro Technique</u> (3)
    - 09: <u>Interview with Michael Hartl, author of the Rails 3 Tutorial</u> (3)
    - 07: <u>Eloquent Ruby Review</u> (6)
    - 01: <u>Jenga Driven Development</u> (15)
- February 2011 (1)

Figure 16—A table of contents

Unfortunately—or fortunately depending on your ideological stance on copyright law—many people online assume that copyright laws don't really apply. Copying images and other content online is pretty common and there is a certain nonchalance about the practice. As a blogger, however, you need to pay attention to and respect other people's copyrights as well as determine what to do if your own copyrighted work is plagiarized.

Avoid Infringing Copyright Laws

Laws can vary drastically from country to country, so you should check what rules apply where you reside. Generally speaking though, most countries have a doctrine of fair use that enables you to quote other works for the purpose of parody, criticism, and similar uses.

We are entering a giant gray zone, where the legality of certain actions is entirely debatable. You can read the Wikipedia entry for an overview of the topic at en.wikipedia.org/wiki/Fair_use. I'm not a lawyer so I'll skip the legalese and give you some practical advice instead that, while not legal advice, is generally accepted to be good online etiquette.

It's usually considered OK to quote a few paragraphs from other blog posts as long as you credit and link to the original source and use them to add your own commentary. Often microbloggers on sites like Tumblr and so-called link blogs highlight quotes or links and rebroadcast them further across the Web verbatim. It's generally fine, but without your insight, doing so won't add much value to your full-fledged blog.

Try to limit the quantity of such quotes to keep their use fair in the eyes of your readers and to the blogger you're quoting. This means that you should definitely avoid quoting a full blog post (unless it's a very tiny one, where quoting only a part wouldn't make sense).

Be extra careful when dealing with mainstream news outlets. AP (Associated Press) made the news a while ago by claiming that quoting five of their words would have required a fee.[3] Of course, this is entirely contrary to the spirit of the Web, but as a blogger it's in your best interest to respect copyright owners' rules so as not to run into a legal confrontation. It's just not worth fighting over such matters.

Don't use images unless they are in the public domain or released under a license that allows republishing. In particular, look for images released under the CC (Creative Commons) license, and observe which conditions apply (e.g., commercial use allowed). (Use Flickr for images and IconFinder for icons.[4])

Alternatively, you can also request permission for their use directly from their respective photographers. Asking nicely usually does the trick when it comes to amateur and enthusiast photographers.

---

3. www.ap.org
4. flickr.com and iconfinder.com, respectively.

Even if you have permission to use the images, you should never hotlink them. This means that you should serve your users a local copy of the image rather than using the original image directly. Among the reasons not to hotlink is the fact that you don't want to have the photographer incur bandwidth expenses on your behalf. As well, keep in mind that the original site may not be configured to handle high volumes of traffic.

Hosting a local copy also prevents your posts from having missing or broken link images if, in a few months or years down the line, the photographer decides to shut down that site, forgets to renew the domain name, or simply moves the image to a different location.

Following these simple rules should help you stay out of trouble. If a blogger with a stuck-up attitude complains to you about being quoted, you can always promptly remove the quoted portion from your post when asked. After that, stop quoting and linking to that blogger. It's entirely that person's loss (who doesn't like a little positive free publicity?) and not yours.

In theory, the worst that can happen for copyright infringement is a lawsuit against you. In practice, however, the more likely outcome would be a DMCA (Digital Millennium Copyright Act) takedown notice filed against you with your hosting company. Depending on the legitimacy of the claim and your hosting company's policies, your site may temporarily be taken offline until you remove the supposedly infringing content.

Issuing DMCA Notices

By following the guidelines mentioned above, you are not very likely to be on the receiving end of a DMCA takedown notice. You are, however, likely to have your content illicitly reproduced elsewhere without any credit being given to you. Lazy spammers need posts for their ad-filled content sites, and they'll get it one way or another—even if that means blatantly ripping it off from you!

Plagiarism can easily be spotted with tools such as Copyscape and Google Alerts.[5] Every single one of my many blogs has been plagiarized at some point in the past. So how are we supposed to deal with annoyances like these?

The easiest way is to politely ask any offenders (by email) to remove your content from their site(s). If you can't find the email address of a violator on a site, try the WHOIS register.

---

5. copyscape.com and google.com/alerts, respectively.

Don't insult offenders, and don't be vulgar or threatening. Simply state that you noticed that they reproduced copyrighted content of yours on their site and that you request its prompt removal. Be specific in your request and point out which URLs are infringing on your copyright.

Many times asking nicely is all it takes. The offenders may remove the content to get you off their case as they go about focusing on lower-hanging fruit instead. Other times this approach doesn't work.

What can you do if your precious, precious content gets shamelessly copied and you can't take it down? You probably guessed it. You can file a DMCA takedown notice with the hosting company or with the blog provider (e.g., WordPress.com). You can see an example of this procedure at the following URL: www.hostgator.com/copyright.shtml.

Remember that you can always use creative thinking and get to them where it hurts: their wallets. You could, for example, report the offenders to their advertisers or ad networks.

There will be times when copyright violators will appear untouchable. They may reside in a foreign country or host their sites outside of the States, and nobody will cooperate with your request. In such instances, it's up to you to decide if you wish to continue pursuing the case or simply let things be.

Don't overly concern yourself with protecting your content, and choose your battles wisely. Spending too much attention fighting copyright violations tends to be a waste of your valuable time and energy.

One positive aspect of getting copied is that if your content includes products you promote, copyright violators will inadvertently spread your message further, thereby doing you a favor.

5.10 Back Up Your Content

You work hard to write your content, so wouldn't it be a shame if it were lost? I can't stress enough how important it is to back up your blog's content.

Your hosting company may offer you backup solutions for a fee. Take advantage of such options if possible. What you are really interested in is saving the database that contains your posts as well as the folders where you store images and other files (e.g., wp-content in WordPress).

To save the database, you can perform a dump of the data (e.g., using mysql-dump) in a file and then upload it to multiple safe places (e.g., on S3, locally, and in a Dropbox folder).

Tip 14

Have at least three backups in different places.

For WordPress, check out a plugin called WP-DBManager, which will even email you your backups at intervals that you've specified in the plugin's settings. You can also consider VaultPress and BackupBuddy.[6]

For Blogger and other hosted services, once you've accrued a significant number of posts, you might want to try a premium service such as Backupify.[7] Google is unlikely to lose your blog's data, but if it kicks you out of the system for whatever reason, it may deny you access to the data you worked so hard to produce.

5.11 What's Next

Congratulations. You are now fully equipped to start writing awesome content for your blog. And that immediately presents you with a challenge: Can you keep up the pace? In the next chapter, I'll provide you with tips on how to keep your writing pace going strong and how to produce large volumes of content in as stress-free a manner as possible. We'll discuss scheduling posts, managing your time effectively, and when and how much to post. After that, we'll move our focus to promoting the great articles you're going to write.

---

6.   vaultpress.com and pluginbuddy.com/purchase/backupbuddy, respectively.
7.   backupify.com

I worked hard. Anyone who works as hard as
I did can achieve the same results.
  ➤ *Johann Sebastian Bach*

CHAPTER 6

Producing Content Regularly

In the previous chapter we discussed how well-written, interesting content is paramount to achieving blogging success. How often and when you post are also two important factors that will influence the growth of your blog, as will whether or not you're able to stick to your schedule.

6.1 What's the Post Frequency, Kenneth?

In theory, you should try to publish as much valuable content as frequently as you can. Doing so, obvious though it may sound, is often the best way to ensure that your blog blossoms and succeeds.

A high publication rate has the ingrained benefit of providing you with plenty of articles to promote, as well as multiple opportunities to be discovered by visitors coming from search engines (i.e., organic traffic).

That's the theory; the reality is that producing plenty of content can take a toll on you. It's not unusual for new bloggers to start producing a great deal of posts during the first few weeks, only to gradually give up on their blogs as soon as they see that the results, in terms of traffic and income, do not justify their huge investment of time and energy. Trying to do too much is the surest path to burnout and failure.

The ideal post frequency then becomes one that you can sustain over a long period of time without it becoming a source of stress in your life. Posting more often than you can realistically sustain will lead you to have diminished interest in your blog and potentially burn out.

The table below shows the current average post frequency per week for a series of successful technical and business-related blogs (as estimated by Google Reader).

Blog	Weekly Posts
Engadget	273.9
TechCrunch	231.7
ReadWriteWeb	164.7
GigaOM	96.4
Daring Fireball	46.2
37signals's SVN	9.8
Seth Godin's Blog	9.3
A VC	7.7
MailChimp's Blog	3.5
Ruby Inside	1.9
Twitter's Blog	1.9
Steve Blank's Blog	1.6
Math Blog	1.4
Programming Zen	1.2
Rails' Blog	0.9
jQuery's Blog	0.7
Joel on Software	0.7
Venture Hack	0.5

As you can see, the frequency varies mostly from a post every couple of weeks to two posts per day. The exception to this sensible range is collective blogs à la *TechCrunch*, which are more news sites than regular blogs and can take advantage of large teams of paid writers.

I can't tell you what your ideal posting frequency is—not without knowing your blog goals, the amount of time you can commit, and how long it takes you to write an average post. But I can recommend that you start with one to three blog posts per week and adjust the pace as it fits your life. If you can only dedicate much less time, try posting once every two weeks at least.

This suggestion assumes that your entries are medium (e.g., above 400 words) to long (e.g., above 1000 words), and not just link collections, quotes, or other forms of microblogging. Your posts shouldn't all have the same word count either, or Google may see your blog as fishy.

Keep in mind that average web readers tend to favor content that is shorter and more frequent rather than longer and less frequent due to the average human attention span being somewhat limited (as briefly discussed in the previous chapter). Nevertheless, don't ignore the power of well-written essays, detailed reviews, or longer HOWTO posts. Lengthy, insightful content may win over quite a few first-time visitors and convince them to become subscribers.

Albeit rarer, it's also possible to be so prolific that your regular readers end up experiencing fatigue and burnout while trying to continually stay abreast of your blog in their feed reader or email client. So long as you stick to the sensible range described in this section, however, reader burnout shouldn't be a real cause for concern.

6.2 Consistency Is Queen

When you have chosen, and perhaps even publicly announced, your posting schedule, you should try to stick to it for a period of at least a few months (after which you can change your schedule again, if required).

Interestingly, there is almost a Pavlovian mechanism at play when you start posting on a regular basis, wherein your subscribers get excited and start looking forward to your next post. This in turn builds loyalty toward you and your blog.

If your articles stop appearing at their usual time, you may end up breaking this cycle of expectation and as a result lose a few readers. Imagine reading a given newspaper every day and suddenly not finding it on your doorstep one morning (or perhaps worse, having it show up on random days). Humans are creatures of habit.

6.3 What Days Should You Post On?

Unless you choose to post every day, you may be wondering just what the best days are to post on your blog.

This is a conundrum that's well known to marketers who manage large newsletters. What's the best day? What's the best time? The difference an opportune choice of day makes can be measured in many thousand of dollars if a marketer's mailing list is large enough.

Bloggers don't have the luxury of A/B testing the same way email marketers do, because you can't publish the same public post one day for 50 percent of your audience and on a different day for the rest and then compare which day was more successful.

What you can do, though, is publish articles on different days of the week and see if over time any clear traffic trend emerges. It's not exactly a scientific approach, but it may give you a better picture of when your specific audience is most receptive.

Generally speaking, I have found that early to midweek days are the most effective days traffic-wise. It's not unusual for technical bloggers who post three times a week to publish their best content at the beginning of the week (Monday and Wednesday) and then publish something lighthearted on Friday. It's the blogging equivalent of Casual Friday. Just don't overdo it, or you may bring the overall quality of your blog down too heavily.

Some bloggers opt to run series of posts on different days. You could, for example, publish a pundit-style essay on Monday, a handy HOWTO on Wednesday, and a roundup of fresh new links to some of the latest articles from fellow bloggers in your niche on Friday.

When it comes to the specific time of the day, I tend to favor early morning (e.g., 7 a.m. ET) for my English blogs that target a predominantly North American audience. This time of day still captures part of the afternoon European traffic while welcoming American and Canadian readers as they sip their morning coffee.

Please note that organic traffic coming from search engines is not directly affected by the day or time you publish your content. All the considerations in this section relate to the behavior of *timely* traffic you receive shortly after publishing a blog post. Indirectly, it still has an impact because the more buzz you generate, the more links you'll attract.

6.4 Schedule Time to Blog

Before getting serious about blogging, you should determine how much time you are realistically willing and able to allocate to researching, writing, and promoting your content.

My recommendation is to set aside no less than four hours per week to your blog. With four hours at your disposal, you should be able to publish, at the very least, one or two blog entries.

Regardless of how much time you allocate to blogging, prepare the majority of your posts the week beforehand and schedule them for publication by using the scheduling feature that most modern blogging software includes (see Figure 17, *WordPress's scheduling feature*, on page 108). By doing so you can write your entries in advance, set them to be published automatically on a certain date and time, and be done for the week. (WordPress users who schedule posts frequently may enjoy the Editorial Calendar plugin.)

If you can't commit the same amount of time every week, I would highly encourage you to take advantage of the good weeks and schedule time for writing as many posts in advance as you can. Then you'll be covered during weeks when you are too busy, are traveling, or encounter unexpected situations that deter your ability to devote as much time as you usually do to your blog.

I like to write down ideas (in the ideas.txt file mentioned before), notes, and even whole paragraphs in a notepad or on my computer as they come to me. But in my experience, it's far better to treat blogging as a serious business and schedule time in your calendar for the sole purpose of this activity.

The good news is that as you gain more experience, you'll become faster at preparing new posts and should be able to get more out of your scheduled blogging time, however long it is.

If you are truly struggling to find the time to write, look into tracking software like RescueTime.[1] You may discover that a nonnegligible amount of your time is spent on unnecessary online activities that can be swapped for some solid focused writing instead.

> **Tip 15**
>
> Schedule empty posts to force yourself to work on them on time.

6.5 Manage Your Time with the Pomodoro Technique

Whatever technique or method you adopt to manage your time (Getting Things Done being a common example[2]), you'll reach a point where you'll settle down to the task of putting together your next post. When you do, you want to gather as much focus as possible to make productive use of the time you've allocated for blogging.

---

1. rescuetime.com
2. en.wikipedia.org/wiki/Getting_Things_Done

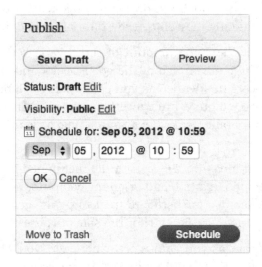

Figure 17—WordPress's scheduling feature

Enter the Pomodoro technique. The Pomodoro technique gets its intriguing name from kitchen timers, which are often shaped like tomatoes (*pomodoro* means "tomato" in Italian).

This productivity hack is extremely simple and can be used when writing for your blog, promoting your articles on social media sites, or doing any task that's important to you.

The basic idea is that each of us can only focus on a given task for so long before we become distracted. This time management technique also weaves in the fact that it's important to take regular breaks as you work (both for the sake of helping you stay focused and for your overall health and well-being). The Pomodoro technique regulates when you are to diligently focus on a task and when you should take a breather.

This technique is centered on breaking your time down into *pomodori* (plural for pomodoro; one pomodoro is equal to 25 minutes). You log a specific task you are going to work on and then sprint your way through that pomodoro. After 25 minutes of dedicated work, the timer goes off and you take a nice 5-minute break from your work.

Once your break is over, you start another 25-minute-long pomodoro. This new pomodoro can be dedicated to the same task as before (if you didn't complete it during the previous pomodoro) or to a new one. After every four pomodori, you can take a longer break (usually a 15-minute one).

It's important not to ignore breaks, as they really help you to stay refreshed when you jump into your next 25-minute pomodoro sprint.

Armed with the Pomodoro technique, you'll start to think in terms of the number of pomodori that a given post might require. Thus instead of allocating four hours to blogging, you may decide to allocate eight pomodori per week. As you gain experience, you'll soon discover how many pomodori you need for your average post.

If you are new to this technique, chances are that you'll be amazed by how much you can accomplish in 25 minutes of unadulterated focus. My average blog post is on the longer side, and it usually takes me no more than two pomodori to write it.

I personally use the Pomodoro for Mac app,[3] which costs only a few dollars from the Mac App Store and is very flexible (older versions are available for free, but they don't offer the same range of features).

If you are not on a Mac, there are other applications for virtually any platform (including Android and iOS) out there. While some of these are less polished and have fewer features than the Mac app, it's important to remember that even a simple timer application and a text editor would do the trick, so you don't actually need all the bells and whistles of the Mac version.

For an in-depth look at this subject, I suggest you read the book *Pomodoro Technique Illustrated: The Easy Way to Do More in Less Time* [Nö09], also published by The Pragmatic Bookshelf.

6.6 Survive Writer's Block

From time to time you may find yourself in an annoying predicament. A new post is due on your blog, but you simply can't seem to bring yourself to write it no matter how much you try. This phenomenon is commonly known as writer's block and can be quite serious if your livelihood depends on your ability to produce new content.

I'm neither a psychologist nor a neurologist, so I won't provide a lengthy explanation of what causes writer's block or how to cure said ailment. Instead, I'll share a few tips with you that work well for me when this situation arises in the hope that you may also find them useful:

---

3. pomodoro.ugolandini.com

- Check your idea file to see if you can write about a different topic that is less challenging or time consuming than the one you're having trouble with.

- If the writer's block is there regardless of the post you are attempting to write, consider changing your environment. Go to a local cafe, the library, a park, or somewhere else that is different from where you normally hang out while writing your posts. Switch to writing with pen and paper if you have to.

- Consider taking a break and going offline entirely for a couple of hours. Go for a walk or to the gym; do anything aside from writing or web surfing. Chances are your brain's background process (your unconscious) will still work on the post for you, giving you more insight and a fresher outlook when you decide to try writing again.

- Using the Pomodoro technique, start writing until the timer goes off, without the intention of publishing your post. Simply write down whatever comes to mind. Nobody will ever see what you write, so you're free to type away without too much concern regarding grammar, sentence structure, paragraph order, and other considerations that make for good writing. You'll quickly realize that polishing these paragraphs and reorganizing them is easier than coming up with the perfect phrasing for each one from the get-go.

- Edit your posts in fullscreen mode to achieve maximum focus. WordPress and several editors offer this feature.

- Rewrite the post from scratch after you try the stream-of-consciousness exercise above. Chances are this time the words will come to you.

- Lower your writing expectations and give yourself a break. What you write doesn't have to be perfect. It can simply be a spontaneous thought, a reflection, or a quick consideration. You'll be surprised at how often posts like this end up becoming extremely popular and well liked by your readers. "Perfect" is the enemy of "good enough."

- Don't write your technical post down. Instead, talk about it with someone else, explaining the subject matter to them in a clear and interesting way. Doing so will help you organize your ideas and express the thoughts you've had tucked away in the back of your mind on a given topic. As you approach the blinking cursor again, you'll probably find it easier to simply rewrite what you just said to your spouse, colleague, or friend.

• Consider having a reserve of unpublished, evergreen posts (such as content that will still be current and useful a few years from now). That way, if you can't snap out of your writer's block in time for a given week, you can use such posts to keep up with your usual schedule nevertheless.

6.7 Get Others to Write for You

One of the best methods for increasing your blog post frequency is to employ help from other people. Having others write content for you as you churn out your own posts will definitely increase the database of content your blog is able to amass.

In this section, we'll explore three free methods you can use to get others to write for you:

• Email (or audio) interviews
• Guest bloggers
• Article translations

We'll cover hiring bloggers in Chapter 13, *Scaling Your Blogging Activities*, on page 227.

Arrange Email Interviews

The premise behind email interviews is straightforward and only requires that you send out one or two messages. The first asks an expert in your field about doing an email interview with you. If that person says yes, you can send a second email with a series of interesting questions tailored to that person that your readers may want to know about.

Coming up with a series of intelligent questions and handling the email communication back and forth may take a bit of your time, but since your interviewee will be doing most of the writing for you with his or her answers, you'll end up with an interesting post that required relatively little work on your part.

From a promotional standpoint, prominent experts tend to have their own audiences who may discover your blog thanks to the interview, assuming said interviewees mention your post on their blogs or on social media sites (not an unusual occurrence). This type of content also has the advantage of lending credibility to your blog if the people you interview are well liked or respected in your field.

In my experience, while you cannot realistically expect to interview Bill Gates, if you email enough people and are polite and mindful of their time, you'll find that sometimes even fairly popular folks are willing to answer your questions.

This works particularly well if your intended interview subject has an ulterior motive for participating. For example, I interviewed Giacomo "Peldi" Guilizzoni, founder of Balsamiq Studio, LLC, back in 2009.[4] This interview exposed my readers to his Mockups software, potentially leading to more sales for him. In fact, if you are a startup owner trying to promote your own products, you should definitely jump at the opportunity to give interviews to fellow bloggers.

I often get approached by companies (and their PR agencies) who are trying to promote their products for free on my blogs. Replying by suggesting an interview by email has been a great way to get rid of the less earnest ones and has helped me score some great interviews with more serious companies.

Finally, consider the possibility of creating a thematic series of interviews on your blog. For example, I used to have a Startup Interviews series on ProgrammingZen.com. A series tells new readers that similar content is on the horizon and can be a big motivational factor when it comes to garnering new subscribers. It may also lead a few experts to contact you to be featured in the series as interviewees.

If you don't dislike the sound of your voice too much, also consider getting a decent microphone and conducting audio interviews or podcasts.

Find Guest Bloggers

Guest blogging is the act of publishing posts on a blog that you don't own. This is typically done in order to obtain some form of free publicity through backlinks to the guest blogger's own blog or site.

In the next chapter we'll see how you can effectively use this technique to promote your blog on other blogs, thereby reaching their audiences. In this section, however, we'll focus on how you can leverage eager promoters to score some free posts for your blog.

The easiest way to attract guest bloggers is to advertise that you're accepting such submissions. You can write a post on your blog that welcomes contributions from your existing audience—a "Write for us" page—as well as put an invite to do guest blogging below each guest post you publish.

---

4.   programmingzen.com/2009/04/13/startup-interviews-balsamiq-studio-llc

I constantly receive emails from prospective guest bloggers and authors simply because my Write for us page on Math-Blog.com does a good job of selling the benefits of doing so (it also clarifies what type of content I'm interested in publishing).

Thanks to that page, I found John F. McGowan, PhD, a scientist and consultant who has become a regular writer for the blog, and as of late has been publishing more posts than I do on a purely volunteer basis. My blog receives high-quality content for free, and he gets a platform to advertise his technical expertise and consultancy business. It's a win-win situation that truly benefits both of us.

Another easy way to find guest writers is to email bloggers you respect, asking them if they are interested in guest blogging for you or in doing an exchange in which you guest blog on their sites and they do the same on yours.

You will want to have established your blog a bit already before attempting to solicit other people to write for you, but tasks like this take little time and can often lead to symbiotic relationships with other bloggers.

Tip 16

Contact people who guest blog on blogs that you follow.

If you're reasonable with your request (don't expect them to write a 10,000-word guide that gets spread out across ten posts) and persuasive enough with your pitch, you may also be able to create guest bloggers from people who have never blogged before in their lives.

Insightful commenters who are already hanging out in the comment section of your blog, valuable technical mailing list contributors that you approach privately, and experts you know from the offline world may gladly take you up on this sort of offer. Going to technical meetups and conferences is a great way to befriend potential guest bloggers.

The only downside to being open to guest bloggers is that you'll have to sort through some rather rubbish proposals to find the quality authors you're seeking. Internet marketers are quite aware of the effectiveness of guest blogging, so you'll likely receive requests from people who are solely interested in getting a backlink to their unrelated—and often less than reputable—sites that were MFA (made for AdSense) or for the sole purpose of pushing specific affiliate offers.

I consider these emails to be little more than spam and tend to reply to them with a polite but candid response about not being interested due to the nature of the links. Alternatively, you may simply ignore them, if you'd prefer.

Translate Other Bloggers' Content

If you speak more than one language, you can easily score great content by translating articles that were originally written by others into the other language(s) that you speak.

The key is to ask for permission before you jump headfirst into translating. In your email to the original content creators, explain that you appreciate what they wrote and that you'd like to make their work available to people who speak the language your blog is in. Reassure them that you'll credit the post back to them and link to the original article(s). Only proceed with translating the post if the original creator grants you permission to do so.

Depending on your mastery of a given language and your skill as a translator, you may find the process to be rather easy. In going this route, you'll be offering a very valuable service and providing high-quality content to your readers. I would not advocate publishing translations only (as your site's sole content source, I mean), but I certainly wouldn't ignore such a valuable opportunity to create worthwhile content either.

If a blogger agrees that it's OK for you to translate a particular article, ask if it's also all right to translate other content from the blog into your language under the same set of conditions (or if you need to ask for permission explicitly each time). This way you'll have another easy pool to draw from should you find yourself temporarily out of good ideas for posts.

Unless you've been instructed not to, let the blogger know when you've published a translation. They may link back to you or mention the translation to their circle of followers.

My programming blog is routinely translated by other bloggers (for some reason, Brazilian bloggers in particular). And if you blog in a language other than English, you are officially authorized to translate any of my blogs' content under the same conditions described above. Namely, credit the original post and link back to it from your post.

6.8 What's Next

This wraps up the series of chapters dedicated to producing content. Having worked through these pages, you should have a clear picture of what to blog about, when, how often to post, and how to get others to write for you for free.

With all that covered, we can move on to the equally important promotional side of things. Starting with the next chapter, you'll see how to promote the content you've worked so hard to produce in order to ensure it receives as much exposure as possible.

Part III

Promote It

Marketing is too important to be left to the marketing department.
> ➤ *David Packard*

CHAPTER 7

Promoting Your Blog

This chapter kick-starts the third part of the book, which is dedicated to the marketing side of your life as a blogger.

Self-promotion and marketing can be touchy subjects among technical audiences, so we'll start by considering why these activities matter, then we'll delve into what you need to do to promote your blog.

7.1 Market It and They Will Come

The 1989 dramatic film *Field of Dreams* popularized the expression "If you build it, he will come" and its variations. When it comes to blogging, the opposite is often true: "Build it, and they won't come."

The truth is that once you have built your shiny blog and published some content, traffic will roll in very slowly unless you actively promote your site. In other words, building is necessary but not sufficient to ensure your blog gets the attention it deserves.

Most bloggers skip this promotional step, and as a result they end up receiving only a handful of visitors. At that point a vicious cycle starts in which seeing so few visitors demotivates the blogger, who in turn publishes less often and consequently attracts fewer visitors (which discourages the blogger further, and so on). The end result is a blog abandoned in a matter of weeks or months.

This disastrous outcome can be prevented. First, you've done your homework regarding subject matter; niche size; on-page SEO; headlines; and the type, quality, and frequency of content. These actions alone put you streets ahead of most bloggers and also partially vaccinate you against a complete lack of readership.

However, there are millions of active blogs in the wilds of the Internet, and standing out and attracting a serious following will require a conscious effort on your part.

Another way to look at this situation is that you've got the first part of the equation right. Now you need to get your marketing efforts right as well. Don't skip this or the following chapters; they are absolutely some of the most valuable ones when it comes to the success of your blog.

7.2 Correct a Self-Sabotaging Mindset

Marketing is bullshit. Marketing is evil. Marketing is everything that's wrong with this world. Marketing is the root of all evil. Marketers should be shot.

I have heard all these statements—and plenty more like them.

If you agree with any of them, you are not alone in your dislike of marketing. I've found that technical people, particularly programmers, tend to have a strong hatred for marketing.

Antimarketing stances stem partly from bad experiences with manipulative marketers and partly from a misunderstanding of what marketing actually is.

Wikipedia defines marketing in this way:

> Marketing is the process used to determine what products or services may be of interest to customers and what strategy to use in sales, communications, and business development.

At its core, marketing is about connecting people to solutions. For example, some people may have an interest in buying an environmentally friendly car. Good marketing involves identifying this segment of the population, then devising a strategy to let that portion of the population know about the existence of your brand-new hybrid car and its benefits (in a style and manner that will appeal to them).

Though the ultimate goal is to sell a car, marketing isn't about convincing people who are not interested in your product to buy it. It's about exposing the right product to the right audience. Done correctly and in an ethical manner, it's possible to promote without deceiving, manipulating, or forcing people to spend their hard-earned money on goods they don't want or need.

It's important to understand that marketing is so much more than just advertising. Marketing encompasses countless aspects of your product, including what you name it before it even exists.

If you still feel that marketing is mostly evil, I encourage you to reflect on the forms of marketing you already do, perhaps without even realizing that they're marketing. Ever applied for a new job? Or dated someone? While you probably didn't misrepresent yourself with your future employer or partner by blatantly lying, you still wore nice clothes and tried to showcase your favorable traits.

In doing so you were marketing yourself.

In blogging, the aim of your marketing is to reach as many people who are potentially interested in your content as possible. As we'll see in future chapters, you may also have related additional goals, such as promoting yourself professionally, marketing yours and other people's products, and so on.

Like all tools, marketing can be used for good or in unethical, obnoxious ways. In this book, I advocate only white-hat marketing techniques that will get your content in front of the people who need to see it. So if you are the stereotypical antimarketing developer, please approach the rest of the chapter with an open mind. I promise that you won't have to sell your soul.

7.3 Perform On-page and Off-page SEO

As amply discussed before, the goal of your on-page SEO efforts is to present your content in the best light possible in the eyes of search engines. You are trying to provide Google and others with positive indicators of the relevance of your content in relation to the search queries provided by end users.

Let's briefly recap some of the most prominent *on-page* SEO factors.

- Create plenty of well-researched, nicely written original content.
- Have a keyword-rich domain name.
- Write catchy headlines containing target keywords.
- Have a keyword-dense slug for your articles.
- Use headings in your content (and include desirable keywords in your headings).
- Interlink your site by using tags, categories, related article plugins, etc.
- Ensure your site loads quickly.
- Have an XML sitemap.

On-page SEO is all about what you can do on your site to better your chances of ranking well with search engines. *Off-page SEO* is the promotional work you do outside of your site to generate backlinks from high PageRank websites (you may recall how a site's PageRank is a number that's assigned by Google to indicate the authority of that site). It's worth noting that an internal page on a high PageRank site won't generally have the same PageRank of its home page. Nevertheless, even internal pages of popular sites tend to attract many links and have as a consequence relatively high PageRanks.

Link building is so fundamental because quality backlinks are one of the strongest signals used by Google's algorithm to determine the authority and relevance of your site. The premise is that if a variety of authority sites that are trusted by Google link to your site with related anchor texts (the words you link), then your URL must be important and trustworthy for that particular set of keywords. Because of this, always use meaningful anchor text in your links. Don't use "Click here" or similar.

When you first launch your blog, link building will help you get found and indexed by Google. To help Google discover you quickly, you should also submit your blog directly at google.com/addurl (you'll be asked to log in first).

The rest of this chapter is dedicated to techniques to perform link building as well as social media promotion. This chapter is really all about techniques that will lead to more traffic for your blog, whether it's of an organic or referral nature.

Tip 17

Check your blog with WebsiteGrader.com.

7.4 Not All Links Are Created Equal

Remember that not all links are created equal. A link to your blog from the home page of *The New York Times* will far outweigh a link from an unknown blog. You should not only strive to build a lot of backlinks but also try to receive them from authoritative sites. These will in fact increase your PageRank, ranking, and possibly send you a stream of referral traffic.

SEO isn't an exact science, so there isn't complete agreement on every factor that determines the value of the backlinks you receive. The ranking algorithm changes frequently as a means of combatting spam, Google bombing,[1] and other such abuses, so that doesn't help matters either.

---

1. en.wikipedia.org/wiki/Google_bomb

Joe asks:
Should I Care About the PageRank of My Blog?

The PageRank of a blog correlates with the authority and popularity of that site. Anything over (and including) a PageRank 4 indicates that your blog is fairly popular. The whole point of link building, however, is not to increase this magic number. The point is to rank well for your target keywords and for as many "long tail" keywords as possible.

Increasing your PageRank is a side effect of link building. In fact, the PageRank of your home page (and internal pages) is only one out of over two hundred signals that are used by Google to determine the rank of a given URL for a certain query.

If this wasn't reason enough not to obsess over it, you should keep in mind that the publicly available PageRank value of your pages will only be updated once every few months. Initially, you won't even see a PageRank value (or it may appear as 0).

You can assess the authority of pages and sites with an SEO browser extension such as SeoQuake, SEO for Chrome, or Mozbar.

Nevertheless, the following are some common characteristics of the ideal backlink that can help improve your PageRank and ultimately your ranking.

- URLs that link to you have a high level of authority (usually measured through the PageRank).

- The domain linking to you is a .edu or .gov. Google values university and government sites.

- The backlink anchor text contains keywords that you're targeting.

- The page that links to your blog contains few other external links. In other words, your URL is one of the main links on that page.

- The page linking to you is relevant to the topic of your blog, and your link is present toward the top of the page (as opposed to a footer link or on the bottom of the sidebar).

Remember that you can't expect the perfect link to your site every time. Most blogs will naturally attract backlinks from a variety of sites in a pyramid-like pattern, as shown in Figure 18, *A plausible PageRank backlink distribution*, on page 125. Google would consider a site that only had high PageRank backlinks to be quite odd and may suspect foul play. (Some people will in fact purchase high PageRank backlinks in bulk, against the Google webmaster guidelines.[2] Read the Google webmaster guidelines in full to fully understand what Google expects from your site.

Also keep in mind that you don't have control over most backlinks. Our discussion about the perfect backlink is meant to help you obtain a few high-quality backlinks. But the majority of backlinks you'll attract will probably not be as a direct consequence of your link-building efforts.

In Chapter 5, *Creating Remarkable Content*, on page 83, we described how to create (good) linkbait that naturally attracts links. Let's dive into how to build high-quality backlinks through off-page efforts.

7.5 Guest Blog on Other Blogs

In the previous chapter we talked about finding guest bloggers to obtain free content. In this section, we'll reverse the tables. We are going to use guest blogging as a tool for promoting your blog.

Guest blogging can be an extremely powerful marketing tool. Compelling content and a dose of charisma can latch onto an existing community that's been created by someone else and quickly attract many followers to your own site. You'll also obtain the high quality backlinks you're working so hard to get.

Here are the three essential ingredients you are going to need to successfully promote your blog via guest blogging:

- A blogger who is willing to accept contributions from guest bloggers.

- A great article, typically comprised of original content that has not been published elsewhere. You'll want to position yourself as an expert on the subject matter you're covering and provide content that is relevant to both the hosting blog's and your niche.

- An enticing biography that includes one or two links to your blog. This biographical content, sometimes referred to as a *resource box*, is typically placed at the bottom of your guest post and may include a small picture of you and a description of who you are as well as a blurb about what you're promoting (e.g., your blog, a book, etc.). The specifics are typically agreed upon in advance with the blog's host.

---

2. www.google.com/support/webmasters/bin/answer.py?answer=35769

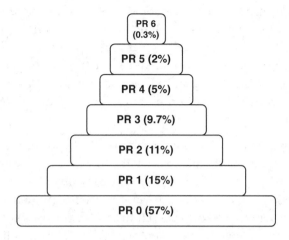

Figure 18—A plausible PageRank backlink distribution

Find Prospective Blogs

As you can probably imagine, the hardest part is finding bloggers who are willing to let you post on their blogs. Guest blogging is a win-win situation no matter which side of the table you sit at. So all you need to do is to explain its benefits to prospective hosts. Compile a list of twenty or so blogs in your niche or field. Give priority to those with a high authority (use an SEO toolbar to assess it) and especially to blogs that have accepted guest bloggers before. This task will be a lot easier if, as you should, you are already following many blogs in your niche via a feed reader.

Tip 18

Establish a relationship with a blogger before proposing a guest post.

Learn more about each blog, including the style, the elevator pitch, and so on. Then individually and sequentially approach each of these bloggers by email, starting from the most valuable and promising one. You can use a customized template message for each of them, but don't just copy and paste the same message for dozens of different bloggers. A message that starts with "Dear Webmaster" belongs in the spam folder.

The key to connecting is being personal and easy to relate to. Address the blogger or editor-in-chief by name. Don't forget some honest praise, including specifics of what you like about that person's approach to blogging. Even if the creator is very famous and you are just starting out, remember that you're dealing with a colleague and you have a fair proposal. Stress the benefits of your contribution, without sounding boastful, and acknowledge that you'll benefit from this relationship, too.

Before you approach the first blogger, ensure that you have a title and rough idea of the word count of the post you'd like to write. Briefly explain what the article is going to be about, what angle you plan to take, and how it's a relevant and welcome addition for readers. If you are feeling proactive, you can even write the article beforehand and send it over with your proposal (however, as you never know who is going to accept your guest blogger offer, do not send out the same article to more than one person until your offer has been turned down by the first blogger you sent it to).

Tip 19

Submit your best content when guest blogging.

Popular bloggers receive a lot of emails, so don't expect an answer in two hours. Give them a couple of weeks before following up with a second email that kindly asks whether they are interested or if you should opt for other blogs instead. If after another week or so you haven't heard back, let them know that you've withdrawn your offer and will now consider other blogs. Thank them for their time. Don't burn bridges with fellow bloggers. If things don't work out, remain as polite, professional, and amicable as possible.

At three weeks or so per blogger, you may assume that it will take you over a year to reach the bottom of that initial list. Thankfully, this is just a worst-case scenario. If your article and proposal are sensible, you'll likely receive a positive answer way before you reach the last name and email on your list. The typical response times will also be much shorter than three weeks.

Once someone shows interest, you can agree on the details regarding how the article should be formatted and submitted, what kinds of links are allowed, whose referral code is used for possible affiliate links, the specifics of your resource box, if this is a one-off arrangement or if you plan to guest blog regularly in the future, and so on.

The survivors from the initial list (those you haven't contacted yet) will come in handy as you proceed to pitch a new article down the road to expand your network of backlinks from other authority blogs. If your niche is very small, you may have to space out your contributions a little or you'll seem to dominate the conversation via multiple blogs.

Repeat the process as many times as you wish. At some point you may see your returns from guest blogging diminish as your site becomes an established blog in its own right within your online community.

Maximize the Effectiveness of Your Resource Box

The resource box is your reward, so you should pay close attention to what you include within it. The main goal should be to sell yourself as an expert on the topic you're blogging about and then get readers to take the action you want (be it buying your product, checking out your blog, whatever).

Don't write a gigantic biography that no one is actually going to read. Include a short, carefully crafted biographical paragraph that highlights your experience without sounding too boastful or like a complete list of everything you've accomplished since junior high.

Your resource box should also include a single, strong call to action. Include many calls, and people will ignore all of them—a pattern, you'll remember, we've seen before in regard to social buttons on your pages.

Carefully select anchor text for your backlinks so that they appear organic yet optimized for your target keyword. Typically you'd be choosing your blog title or a variation of it as the anchor text for the link to the home page of your blog.

When you discuss the resource box with the blogger who'll be hosting your guest post, ensure that you are allowed to have regular links and not nofollow links. The nofollow value in the link below tells Google that it shouldn't positively influence the PageRank of the linked site (e.g., *Math-Blog*).

```
<a href="http://math-blog.com" rel="nofollow">Math Blog</a>
```

Nofollow links were invented as a way of discouraging the rampant comment spam on blogs, so they have a legitimate use (just not for guest blogging purposes). As you work through your link-building efforts, remember that nofollow links are essentially useless for search engines (however, people may still click those links, of course).

I have heard the argument before that people doing massive link building for very competitive keywords should also include nofollow links in the mix to make the link building process appear more natural over time. We are not taking that approach here, so you shouldn't worry about that. Focus on obtaining high-quality *dofollow links* (i.e., links that don't have the rel="nofollow" attribute).

7.6 Other Forms of Article Marketing

Guest blogging is a specialized form of article marketing. Try it out because when you guest blog, you're adding value to your community with content that has been reviewed by at least two bloggers (you and the host of the blog you're publishing on). In other words, it's a form of promotion that ends up benefitting everyone involved.

Other forms of article marketing, while still technically white hat, can't truly make that same claim in regards to adding value to a community. I'm referring to the more traditional forms of article marketing that are carried out through article directories and press releases.

How Article Directories Work

Article directories are sites that accept article submissions on a variety of subjects. In exchange, they usually provide you with a resource box at the bottom of your articles in which one or two links of your choice can be embedded. Most directories review your articles before approving them.

Such sites make money via AdSense and other advertising forms and give you backlinks from high PageRank directories. Win-win situation once again, right? In theory, yes; this is very similar to the experience of guest blogging. In practice, though, things are rather different.

The average quality of articles on the most popular directories leaves a lot to be desired. The articles are full of typos; they're bland and often commissioned for a few dollars from people who know nothing about the subject matter they're writing about. Not only are the approval standards much lower than the average blogger who accepts contributions, but the people reviewing your articles will usually have no clue about your subject matter.

The majority of articles, you'll find, are poor, commercial in nature, and published under pen names by people who do not want to be associated with what they've written. I understand that this may come across as elitist, but if you've ever stumbled upon any of the following sites, you'll probably know what I'm talking about and will share similar feelings: Ezine Articles, Articles Base, Hub Pages, or Squidoo.

Incidentally, Google recently downgraded the ranking of most of these directories because it, too, perceives them as poor-quality content (i.e., *content farms*) that adds little value to the user.

The audience of these directories is mainly comprised of random people arriving from search engines and other fellow article marketers. It's not the cohesive, tight-knit kind of community you can expect from a blog niche that specializes in topics similar to yours. So while you may receive some PageRank juice from article directories, you won't get all the benefits you can typically expect from posting on the high-quality blog of a fellow expert.

Affiliate marketers love article directories because they offer an easy way to obtain hundreds of backlinks. In fact, most of these marketers outsource the creation of a handful of articles (for a few dollars apiece), and then use synonym-based software (i.e., *article spinners*) to automatically rewrite hundreds of combinations of those articles in a way that is difficult for duplicate filters to detect. Other software is then used to submit a rewritten version of each article to hundreds of directories.

Does it work? Yes, for the most part, or SEOs wouldn't use it. But you have to ask yourself how much value are you adding to the world by polluting Google with hundreds—if not thousands—of copies of the same article that was, in many cases, poor to begin with. This isn't technically a black-hat SEO approach, but Google doesn't appreciate it either. (Assuming you spun an article you created or commissioned and didn't scrape or copy it outright from a competitor.)

Keep in mind that you don't need hundreds of backlinks every month to rank in search engines for your average technical topic. The reason Internet marketers end up relying so heavily on automatic link building of this kind is because competition is fierce for commercial keywords such as *insurance quote* or *make money online*.

You can take a more time-consuming approach and manually write high-quality articles for these directories, ignoring spinners and similar software. But at that point, the effort and time required will not make article directories any more appealing than guest blogging.

In short, focus on guest blogging and leave article directories as a tool of last resort for link building (if guest blogging isn't panning out well for you).

Use Press Releases for SEO

Press releases have traditionally been used to announce news about a company or product launch to members of the media. Much like article directories, there is nothing evil or inherently wrong with using them in the hopes of attracting the attention of journalists and other media.

In practice however, you'll find that most journalists are not interested in your new blog unless it has a novelty factor that is well suited to attention-grabbing headlines about the hot topic of the moment (e.g., "New Blog Showcases the Worst of Facebook").

Nevertheless, press releases can be used for SEO purposes. In fact, every time you use a PR service such as prweb.com, you'll see your press release reprinted across hundreds or even thousands of sites. Include links to your site in the press release, carefully select your anchor texts based on your target keywords, and you'll magically receive a boost in the SERP. Just don't expect your story to be picked up by AP or Reuters, even with the most expensive press release plan that these sites offer.

In my experience, such services won't send much traffic your way, but they will generate many backlinks for you. Are they worth the price of admission? It's up to you to decide that, but search around the Web before plunking down your money, and perhaps start out with a free service with a more limited distribution. (Search online for a good tutorial on writing press releases, or commission them to someone more experienced.)

It's worth considering the argument that PR services, particularly low-cost ones that are distributed throughout the Web, are little more than spam. Whether you buy this argument or not, it's important to stress that we are not in black-hat territory by any means. But how much value are you adding to users by polluting Google with your press release?

For the record, I've experimented with PRWeb's most expensive distribution plan for my new book notification service, *Any New Books*.[3] Using Google, I can verify that the press release was reprinted online 210 times, including on Yahoo.

In short, feel free to skip press releases for your blog for now, but be aware of their existence for those times when you're short on ideas to further promote your site.

7.7 Participate in the Community

One easy way to boost your link-building efforts is to actively and genuinely participate in the blogosphere. Follow blogs that are relevant to your field and

---

3. anynewbooks.com

Add Your Blog to Planet Sites

Planets are feed aggregator sites that display a list of posts from a variety of blogs on the same topic on a single page (and in a single RSS feed).

For example, Planet Python (planet.python.org) aggregates a large number of posts from blogs by Python programmers.

If a planet site exists for your niche, you should consider contacting the owners to add your feed to their list. The perks of doing so include greater exposure for your posts and SEO advantages because you are receiving backlinks from the planet site.

You can check out a few sample planet sites at planetplanet.org. If you intend to start a planet for your niche yourself, I recommend using Planet Venus at intertwingly.net/code/venus.

actively engage in commenting the stories they feature. Book fifteen to thirty minutes a day for this activity if doing so doesn't come naturally to you.

Commenting will foster your diplomatic relationships with other bloggers and provide you with plenty of backlinks. Albeit some of the backlinks will be nofollow, you'll still receive many new visitors because of them.

As you probably know, most blog engines allow your name to be linked to a URL of your choice when leaving comments. The key point here is to add value with your comments, though. Don't leave comments just to obtain a backlink. Instead, read what the blogger has to say and then comment with your own insight. Few things will attract readers to your blog like excellent comments by an expert voice.

The difference between comment spam and an active reader who's trying to be useful lies in the words used. Responding to a post with a comment such as "Great post" while filling the URL field of the form with your blog URL is not that different from what comment spammers do (OK, they automate the process to scale, but conceptually it's not that different at all).

Always add value to the topic at hand, and take the time required to leave an insightful comment that is at least a paragraph or two long. Don't speak solely because you want a backlink. Comment because you have something valuable to say. And by all means forget SEO when commenting. The name field should include your name, not target keywords.

At times it may be appropriate to link to your blog directly within your comment. In fact, if you are the first or second person to comment with a link, people may click your link even more than on the links within the post itself.

For example, the following comment would probably be OK with most bloggers:

> Brilliant post, Richard. I expressed very similar thoughts about the behavior of subatomic particles here: <link>. I must say however that your diagrams are an extremely clever representation of quantum electrodynamical interactions. They may catch on.

Be very careful with this, as it's easy to come across as a spammer or as too aggressive of a self-promoter. Step back for a second, and think about how you'd react if the same comment was made by another blogger on your own site. Would you approve it or reject it? Would it upset you?

Tip 20

Remember the golden rule: treat others as you'd like to be treated yourself.

7.8 Leverage Foreign Blogs

When your blog acquires enough visibility, you may be approached by foreign bloggers who will ask you to translate some of your content into their own language.

Let them publish your translated content (for free). You'll get further distribution of your ideas and/or products as well as a backlink from a potentially popular blog or online magazine. The only condition you should have is that the article is credited to you and that it links back to your original post. In fact, you may even go so far as to actively scout for related blogs in other languages, then propose such an arrangement.

Most of the people who approach you and offer to translate your content are genuine bloggers who are interested in propagating your content in other languages.

When a translation is published on someone else's site, you can decide if you want to link back to the translation from your original article or not (e.g., "This article is also available in Spanish, Japanese, and Chinese."). You don't have to. Some bloggers opt to do so, however, and this is where scammers see an opportunity.

From time to time you may be approached by scammers who ask you if they can translate a highly popular article of yours. You'll say it's OK, and they'll supposedly work on a translation. Then they'll send you a link to a page that seemingly includes your translation and in turn they'll ask you to include a backlink to their translation from your article with a high PageRank.

The scam factors in when the page you've been pointed to is not an actual translation of your article. Scammers may keep the title, but the content will have nothing to do with what you wrote. Even if they do translate your content, perhaps badly via Google Translate, don't be afraid of saying no to the request of linking back to the translation.

Link back only when you receive a link to a quality translation of your actual content. Again, Google Translate can help you figure that out, but a friend or reader who speaks the language would be better.

Evaluate the overall quality of their blog and not just the translation. If the foreign site is not in your niche, contains translated content about all sorts of unrelated topics, or is plastered in ads, an offer to translate your content may have little to do with admiration and a whole lot to do with SEO and link building. Don't be afraid to say no to requests for backlinks to translations from your original article or page.

7.9   The Dark Side of Link Building

If you pursue link building and SEO education further on your own, you'll quickly discover what I call the dark side of online marketing.

I'll refrain from teaching you black-hat techniques and opt instead to list a series of borderline activities you may come across and be tempted to partake in. Don't. They are not worth your time.

- *Buying high PageRank links*: As mentioned multiple times, buying links will get you blacklisted or penalized by search engines.

- *Renting email addresses*: At best this is a waste of time; at worst you end up spamming people who don't know you or your blog.

- *Buying social media votes*: You can artificially boost your popularity on social networks like Reddit and StumbleUpon by buying votes for $0.10–$1.00 USD each. In many cases, doing so will get your blog banned from or penalized on social networking sites.

- *Three-way link exchanges*: Reciprocal links between two sites don't offer much in the way of SEO benefits, so there are services that take advantage of intermediary sites in the link chain to generate nonreciprocal links among those who participate in their network.

- *Fake blogs*: You can create a series of dummy blogs through free services like Blogger or WordPress.com, and then have all of them point back to your blog. Such services routinely ban fake blogs and accounts in an effort to keep down spam.

- *Link wheels*: This is a linking scheme involving fake blogs and article submissions that are organized so as to boost the PageRank of the URLs linking to your money page (the URL you want to promote), with the ultimate goal being to greatly boost the PageRank and relevancy of your money page for target keywords.

- *Mass article submissions*: Spun content is submitted not just to article directories but also to networks of low-quality blogs and is set up only to attract the content of other bloggers and to earn money via AdSense and other advertisements.

- *Automated submission to a variety of directories*: This is when you use software to automatically submit your site and feed to hundreds or thousands of crappy directories that no human will ever truly find useful.

While some marketers do pretty well with these techniques, which are not actually illegal, they're still trying to game the system. Focus on adding value to your readers and your online community. The rewards and efforts will be far greater, and you won't risk being penalized by search engines and social media sites.

7.10 Promote Your Articles on Social Networks

In this section (and the next), we'll talk about promoting your articles on a variety of social media sites.

The same principles can be applied to new social networks that will pop up in the future as well as to specialized social media sites for your particular sector that are not represented here.

General Social Networks to Promote On

General social media sites you should promote your content on are as follows:

- Twitter
- Facebook
- Google+
- StumbleUpon
- Delicious

If your content is any good, it will see its way through these five channels naturally. Yet it's important to ensure that all your valuable articles are promoted on these sites.

The visibility you can obtain on Twitter, Facebook, and Google+ will largely depend on your network of friends, as well as on those friends or followers of anyone who sees your content and decides to post it on Twitter, Facebook, or Google+. In fact, whatever you post on these sites will appear on the stream/wall of those who follow you or befriend you on such sites.

If you don't have existing accounts on the sites mentioned above, now would be a good time to create them and start adding friends, colleagues, and acquaintances.

StumbleUpon and Delicious work differently. With StumbleUpon, your article, once submitted, is randomly shown to a series of toolbar users who are interested in the categories you've selected for your article. If they like your content, they can give it a thumbs-up in the toolbar, which will increase your page's score and consequently lead StumbleUpon to show your link to more people.

Delicious is a bookmarking service. If enough people bookmark your article in a short time frame (a few hours), your link may appear in the frequently bookmarked area of the site. The quicker this process and the more bookmarks you receive when first bookmarked, the higher the likelihood of appearing in the popular page for a given tag or on the list of popular links on the home page.

Your Promotional Workflow

As soon as you publish a new article on your site, you should take the following steps:

- Google +1 your article by using the counter/button we previously installed. Share your post on Google+ by pasting your link as an update.

- Tweet the title plus a shortened URL on Twitter. Add a prefix such as "New blog post:" if you want to stress that it's a link from your blog.

- Facebook Like your article and then post the URL on Facebook to share it with your friends.

- Submit your URL to StumbleUpon. Ensure that you pick up to five large categories (the maximum that StumbleUpon permits per page submitted). As an example, aim for Databases, not for Transactions.

- Bookmark your article on Delicious using a few relevant tags. Many people will be shown these tags when they bookmark the page too, so ensure that you select several appropriate tags that include a couple of generic ones like "programming" or "development."

Using services such as StumbleUpon's su.pr,[4] it's possible to automate the submission of your articles on Twitter, Facebook, and StumbleUpon directly from your feed. Automating your social media promotion workflow is a good idea so that you have fewer steps to worry about once you hit the Publish button.[5]

Resist the urge to create your own voting ring with close friends or colleagues on StumbleUpon. Instead, tell them about your new blog and perhaps introduce them to StumbleUpon. If they become active users of the site and follow your blog, they may thumbs-up your content from time to time.

On the other hand, feel free to encourage them to share your content with their friends on Twitter, Facebook, and Google+, as well as bookmark your articles if they find them interesting. There is no penalty of any kind for doing so with just a few friends. (Intentionally getting a couple of hundred people to bookmark your site, as per your instructions to do so, would constitute manipulation of Delicious.

Tip 21

Image-rich articles and infographics tend to go viral.

General Social Network Traffic Expectations

Earlier on I mentioned how you can only expect so much traffic from Twitter, Facebook, and similar sites. The reason for this is that people who are using such sites generally follow or befriend a great deal of people. They simply can't keep up with the continuous stream of links, updates, jokes, pictures, etc. From time to time they'll check their stream and click what interests them.

---

4. su.pr
5. HootSuite and dlvr.it are also solid choices.

So even if you have more than two thousand people following you on Twitter like I do, only a few of them will actually click or retweet your messages. You need massive followings, or retweets by those who have large followings, to originate even so much as a few hundred hits from your Twitter and Facebook accounts.

Delicious will bring you a few hundred hits—if you are lucky, even a couple of thousand—as long as you hit its popular list. This won't happen naturally unless you manage to first catch the attention of users on other sites. In turn, a percentage of these viewers will bookmark the site on Delicious, therefore raising your position in the popular list for that day. The bulk of your traffic from Delicious will arrive on the same day you hit the popular page, but you may see a trail of smaller volumes of traffic continue to trickle in over the next several days.

StumbleUpon has the ability to send you what seems to be an unlimited amount of traffic. My blogs, as well as the blogs of many others, have received hundreds of thousands of visitors from StumbleUpon over the years. The beauty of StumbleUpon is that you'll periodically receive waves of traffic from new users who discover and thumbs-up your content. Unlike the other sites mentioned in this section, StumbleUpon is not just an instant traffic generator but a long-term means of bringing new visitors to your site.

7.11 Promote on Technical Social News Sites

As a blogger who is focused on technical or business topics, promoting on the sites discussed in the previous section will only get you so far. You also need to promote your best articles where technical audiences gather the most. In particular, while I don't know the details of your blog, I suggest that you sign up with the following sites:

- Reddit
- Hacker News
- DZone[6]

These three technical news sites should have you covered. I would recommend Slashdot as well, but only when you've just broken an important or immensely fascinating story. It's not exactly the kind of place where you'll routinely promote your blog.

---

6. dzone.com

Feel free to search for and explore more social news sites on your own. For example if you are into Ruby development and blog about it, you can promote your best articles on *RubyFlow*.[7] If you are into Internet marketing, there is *Sphinn*.[8]

Social news sites tend to operate by accepting stories that have been submitted by their users. Then they order them so that the "best" ones end up at the top of the home page—*best* as it's used here is a very relative term, given that each site uses a different algorithm to determine what floats to the top and what never ends up seeing the light of day and is shown only to the few people who check the queue of new stories or check stories on page 2, 3, 4, 5, or beyond.

The most common factors that influence the popularity and visibility of your links on these sites are the numbers of upvotes you receive (as opposed to downvotes or other forms of negative flagging/reporting) and how quickly you receive them. Old submissions will not randomly make the front page of these sites, even if they receive a lot of votes all of a sudden. A story either receives a lot of votes shortly after being submitted or it'll never stand a snowball's chance.

The majority of stories will only attract one or two votes and never move from the new queue to the home page/popular one. This is simply the nature of such sites. Only the best stories are supposed to surface. The difference between your story hitting the front page of one of these sites or not can often be measured by the several thousand visitors you'll likely receive. Your objective is definitely to hit the front page of as many of these sites as possible.

Add the act of submitting your most relevant new articles to these three social news sites as part of your blogging workflow. If you have a blog already that has numerous articles in it, don't submit past stories all at once (or your home page for that matter). You'll be seen as a spammer. Instead, pick your three best articles and submit them over the course of a week. Then submit your best new posts as soon as you publish them from then on out. Always ask yourself, is my article really a good fit for these social news sites? Sometime the answer will be no, even if your article's content will be loved by search engine users.

To speed up the submission process, install site specific bookmarklets.

---

7.   rubyflow.com
8.   sphinn.com

Tip 22

Submit your stories between 9 a.m. and 1 p.m. ET to maximize votes and exposure.

Submit Your Posts to Reddit

Reddit has the largest audience of the three sites discussed here, and there is a series of popular subcommunities called subreddits from which you can select when submitting a story. Occasionally you can submit the same story two or three times to different subreddits, but it would be better to stick to a single submission per post that you publish.

reddit.com/r/programming is the largest community for developers, with hundreds of thousands of subscribers. Depending on the topic you blog about, there's a good chance you can find relevant subreddits at reddit.com/reddits.

Other large geek subreddits to consider are /r/gaming, /r/technology, /r/science, /r/apple, /r/android, /r/math, and so on.

Always check the number of subscribers a subreddit has before deciding to submit your story there. (You can do so by looking at the number shown in the right sidebar.) A story about NoSQL databases may as well belong more to /r/nosql than /r/programming, but its current 395 subscribers means that you'll receive virtually no traffic (even if the story hits the customized home page of these subscribers).

/r/database with its current 2,500 subscribers would be a bit better, and you'd automatically be on the front page of the subreddit given its slow submission rate, but it's still a small community. Unless your story is of no general interest to /r/programming, I would try there first.

If a subreddit has 10,000 subscribers or more, however, it may make more sense to opt for it over a larger, more generic one. For example, a HOWTO about Ruby will most likely be killed instantly on /r/programming, whereas it might receive several upvotes on /r/ruby. Evaluate each case, and if you are truly in doubt, try submitting to both. (As long as you don't do it too often.)

Reddit won't admit to it, but it tends to like a bit of sensationalism. So make your submission headline attractive and interesting (it does not have to be the same thing as your actual blog post title). If you quickly attract a few votes on /r/programming, you may get some ego-killing comments (regardless of your content), but you'll also receive thousands of visitors. In the past I have received up to 50,000 visits within forty-eight hours from /r/programming for a single article of mine.

Some users may complain that you submit your own stories there, but it's considered fair play by the admins of the site as long as you do the following:

- Pick relevant subreddits.
- Don't flood the site with your submissions.
- Participate in the community by submitting stories from other sites and by commenting as well.[9]

> ## Tip 23
>
> ## Participate; don't just submit your own blog entries.

For an in-depth look at Reddit voting patterns and stories that made it big, check out Reddit's own analysis at blog.reddit.com/2011/07/nerd-talk-tale-of-life-of-link-on.html.

Hacker News

Hacker News (HN) is currently my favorite community. It's smaller than Reddit, but it's growing quickly and tends to be much more friendly than communities such as /r/programming. If you hit its front page, you'll still receive several thousand visitors (and quality ones at that).

On Hacker News, you can submit any story that's relevant to programming, technology, business, and the world of startups. War stories about your entrepreneurship or development experiences are particularly loved by this community. The audience tends to be smart, so the standard for your submissions is higher than the average site.

Stories that the community sees as fluff, off topic, or devoid of real content are routinely killed by users who flag them. Politics is also another no-no.

Take a look at the existing stories on the front page and their comments to help you figure out the type of content and headlines that are appreciated on

---

9.   www.reddit.com/r/Moderating/comments/cz6zu/identifying_spammers_101

Hacker News. Then read their guidelines in full at ycombinator.com/newsguide-lines.html.

If your link receives several upvotes, it will also be converted from nofollow to a regular link that receives PageRank juice (but the real value is in the instant referral traffic potential). For the record, Hacker News's home page is currently a PageRank 8 page.

It's extremely important that you spend some time understanding the site before you make your first submission. If you submit your blog for the first time and your story is flagged and killed, your blog's submissions will auto-matically be killed from there on out. Not being able to promote your quality content on Hacker News would be a great shame that translates to the loss of several thousand valuable visitors each month.

Your first submissions from your blog must categorically be very high quality to ensure that the community welcomes your blog and doesn't flag it. If you are even remotely in doubt, don't submit your own blog posts yet. Submit other relevant stories you find interesting.

Just like StumbleUpon and other social sites, you should avoid gaming the system by having all your friends upvote your stories. And if you send a link to your submission to a friend on Twitter or elsewhere, know that direct visits to item pages are valued less than organic votes obtained in the "new" page by HN's ranking algorithm.[10] (Yeah, this can be easily worked around by pointing your friends to the new page instead of to your submission. But don't do it.)

DZone

DZone is the smallest community of the three and will only give you a few hundred hits on average, if you make its home page. It's exclusively dedicated to programming, so if your posts are not about programming, you should not take advantage of this channel.

One of the advantages of DZone is that it's relatively easy to have one of your submissions become a popular link on that site.

While you shouldn't expect grandiose traffic from it, it would be foolish not to pursue this community if it's relevant to what you're blogging about. Sub-mitting a story takes a couple of minutes because you are required to provide a short description of your article. I don't know about you, but I'll gladly trade two minutes of my time for a few hundred visitors any day.

---

10. news.ycombinator.com/newest

7.12 Case Study: ProgrammingZen.com's Referral Traffic

In order to provide you with a more realistic idea of how much all these social media sites respectively contribute to a blog about programming, I have included the top ten referral traffic sources over the past year for my own programming blog.

The percentages are based on the total referral traffic only (i.e., link traffic), and not on organic traffic or other sources.

Rank	Referral Site	Percentage (%)
1	Reddit	49.29
2	Hacker News	10.79
3	Slashdot	6.83
4	DZone	2.73
5	StumbleUpon	2.57
6	RubyFlow	1.79
7	Twitter	1.74
8	Facebook	1.46
9	StackOverflow	0.60
10	Delicious	0.25

As you may recall, the referral traffic distribution here is quite different from that outlined for Math-Blog.com in Chapter 5, *Creating Remarkable Content*, on page 83. The most striking difference is StumbleUpon, which copiously provided traffic for Math-Blog.com but nowhere near as much for Programming Zen.com. That community demographic tends to be more interested in math than programming, and my long essays on programming certainly didn't capture the short attention span of most Stumblers.

You'll also notice how Reddit was crucial for the promotion of my programming-related blog, with nearly half the referral traffic coming from it. In total, all traffic sources considered, one in five visitors came from Reddit in the past year.

7.13 What's Next

Use the techniques outlined in this chapter, and you'll no doubt promote your blog well into the realm of being successful.

An important step after promoting your content—and submitting your blog to the various social media sites discussed—is to measure your results. This way you'll be able to concentrate on what works and ignore or adjust your strategy for what doesn't.

The next short chapter is entirely dedicated to the subject of analyzing the traffic resulting from your link building and your social media promotion.

Not everything that counts can be counted, and not everything that can be counted counts.

➤ *Albert Einstein*

CHAPTER 8

Understanding Traffic Statistics

Immediately after you publish and promote an article, visitors from all over the world will start coming to your blog. This is a very exciting moment. It's important, however, to fully understand the traffic figures from your web analytics suite as well as to keep track of them over time.

Analyzing statistics is particularly important because you should strive to take an Agile/Lean approach to blogging. When you try something out—a new type of article, a new style of headline, changes to the layout, anything really—you need to validate your hypothesis. You assume that a change (or perhaps a new article) will be welcome and ultimately end up improving your blog, but you don't know for sure until you try it out and verify the results.

8.1 Baseline vs. Spike Traffic

The immediate flow of traffic you receive upon releasing and publicizing a new post will appear in your statistics as a noticeable spike. If you publish once a week on the same weekday, for example, you'll notice a more or less constant amount of traffic (i.e., your average traffic, or *baseline*) and then a jump around the day your new posts usually go live.

As you can see in Figure 19, *A traffic spike*, on page 147, the effect lasts for a few days. This spike will eventually disappear from your charts, but the baseline of traffic you receive should increase slightly in the long run as a result of it. Every post you add to your blog will contribute to the ongoing growth in the average amount of traffic you receive without any further effort on your part.

If I were to quit blogging for six months, I would still receive a great deal of baseline traffic every day, thanks to my wealth of existing articles. People will find such posts through search engines, links from other blogs, social media citations, and so on.

Of course, ceasing to blog would cause the average number of visitors per day to slowly but surely go down over time. More importantly, my feed subscribers would probably begin to vanish as well as they begin to notice that I haven't published anything for months.

To grow your baseline, keep adding spikes with new posts. Think of it as adding logs to a fire to keep the flames roaring.

8.2 Key Site Usage Metrics You Need to Consider

Traffic is a generic term. Let's get more specific and consider some of the most common metrics used to describe the amount of visitors you receive. (This section also acts as a nonalphabetized glossary.)

- *Visits*: The total number of times your site has been visited by all your visitors. If the same visitor comes back to your site multiple times over a given timeframe, all of these visits will be counted. A visit corresponds to the duration of a session. The session is started when the user arrives on your site and ends when the user closes the tab/browser or is inactive for a certain amount of time. (In the case of Google Analytics, that's thirty minutes by default, but this number can be customized.)

- *Unique visitors*: The total number of visitors who arrived on your site, excluding duplicates. Unlike visits, this figure ignores multiple visits by the same visitor over a time period. This value is an approximation due to the fact that the uniqueness of a visitor is determined via cookies, which can obviously be cleared from time to time.

- *Pageviews*: The number of times your pages have been loaded. If ten visitors visit your site five times each, and each of them browses two pages per visit, your pageview count will be 100 (i.e., 10 x 5 x 2). If the same visitor reloads a page multiple times, each of those refreshes will be added to the counter.

- *Average pageviews*: The ratio between your pageviews and your visits. This roughly indicates how many pages are viewed on average each time someone visits your site. If your average pageview count is 3.0, it means that, on average, people come to your site, see that page, and then explore another two pages before leaving.

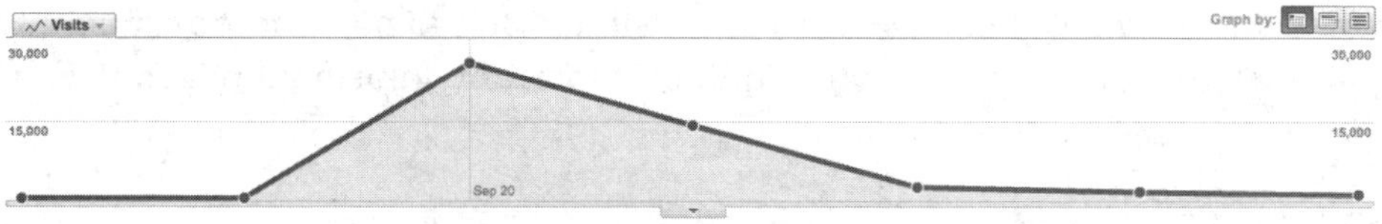

Figure 19—A traffic spike

- *Time on site*: The average amount of time spent on the site by your visitors. This, too, is a very approximate figure, because leaving a window or tab open will influence this value, even though the user may not necessarily be reading or engaging with the site in any active capacity.

- *Bounce rate*: The percentage of visits that lead to a single pageview. It's a measure of how many visitors leave after landing somewhere on your site directly from that page versus those who stay and explore other pages before leaving. This number can vary wildly from one analytics suite to another.

- *New visits*: The percentage of visits from new visitors versus visitors who have already visited your site within a given time frame.

The exact implementation of these concepts by your web analytics tool will affect the numbers you see. Google Analytics' figures are generally accepted as a standard of sorts in the industry.

A good analytics solution will show you these site usage details as well as plenty more about the profiles of your visitors (network, country, language), their browser profiles, your site's traffic sources, which search engine keywords were used, and so on. You can learn a lot about your visitors by taking a look at these less frequently used metrics from time to time.

8.3   Interpret Visit Quantity and Quality

It's important to regularly keep an eye on your site's usage stats. Some of these will tell you how good a job you are doing in attracting visitors to your site. Others will give you a glimpse of how satisfied your visitors are likely to be with what you're providing them.

Visits, unique visitors, and pageviews are *visit quantity* metrics. Average pageviews, time on site, bounce rate, and new visits are *visit quality* indicators.

Generally speaking, people pay attention to visit quantity but very little to visit quality. If you were to express the popularity of your site to other people, you would normally list pageviews and visitors. But do not ignore visit quality parameters. They can give you equally important information about your visitors' behavior.

Visit Quality Statistics

Aim to have high values for average pageviews and time on site. These numbers correlate to the amount of exploration and reading that your visitors do once they land on your site. If these figures are decreasing over time, you may have to work on the quality of your content and the way you interlink so as to facilitate the easy discovery of other pages and posts on your blog.

Conversely, aim for a low bounce rate. A high number often correlates to visitors who are disinterested in your content. For example, their landing page (or entrance page) may not be that relevant to what they came looking for. Or perhaps your layout, eclectic font, unique background choice, ads, etc. are putting your readers off straight out of the gate.

The issue of new versus returning visitors is a bit more complicated. Here you want a high number because it means that you are attracting a lot of new visitors. Unfortunately, a very high number also implies a low number of returning visitors, which in turn could be a red flag regarding your visitor retention and engagement ability.

For technical audiences, a lot of returning visitors will do so via feed readers, which wouldn't be accounted for in your statistics suite. Technical users also tend to clear their cookies more often. Due to these points, I wouldn't worry too much about a low percentage of returning visitors. Instead, strive for a very high number of new visitors (e.g., 70 percent or more) to help accelerate the continued growth of your site. If your conversion rate from visitor to subscriber is good, your main goal unequivocally becomes recruiting new visitors.

Tip 24

Use the PostRank browser extension to assess the popularity of your RSS entries.

How Social Media Affects Your Stats

As you analyze your statistics, you should always keep the nature of your site and traffic in mind. For example, song lyric sites—which everyone seems to hate—probably have an average pageviews value approaching 1.0 and a bounce rate nearing 100 percent.

People come to such sites in order to read the lyrics to a song and then leave immediately. It's hard to engage users further, due to the very nature of these sites, so their owners opt to be ruthless in their monetization strategy instead, which further alienates users who land on these ad-ridden sites.

In the case of a technical blog that's been promoted as described in the previous chapter, visit quality metrics will primarily be affected negatively by the fickle nature of social media traffic. Your blog will most likely be relatively popular and grow quickly, but you'll also have relatively low average pageviews and time-on-site figures and a high bounce rate. (As we'll see soon, Clicky addresses the issue of social media affecting bounce rate by redefining what a bounce is.)

For example, ProgrammingZen.com's global statistics for this month show 1.18 average pageviews, 36 seconds average time on site, and an 89.40 percent bounce rate. Filtering the statistics for search traffic only shows a much higher average pageviews value, triple the time on site, and a noticeably lower bounce rate. Conversely, the new visits percentage is an excellent 86 percent, regardless of traffic source.

In fact, the typical use case for social news users would be to click your site link, skim the post, and then go back to the social news site they came from to read the comments and perhaps share thoughts of their own there. For other social networks, such as Facebook and Twitter, the pattern is not much different.

These low values, affected by the nature of my traffic, are not cause for concern per se. What really matters is the trend. Are they getting better, worse, or staying about the same over time? If yours get significantly worse, then you need to investigate why this is and figure out what changed.

8.4 Where Do They All Come From?

OK, you've published a great post, promoted it everywhere you could, and your site usage statistics are now showing a great deal of traffic rolling in. Awesome. But how do you know which promotional channels worked? Was

Alerts and Goals

Both Google Analytics and Clicky allow you to set alerts and conversion goals.

Alerts are useful for receiving emails (or SMS) when traffic levels reach a certain target or goal. When you are starting out, set your alert to something low, like 500 visits per day, depending on your expectations. Figure 25, *Setting up a custom alert in Google Analytics*, on page 157, shows an alert I have for *Math-Blog*.

Conversion goals help you keep track of specific events, such as a reader visiting a particular thank-you page after signing up for your newsletter. These are particularly useful to quickly get conversion statistics on events such as downloads, email subscriptions, sales, etc.

As we'll see in Chapter 11, *Promoting Your Own Business*, on page 199, if you run a startup that sells products or service subscriptions, you'll need to keep track of your conversion funnel. You can do so through custom reports in Google Analytics or through a specialized solution such as *KISSmetrics.com*.

it Reddit or Hacker News that brought in the masses? Perhaps you made it big on StumbleUpon.

And for that matter, how do you even know that all these new visitors are coming for the sake of your latest article and not from an older one that suddenly got popular? (This certainly does happen sometimes.)

Any traffic analytics suite worth its salt is going to be able to answer these two important questions for you. You should monitor where your traffic is coming from (i.e., your *traffic sources*) and what it's coming for (i.e., your *top content*). Doing so tells you where it's worth promoting your content and what kind of content and headlines are working for your blog.

Note that with most analytics software it's possible to drill down or filter statistics by a given URL. By doing so you can see where the traffic came from for a specific article, as shown in Figure 20, *Entrance sources for a single page*, on page 151. Likewise, you can filter by traffic source to check out which articles and pages are popular among visitors coming from a given source.

8.5 Analyze Google Analytics and Clicky Statistics

It is ultimately outside of the scope of this book to illustrate every corner of either Google Analytics or Clicky, but in order to help you get started with them, let's see how to use the most fundamental statistics discussed above through these two tools. If you haven't installed trackers for either of these

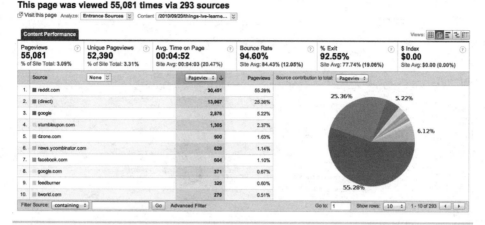

Figure 20—Entrance sources for a single page

two suites yet, as discussed in Chapter 4, *Customizing and Fine-Tuning Your Blog*, on page 55, do so now.

Get Statistics Out of Google Analytics

Note: I have opted to present instructions and screenshots for the new version of Google Analytics. If your layout looks significantly different, ensure that you clicked the New Version link at the top of the suite.[1]

When you check out the statistics of your blog in Analytics, you'll be prompted with a dashboard that looks similar to the one shown in Figure 21, *Google Analytics's dashboard*, on page 152. The data shown will cover the past thirty days, but you can change the range to whatever you like.

As you can see, Google tries to provide you with all the key site usage statistics for the chosen period in one spot. Namely, these are visits, unique visitors, pageviews, average pageviews (shown as Pages/Visit), average time on site, bounce rate, and percentage of new visits (shown as % New Visits).

In the left sidebar you should see Visitors, Advertising, Traffic Sources, Content, and Conversions groups, with many links below each of them. Explore all of these to discover the default reports offered by Google Analytics. In particular, check out the Traffic Sources and Content tabs.

Both of these menu groups contain an Overview link that acts as your dashboard specific to Traffic Sources and Content, respectively. By using other

---

1.   www.google.com/analytics/web

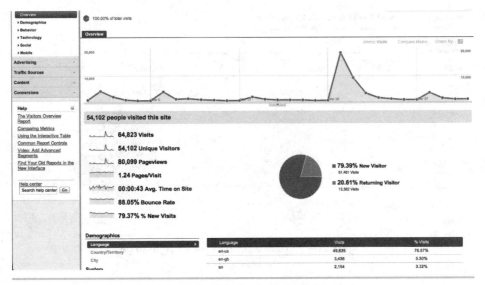

Figure 21—Google Analytics's dashboard

submenu items, such as All Traffic, Referrals, Search, Pages, and Content Drilldown, you'll be able to get more specific information.

Keep in mind what we've discussed in previous sections. You are free to go as deep as you wish and find out all sorts of details, but we are mostly after site usage statistics, traffic sources, keywords, and top content. The whole process of checking such things out via the aforementioned links shouldn't take any more than five minutes.

Figure 22, *Traffic sources*, on page 153, shows the Overview link for Traffic Sources.

Understanding what keywords, content, and traffic sources are working will give you the edge when deciding what other kinds of content you'd like to publish and how to go about promoting it.

(Searches by logged-in users coming from Google are no longer reported. This means that "(not provided)" will appear in your organic search traffic reports.)

Keep in mind that most blogs receive the majority of their traffic from Google. When you check out your statistics, you'll probably learn that you are not one of them.

Thankfully, that's not cause for alarm. With the techniques described so far you'll attract so much referral traffic that it will be very hard for organic search traffic to match it. Search traffic will help you have a healthy baseline of

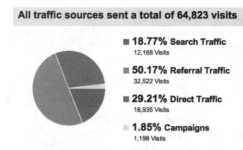

All traffic sources sent a total of 64,823 visits

■ **18.77%** Search Traffic
12,168 Visits

■ **50.17%** Referral Traffic
32,522 Visits

■ **29.21%** Direct Traffic
18,935 Visits

■ **1.85%** Campaigns
1,198 Visits

Search Traffic

Keyword	>
Matched Search Query	
Source	

Referral Traffic

Source

Direct Traffic

Landing Page

Keyword	Visits
ruby books	233
best ruby on rails book	122
best ruby book	109
best ruby books	108
ruby on rails book	89
ruby on rails books	87
rails hosting	84
rails performance	76
technical marketing	74
ruby book	69

Figure 22—Traffic sources

traffic every day, but the big numbers you will see each month will definitely be inflated by social media traffic spikes.

Explore Clicky

Clicky works quite similarly to Google Analytics. There is a dashboard, shown in Figure 23, *Clicky's dashboard*, on page 154, which contains most of the info you'll want to know. You can customize the date range (by default, today's stats are shown), and the navigation bar offers a variety of menu items to provide you with all kinds of statistics.

You can filter by virtually anything (including by URL and by visitor), and as mentioned before, Clicky is also in real time. You can use the Spy feature minutes after promoting your posts to literally see traffic as it arrives on your site. In the beginning, this is a captivating experience and may lead you to waste too much time basking in the excitement of seeing your first visitors.

What is different from Google Analytics, aside from quite a few extra features, is the nomenclature. Instead of pushing pageviews, Clicky likes to refer to *actions*. The two concepts are not very different, except for the fact that an

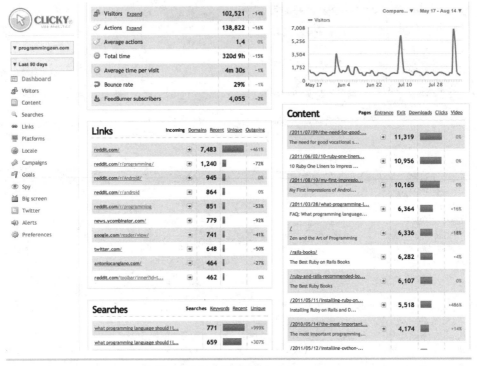

Figure 23—Clicky's dashboard

action such as downloading a file or clicking a link will be counted as an action but not as a pageview.

The bounce rate is calculated in a drastically different way, however. Whereas Google might show me an 85 percent bounce rate, Clicky tells me that it's 25 percent. The difference lies in the fact that the smart team behind Clicky has redefined the concept of bounce rate to better describe the behavior of the user.

According to Clicky, a user that lands on your page and then stays there for a while to read it (before leaving) should not be seen as a bounce. I tend to agree and like to use Clicky's metric because it gives me a better sense of how many people really were put off by my site/article, and how many were engaged by my page but didn't stay to explore the rest of the site. In an era of social media traffic, this is an important distinction.

I find Clicky to be particularly useful when I truly want to understand the behavior of users. In fact, if I wanted to, I could select a single user and see the complete set of actions that person took, as shown in Figure 24, *"Stalking"*

How Reliable Are Traffic Comparison Sites?

As the owner of your blog, you'll have exact, detailed statistics. However, unless you share these numbers, other people won't know about them. Likewise, you won't know about the actual statistics of most other sites that you're not in charge of.

There are websites such as compete.com and alexa.com that attempt to compare sites in terms of traffic based on a series of heuristics. In Alexa's case, for example, it mostly relies on the sites that have been visited by users who installed the Alexa toolbar.

In my experience, these sites tend to be wildly biased and inaccurate. If you decide to compare sites this way, remember that the results you get are only a vague indication of the true popularity of the URLs you test.

Compete believes that this month ProgrammingZen.com only received 375 visits and Math-Blog.com received 3,676. It's off by at least a couple of orders of magnitude in the first case, and easily one in the latter. The sites receive comparable amounts of traffic, but Compete would lead you to believe that my math blog is ten times more popular than my programming blog.

Part of the reason for this is that very technical sites are penalized by Compete and Alexa, given that very few techies are willing to install a toolbar that keeps track of what they do on the Web (even though those toolbars are not the only source for such sites' stats).

visitors with Clicky, on page 156. This user came from Google looking for information on how to learn programming and then went on to explore a series of articles on my programming blog.

Do I have enough content to satisfy what that user is after? If not, what sort of articles could I write to help that person out? More commonly, you'd think about this when checking out what keywords brought you traffic rather than by stalking an individual user. Nevertheless, that's the kind of thinking this exercise should lead one to.

8.6 Keep Track of Your Blog's Growth

In the business world there is a common expression that says that what can be measured can be improved. In my experience, there is a lot of truth to that observation. It's important to assess the current statistics and verify how they evolve over time as a result of your efforts when you start a blog or try to revamp an existing one.

Some entrepreneurs, particularly in startups, like to use a KPI (key performance indicator) dashboard or spreadsheet. As a blogger, regardless if you have a company or not, it's a good idea to do something similar.

Actions from this session, oldest to newest:

Time	User	Action	Referrer
Aug 14 2011 5:32:39 pm	Comcast Cable	/2011/03/28/what-programming-language-should-i-learn-first/ FAQ: What programming language should I learn first?	google.com → learning programming
Aug 14 2011 5:34:08 pm	Comcast Cable	/2008/12/13/learn-merb/ Learn Merb	
Aug 14 2011 5:34:47 pm	Comcast Cable	/2011/03/28/what-programming-language-should-i-learn-first/ FAQ: What programming language should I learn first?	
Aug 14 2011 5:34:52 pm	Comcast Cable	/2010/05/14/the-most-important-programming-language-today/ The most important programming language today	
Aug 14 2011 5:36:19 pm	Comcast Cable	/2011/03/28/what-programming-language-should-i-learn-first/ FAQ: What programming language should I learn first?	
Aug 14 2011 5:36:25 pm	Comcast Cable	/2010/07/09/thoughts-on-clojure/ Thoughts on Clojure	
Aug 14 2011 5:38:08 pm	Comcast Cable	/2008/09/14/django-turns-10/ Django turns 1.0	
Aug 14 2011 5:39:08 pm	Comcast Cable	/2008/03/04/rails-is-the-best-thing-that-ever-happened-to-py... Rails is the best thing that ever happened to Python	
Aug 14 2011 5:42:25 pm	Comcast Cable	/2007/11/28/holy-shmoly-ruby-19-smokes-python-away/ Holy Shmoly, Ruby 1.9 smokes Python away!	
Aug 14 2011	Comcast Cable	/2010/07/09/thoughts-on-clojure/	

Figure 24—"Stalking" visitors with Clicky

Use Excel or Google Docs to keep track of your blog KPIs. Which ones? The choice is up to you, but definitely include your site usage metrics (as described in this chapter), your FeedBurner, and your email subscription numbers. Eventually you may also want to keep track of conversion rates (e.g., from visitor to subscriber), revenue, and so on.

For the time being include a column for the date when you checked your stats, then have columns for pageviews, unique visitors, average pageviews, time on site, bounce rate (from Clicky, if possible), total number of articles on your site, feed subscribers, and your email subscribers. Update your spreadsheet once a month to see how your site is growing and evolving over time. At some point you'll even be able to plot some of these metrics to better visualize your progress.

A final word of advice: don't obsess over statistics. By all means check your stats for five minutes a few hours after publishing an article, but don't let doing so become an addiction. Checking your global stats once a month to

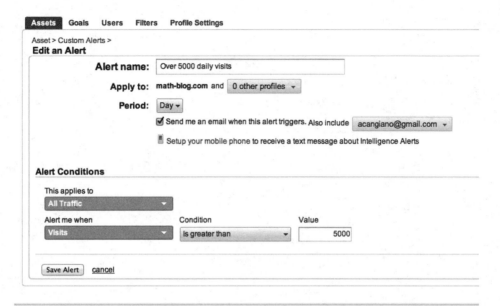

Figure 25—Setting up a custom alert in Google Analytics

fill your KPI spreadsheet is plenty. It's a fun and useful process, but remember that checking your stats continually will not help them grow or be a very productive use of your blogging time.

8.7 What's Next

With this chapter we have added another piece to the puzzle. At this point in the book, you're ready to go out there and get noticed.

What's missing from your tool belt is one more chapter about user engagement and then the last two parts of the book, which are dedicated to benefitting from your hard work and further scaling your blogging initiatives for your plans of world domination.

For the time being, wax on, wax off.

Great spirits have always encountered violent opposition from mediocre minds.

> ➤ Albert Einstein

CHAPTER 9

Building a Community Around Your Blog

As a blogger you bother with promotional activities because you want to attract a following. You can then expose this group of readers to your thoughts and writing. Once again, it's all about getting your content in front of the right audience.

The next logical step in this process is to take a closer look at this readership. You aim for a large pool of readers, sure, and that gives you quantity. But what about quality? Ideally you want a loyal, engaged public who is receptive to your ideas, content, and projects. You want readers who are fans of your work, who share it with their friends, and who are ready to do word-of-mouth work both online and offline for you. You want readers who feel like they're part of a like-minded community that they enrich via their active participation, comments, and presence.

In this chapter we'll focus on how to build such a community. The emphasis will be on your blog itself rather than on social media, because we'll further discuss how to attract fans on sites like Facebook and Twitter in the last part of the book (called Scale It). We'll also spend time discussing some unpleasant aspects of being a successful blogger—chiefly, dealing with criticism and trolls.

9.1 Engage Readers

Your main aim is to transform silent spectators (also known as *lurkers*) into active participants of your community. Users who interact with your site and feel like they're part of a community are far more likely to contribute and promote your site (as they feel it's *their* community).

Below I've listed a variety of effective ways to achieve a greater level of active participation from your readers. You are not expected to do these activities all at once. Instead, try some and, as usual, measure the response from your community. Then iterate. Each blog is a unique snowflake, so you need to verify what actually works for you and your site.

Also keep in mind that your time is limited, so you may not be able to carry out many of these activities on an ongoing basis, even if they've proven to be effective for you. Prioritize and aim for tasks that have a great reward-to-effort ratio.

- Write great content. Remember how it's all about your content? Compelling, interesting, unique, useful, and/or controversial content will always attract comments, engage readers, and help you build a community. For a good example of how unique, noteworthy content helps you build a community, check out *LessWrong*,[1] a blog that attracts a large community of people who are interested in rationality.

- Ask for comments. As we've touched on before, calls to action are a very powerful tool. In your posts, explicitly ask your readers to share their opinions or ideas in the comments section. Some folks will do just that, simply because you suggested it. The sole inclusion of the word *comment* or *comments* in your post will statistically increase your blog's commenting rate.

- Reply to questions. If you receive questions or requests for clarification in your comments section, try to be helpful and reply to those queries with a comment of your own. Nobody likes to be ignored.

- Credit updates and corrections. We have discussed this before, but always credit commenters when updating or correcting a post thanks to their suggestions.

- Praise insightful comments. Don't just reply to commenters who ask you a question. Instead, take the time to publicly thank insightful commenters for their participation and contribution by replying to them. Acknowledging those who share valuable information will encourage them to continue contributing (and others to join in). Positive reinforcement can do wonders for your community.

- Don't provide all the answers. In your posts, leave some space for people to add more to the discussion.

- Ask questions in your posts. Get people to interact with you by letting them answer questions you may have. These can be generic ones, such

---

1.   lesswrong.com

as, "What do you think about this?" or specific ones, such as, "And that's my story. At what age did you start programming?"

- Ask for feedback. This tip has been mentioned before in the book, but it warrants repeating. Engage your readers by asking them for feedback about how you are doing and what sort of material they'd like to see more of. Don't do this weekly, just every once in a while, as it can help bring out lurkers that you haven't heard from before. Don't forget surveys either.

- Poll your readers. Along the same train of thought, you can poll your readers about topics that they're interested in on a fairly frequent basis. Just remember to share the results of such polls with your community in a new post, adding your own reflections on the results and inviting readers to share theirs.

- Answer commenters' questions in new posts. If a particularly good question has been posted by someone in the comment section, you may want to provide an extensive answer in a new post. Always credit the commenter with the original question and thank him or her for the question in your post. This will make the commenter feel special, and you may be rewarded with a backlink (if the commenter also has a blog).

- Showcase commenters. Check to see if your blogging engine has a plugin or feature to showcase your top—and more recent—commenters on your home page or sidebar. People may try to game this for a backlink, but overall you'll still get an increased level of participation.

- Promote commenters to bloggers. Publicly or privately invite your best regulars to become guest bloggers or to contribute as coauthors for an article on a topic they have shown expertise in.

- Post a collection of the best comments your site has received. Once your blog is well established, consider periodically publishing a digest of the most insightful and informative comments you've received on your blog. Credit the authors and link back to their blogs or sites, if provided.

- Comment on your commenters' blogs. This can be time consuming, but you can greatly increase the chances that commenters will be back if you visit their own blogs and leave comments there (assuming their blogs are in the same niche). The concept of reciprocity is practically hardwired in the human brain.

- Reply to emails. Fans of your blog will feel a personal connection to you. Much like a celebrity, you may not know your fans, but they know you.

So do not ignore their emails. Instead, try to be kind, friendly, and appreciative of their enthusiasm for your work.

- Create a serene environment. Use comment moderation and reminders to keep discourse civil so as to keep any form of harassment at bay. If your blogging engine doesn't support comment moderation and you are not opposed to it, you can always remove harassing comments immediately after they are posted. (More on these types of comments in Section 9.3, *Forms of Criticism*, on page 164.)

- Help your commenters. If a commenter of yours has a site or product that is particularly relevant to your audience, feel free to mention or review it as a means of showcasing the commenter's work to your readers. Acknowledge that you are mentioning/reviewing—unsolicited—a site or product you found by checking out a commenter and that you will continue to do so in the future. The commenter will no doubt feel appreciated, you may gain a business connection, and this generous act may motivate more people to stop by and comment.

- Challenge your readers. Ask your readers engaging, difficult questions or puzzles for which you have devised an interesting solution. Make such questions relevant to your niche, and they will no doubt generate a series of responses on your blog and elsewhere. (Your readers may also show you a much better solution than the one you came up with initially.)

- Organize contests and giveaways. Readers love these kinds of posts, as they provide them with a chance to benefit directly from your blog. As you'll learn in Chapter 12, *Taking Full Advantage of Your Blog*, on page 215, these are easier to organize when the product you're giving away is provided to you for free. Regardless of how you obtain the goods, you can further engage your commenters by selecting judges for your contests from among your best commenters.

- Highlight your commenters' expertise. Organize an Ask Me Anything (AMA) or Ask an Expert series of posts with the most insightful experts who hang out on your blog. Once a month, you could solicit questions from your readers on a specific topic that will then be answered in a post by an expert you picked from your commenters. This encourages commenting all around, but it's best done when you already have a decent following.

- Go where the comments are. By following the promotional workflow described in the previous chapters, you will sometimes end up attracting more comments on social news sites like Reddit and Hacker News than on your own blog. A recent article of mine, for example, attracted over four hundred comments on Reddit but only thirty or so on my blog. That's OK. Those are huge communities whose members may have higher loyalty to fellow members than to you. Read those offsite comments and, if necessary, feel free to occasionally engage commenters on such sites too. (Just keep in mind that you are now playing an away game.)

- Tell readers that they are part of a community. Use words like *we*, *this community*, *participants on this site*, and so on. This will help readers identify more with the inevitable community that will form around your blog. Then lead the community by organizing events that help participants bond and feel like they're a part of something meaningful.

9.2   Supplement Your Blog with Community Tools

In addition to the suggestions above, you should also consider the following tools and activities that go beyond a regular blog:

- Start a forum. Comment sections limit the discourse to the topic at hand. Having a forum can greatly increase the level of interaction among your visitors, with a much greater degree of freedom when discussing topics within the borders of your niche. You may even use the forum's questions and answers as a way of generating more content for the blog itself. Just relentlessly credit people when you do so. Select your most active forum users and commenters as moderators to further reward them, but always keep an eye on their behavior (some people can single-handedly destroy a community with their power trips). Finally, don't start a forum until you have a large audience. Dead forums (fora, if you prefer) with very few participants just come across as pathetic to most new visitors.

- Start a wiki. A well-organized and curated wiki for your niche can bring lots of traffic to your blog, provide a useful service to the community at large, and make your readers more prone to produce—and not just consume—content. Encourage your readers to contribute to the wiki and reward them by highlighting the best contributions by your readers in your blog posts and on key spots on your site.

- Hold office hours. In order to further connect with your community, why not have a couple of office hours once a week during which readers can call you up to discuss whatever they wish for fifteen minutes? Be very clear about the time zone and rules of conduct, and you'll be surprised about the connections you'll make and the opportunities that this can open up for you. Plus, you'll come across as extremely approachable and serious about your site.

- Organize group chats. Using tools like Google+'s Hangouts or even good old-fashioned IRC (Internet Relay Chat), you can organize monthly chats with and among your readers. Announce such chats in your blog posts well in advance, and again, make the exact time of the chat clear for people who are located in different countries. You can even set a specific, relevant theme for each chat.

- Infiltrate other communities. Without spamming in any way, don't be afraid to mention or link to your blog/community from other forums and communities. Before you can do this, however, you'll need to become a respected member of such communities or you'll be seen as a spammer. Contributing to other communities without hiding the existence of your own is an easy way to increase the size of your community.

Remember to use this and the previous list as a reference to be inspired from and not as a To Do list. You'll quickly become overwhelmed otherwise.

9.3 Forms of Criticism

As you work at increasing reader engagement and comments, you'll quickly discover something unpleasant. Almost regardless of what you write, attracting a large audience means being on the receiving end of criticism.

People are going to take issue with what you say, because any content that is worth sharing is worth discussing and debating. Even if you don't try to be controversial, you will inevitably end up being the target of a small percentage of vocal detractors of your content.

The following are some forms of criticism you will encounter when running a successful blog. For each of them, you may see a rude or a nice version, depending on the mood and attitude of the commenter.

- *Constructive criticism*: The commenter will point out flaws in your reasoning, argument, or the facts that you present. It's not pleasant to be wrong, but this is the best kind of criticism because you can deal with it by simply admitting to being mistaken or by rationally and factually defending your position. You may end up "standing corrected," agreeing to disagree, or convincing the commenter that you were right in the first place. The focus of this commenter is the truth and adding value to the discussion, so an intellectually honest debate can be had. It's an occasion to grow that you should cherish.

- *Disagreement criticism*: Particularly for controversial or opinion-based content, you may encounter commenters who disagree with your viewpoint or observation. None of you will be objectively right or wrong, because both stances will be valid and defensible.

- *Nitpick criticism*: The commenters will focus their criticism on marginal issues that don't really affect the validity of your article. This may lead the conversation in unpredictable directions that veer far off the original topic.

- *Misguided criticism*: People don't always pay attention to what you say and may start commenting on articles they haven't read or understood carefully. As a result, you'll see comments about points you already addressed in your article or against arguments you never made yourself. Your position will often be misrepresented with this type of commenter, and you'll experience the annoyance of dealing with the straw man logical fallacy.[2] It will also teach you *defensive blogging*, wherein you address the most likely objections to the topics you cover, and you try to be as clear as possible so as to make it really hard to miss the point of your articles, though some people will still manage to.

- *Personal criticism*: Sometime the focus of the reader's criticism will be you rather than the content itself. This is one of the most annoying types of criticism because it questions you personally as an individual or professional rather than disagreeing with one of your stances. It's also much easier to defend a viewpoint than to try to justify that no, in fact, you are not stupid, evil, a shill for a corporation, an idiot, or a [insert insult of your choice here]. Thanks to these comments, you'll get acquainted with another common logical fallacy known as an ad hominem argument.[3] (Insults are not ad hominem arguments per se, though.)

- *Meta criticism*: This type of criticism will not focus on the actual details of your content or on you personally. Instead the commenter will question the whole existence of your post or blog. Among technical audiences this is not uncommon, as some commenters will take issue with the commercial nature of your blog, your inclusion of affiliate links, the presence of ads, your moderation of comments, or perhaps the fact that you are reviewing a book that was provided to you for free.

---

2.   en.wikipedia.org/wiki/Straw_man
3.   en.wikipedia.org/wiki/Ad_hominem

- *Trolling*: The sole purpose of these comments is to stir up controversy or intentionally rile you up. They usually lead to drawn-out, pointless debates known as *flame wars*.

Examples of Criticism

Let's see how each of these types of comments pan out with an example. Imagine that you published an article in which you compare Android devices and the iPhone on your gadget blog, and you praise Android for being surprisingly good.

Constructive Criticism

Here's some constructive criticism:

> I don't think it's fair to draw conclusions about how responsive the two operating systems are when you are using two devices with substantially different hardware specs. The iPhone is clearly disadvantaged here.

Reply to these types of comments and address the issue without getting emotional. Admit when you are wrong and argue back when you are not. Sometimes this type of justifiable criticism escalates to other types of unacceptable criticism or overly long discussions, at which point it is no longer worth engaging.

Disagreement Criticism

Disagreement criticism looks like this:

> I don't agree that the Android Marketplace has lots of applications. I had to bring my Android device back because most of the apps I was used to on the iPhone were not available for it. I couldn't even find an app to do online banking with my bank, for Pete's sake!

Generally speaking, don't reply unless you see a gaping hole in the logic or you think you can add more to what you already wrote by addressing the objection. People have a right to disagree with you, as long as they are not complete jackasses about it.

Nitpick Criticism

A nitpicker may say this:

> Why would you need a smartphone for your bus commute? Can't you read a book or something, like most people do?

Here the aim of the critic is not the same as the point of your article. If your blog is moderated, publish such comments, but generally ignore them. If it's been posted elsewhere, like Reddit, ignore it as well. Yes, you want commenters, but quality trumps quantity every time.

Misguided Criticism

Misguided criticism may present itself as follows:

> How can you say that Android has better battery life than the iPhone if you haven't tried both?

Assume, for the sake of this example, that the article actually explains how battery life was tested for both over the course of a week in a fair manner. The commenter here would then have skimmed the post and posted a knee-jerk reaction to your claim about battery life without reading the details.

Feel free to rectify commenter misunderstandings, but don't let it escalate into a long argument. Reply once. If they take the hint, good. If they persevere, ignore it.

Personal Criticism

Personal criticism can be unpleasant and may look like this:

> Color me shocked! A Google lackey finds an Android phone to be better than the iPhone. News at 11. Why don't you just stop blogging, moron.

You are free not to even let a useless personal attack like this get past the moderation. Unfortunately, when a comment like this is posted on Reddit, you have no control over it. It's extremely tempting to reply, but don't. You don't have to prove yourself to anyone who attacks you (provided you disclose any affiliations you have in your post, of course).

I remember one time when I entered into a heated debate with a very young commenter on Reddit. The argument started about a trivial point and escalated all the way to questioning me as a programmer, my choice of programming languages, and even my motivation for blogging.

It got ugly fast, and I really should have known better. You rarely can convince someone who immediately thinks you are an idiot (because he or she disagrees with your post) that you are not one. There is no point in even trying. Eventually that kid ended up deleting most of his responses, leaving a long list of my replies to [deleted] comments. What a waste of time for everyone involved. And he occasionally questioned me again. It's simply not worth creating this kind of situation.

Meta Criticism

Back to the examples. Meta criticism could be any of the following comments:

> Stop submitting crap like this. This is just blogspam.

> This article was written to sell you on the affiliate links.

> You are too much of a coward to publish my comments.

If you have control of the channel (e.g., the comment was posted on your blog), you have a choice. You can either approve the comment or opt not to publish it, depending on your stance on moderation. Just know that if you approve such a comment, it rarely makes sense to engage in argument over it.

Trolling

Finally, here's an example of trolling:

> Nobody in their right mind would buy an Android phone. Stop being a bunch of commies, and get yourself an iPhone.

The comment doesn't have a genuine counterpoint to the article. But the end result is that people who have an Android phone will feel personally attacked and will want to reply to this commenter. Do not let such comments through unless you are ideologically opposed to any form of moderation. Above all, ignore them when you see them on social media sites. No good can come from replying to them.

So-called trolls feed on replies. The good old Usenet mantra says, "Don't feed the trolls." Ignoring them is the best thing you can do. The most challenging part is figuring out if the person is trolling or is just misguided. The example above is obvious, but successful trolls are subtle and make you think you are dealing with a person who is "wrong on the Internet."[4] When in doubt, let them be wrong.

You'll need a particularly thick skin to stomach the comments on Reddit. It's a wonderful community, but criticism, sarcasm, and cynicism are highly rewarded. From time to time what you write—as well as you personally—will be shredded to pieces in the Reddit comments. Ignore the negativity as much as you can, and you'll discover that it's worth submitting there for the sheer number of new readers you'll attract. (If you've never been likened to Hitler at least once on Reddit, you're probably not submitting enough.[5])

---

4. xkcd.com/386
5. en.wikipedia.org/wiki/Godwin's_law

9.4   Your Mantras When Dealing with Criticism

The way you handle comments and moderation is highly personal, so you may disagree with some of my suggestions. That's okay. Try to stick to the following principles though, as they will serve you well:

- Welcome constructive criticism as an opportunity for growth.
- Haters gonna hate. Accept it.
- Don't feed the trolls.
- Consider all criticism, but reply only when strictly necessary.
- Report serious abuses.
- Keep writing.

Remember that in most cases it's not you, it's them. You can't be liked by everyone, and sometimes in life people will act like real jerks. This is particularly true when large audiences and anonymity are involved.

If you receive death threats or have serious concerns about your safety, report such abuse to the authorities. It's rare that you'll have to deal with drastic situations like this, but it does happen occasionally, depending on how controversial you are with your opinions. Also, if you are a woman, gay, transgender, a minority of any kind, or strongly unconventional in some sense, your chances of being harassed as a blogger are even greater. Take care of yourself, and consider using a pseudonym if you are concerned about being the target of hatred or abuse.

As a final word of advice on the topic, don't become another victim of criticism. Criticism will ruin your day in the beginning, and it's tempting to give up writing and promoting articles when you're met with such hurtful words. You are not alone in this struggle.

Most readers will love the fact that you share your knowledge and thoughts with them. They'll side with you. Don't deprive 99.99 percent of your readers because 0.01 percent are made up of haters, lunatics, harassers, trolls, stalkers, fanatics, racists, homophobes, sexists, people jealous of your success, and other undesirable, sad people. With any large audience comes a small percentage of people who haven't learned about the importance of the golden rule yet.

If you are truly struggling with some members of your personal anti-fan club, consider Googling resources for dealing with harassment, cyberbullying, and stalking. Plenty of help is out there.

Also, if you are at the point of giving up on blogging due to the nasty comments you receive, as a last resort you can consider turning comments off on your blog. It won't make comments people leave elsewhere regarding your post disappear, but at least you won't receive notification of such comments in your inbox.

We'll talk further about preparing for success, including some more positive side effects, in Chapter 12, *Taking Full Advantage of Your Blog*, on page 215.

9.5 What's Next

This section concludes the part of the book that's dedicated to promoting your blog. Promotion is a never-ending process and something you'll wind up experimenting with throughout your career as a blogger. These chapters, however, should give you the foundation that's required to get your content out there in front of people and for you to be better equipped to deal with the occasional negativity that comes your way.

We'll touch on promotional activities again in the final part of the book, which is dedicated to growing and scaling your blogging endeavors.

Back to the immediate future. Turning the page will lead you into the fourth part of the book, which is devoted to reaping the benefits of your work as a blogger. This is the fun part, where you'll learn how to maximize your reward as well as experience the satisfaction of having your content be widely read and appreciated.

Part IV

Benefit from It

For I can raise no money by vile means.

> ➤ *William Shakespeare*

CHAPTER 10

Making Money from Your Blog

This section of the book is where you learn strategies to reap the benefits of your blogging activities. We'll start by looking at direct, easy-to-implement ways you can earn money from your blog.

I realize that you may have zero interest in making money from your blog. That's fine. Feel free to skip this chapter as well as the next chapter on promoting your own products. But if you'd like to get paid for your blogging efforts, pay close attention and get ready to earn some extra cash.

10.1 Common Monetization Strategies

The following are some of the most common direct monetization strategies for blogs. We'll discuss indirect ways, such as selling your own products or promoting your consulting practice in the next two chapters.

- Ads
- Sponsorships
- Affiliate links
- Subscriptions
- Donations
- Merchandise

We'll dissect each of these, focusing on best practices and profitability.

10.2 Make Money with Ads

Advertising is the first strategy to consider to start monetizing your blog. Thanks to ad networks such as Google AdSense,[1] placing ad units on a blog

---

1. google.com/adsense

is very straightforward. Such networks act as intermediaries between advertisers and publishers (i.e., you). The details vary, but essentially ad networks aggregate a series of ad spots on a large number of sites and let advertisers pay to place ads in them. This frees you from the burden of finding advertisers, agreeing on a fair price, collecting payments, and so on.

How Google AdSense Works

If you intend to place ads on your blog, you can sign up for free with Google AdSense (the most common choice among bloggers) and then set up one or more ad units, as shown in Figure 26, *Setting up a Google ad unit*, on page 177. AdSense is the site owner (i.e., publisher) counterpart to the Google AdWords program, which is the interface used by advertisers to buy ads on search results and sites belonging to the Google AdSense program.

You will be provided with an embeddable snippet of JavaScript code for each ad unit you create, which you then place in strategic spots on your blog. You could, for example, select a full banner above each of your posts, a vertical skyscraper for your sidebar, and a box ad unit at the bottom of each post.

Ads that are relevant to your content will automatically be displayed inside such spots on your blog, and your account will earn a variable amount of money each time a visitor clicks one of those ads. This is called *contextual advertising* because the ads that are served vary depending on the content of the page.

The amount of money you receive will be what the advertiser paid to have an ad displayed on your site minus a substantial cut that Google takes. Realistically, this means putting anything between a few cents to a few dollars in your pocket for each click. Such numbers really depend on the competition level and niche you're in, but for technical blogs the CPC (cost per click) you'll earn tends to be well below a dollar.

Google will display a maximum of three ad units regardless of how many units you place on a given page. This means that you shouldn't place more than three ad units on any page of your site. (Each unit may contain a multitude of ads, however, and this is handled automatically by Google.)

WordPress users can include ads in the sidebar by adding a Text widget containing the JavaScript ad code provided by AdSense. For other spots, such as below each post, users can choose their theme's ad options (if provided by the theme) or use one of the many ad plugins available, or they can edit the theme's files directly. Common theme files to edit are header.php, footer.php, and single.php (for adding content above or below each post).

Blogger users can take advantage of the AdSense gadget, which is available in the Page Elements pane within the Design tab.

Regardless of your blogging engine, you can add a search box powered by Google AdSense if you wish. When users search your site with it and end up clicking any ad that's displayed on the results page, you get a cut. Google also enables you to include ads at the top and/or at the bottom of your feed.

Using fonts and colors in your ad units that match your theme will increase your CTR (remember, click-through rate). Squares and rectangles also tend to have good CTRs. Likewise, choosing key positions in your template will help you achieve a higher CTR. In my experience, visitors are significantly more likely to ignore AdSense units that are located in the sidebar than those placed before (much more so) or after your posts, as shown in Figure 27, *A high CTR ad unit*, on page 178.

To increase your revenue you can either bring in more visitors or up the number of clicks you get from the current volume of visitors you receive (your CTR). Ideally you'll be able to do both.

Avoid positioning your ad units in a way that makes them appear to be actual content, such as horizontal ad units containing a few links that resemble a list of categories or pages for your blog. Such ads should not be placed where your navigation bar would normally be. Misleading your visitors is never acceptable, and Google will sometimes intervene in situations where such behavior is reported.

Detailed reports will allow you to figure out which ad units and products (e.g., AdSense for Content, Search, and Feed) are performing well. These reports include details such as the number of ad impressions/pageviews you served, the CTR, CPC, and RPM (revenue per mille; *mille* is Latin for "one thousand"). RPM is often called CPM elsewhere, where the *C* stands for cost.

Don't try to game the system or you'll be banned, and all of your unpaid earnings will be frozen. Avoid clicking your own ad units, and never invite your readers (or friends) to click them either.

In your account settings, you'll be able to specify how and when you get paid, but by default you'll receive one payment per month provided your account balance reaches at least $100 (if it hasn't, then the balance will be carried forward until you reach $100 or more, after which you'll receive a payment for the month in which that occurs).

Finally, it's important to note that Google requires you to have a privacy policy on your blog (as do many other networks). You can obtain one by searching Google for a privacy policy generator and then adding the text (customized for your domain and email address) to a Privacy Policy page that you link to from your blog's menu bar or from the footer.

Alternatives to AdSense

AdSense may be the most common ad provider for bloggers, but it's certainly not the only option available. A wide variety of ad networks exist, and some of them may be good matches for your blog. Here's a list, by no means exhaustive, of a few of the most popular choices you may want to check out:

- adBrite (www.adbrite.com/mb/exchange_publishers.php)

- Burst Media (burstmedia.com/publishers.html)

- Project Wonderful (projectwonderful.com)

- Advertising.com (www.advertising.com/publisher/overview)

- Bidvertiser (bidvertiser.com)

- Chitika (chitika.com/publishers)

- Kontera (www.kontera.com/publishers)

- Value Click Media (www.valueclickmedia.com/publishers)

- Federated Media (federatedmedia.net/publishers)

Some of these networks pay publishers in the same way AdSense does, on the basis of the actual clicks received (CPC-based), whereas others sell you ad spots at a fixed rate per thousand impressions (CPM-based) or per given time period. For the latter two types of ad networks, the ads' click-through rate does not affect your earnings.

Keep in mind that if you opt for an ad network as a technical blogger, you may be better served by niche networks that specialize in the area of your blog, if such is available. For example, in the creative and design field, both Fusion Ads and The Deck will generally perform much better than AdSense.[2]

Likewise, a world-class Ruby blogger may try to join the exclusive Ruby Row niche ad network.[3] The author of a humorous, comic-centered blog might look into Blind Ferret.[4]

---

2. fusionads.net and decknetwork.net, respectively.
3. rubyrow.net
4. blindferret.com

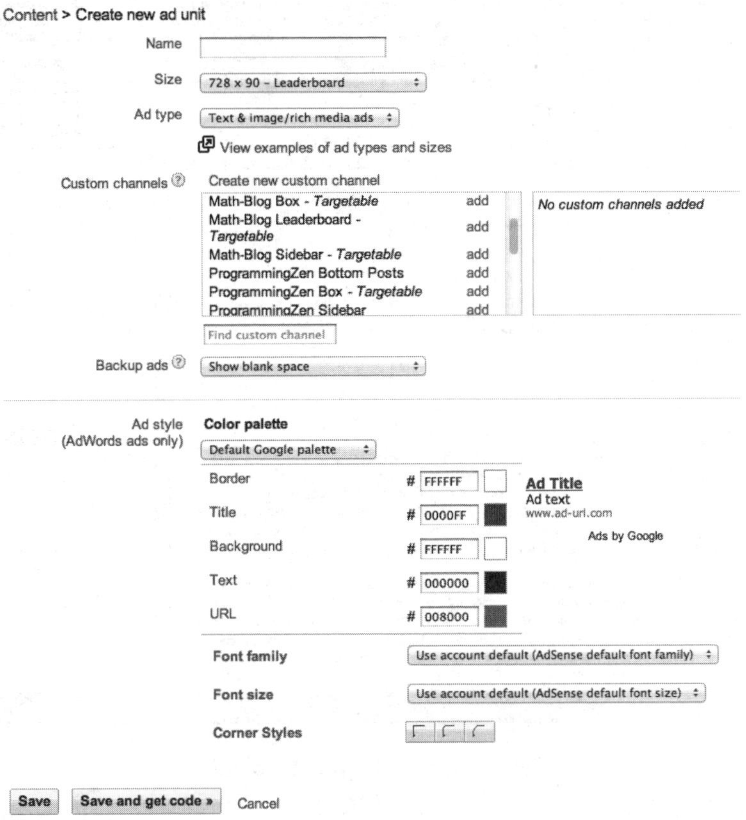

Content > **Create new ad unit**

Name	
Size	728 x 90 – Leaderboard
Ad type	Text & image/rich media ads

View examples of ad types and sizes

Custom channels ⑦ | Create new custom channel

Math-Blog Box - *Targetable*	add	No custom channels added
Math-Blog Leaderboard - *Targetable*	add	
Math-Blog Sidebar - *Targetable*	add	
ProgrammingZen Bottom Posts	add	
ProgrammingZen Box - *Targetable*	add	
ProgrammingZen Sidebar	add	

Find custom channel

Backup ads ⑦ | Show blank space

Ad style (AdWords ads only) | **Color palette**

Default Google palette

Border	# FFFFFF	**Ad Title**
Title	# 0000FF	Ad text
Background	# FFFFFF	www.ad-url.com
Text	# 000000	Ads by Google
URL	# 008000	

Font family	Use account default (AdSense default font family)
Font size	Use account default (AdSense default font size)
Corner Styles	⌐ ⌐ ⌐

Save | **Save and get code »** | Cancel

Figure 26—Setting up a Google ad unit

Keeping an eye on fellow bloggers in your niche is a good way to spot niche-specific ad networks that could potentially lead to decent rewards.

For my programming blog, I personally use Federated Media, which has a strong technology subnetwork (a *federation* in its terminology). In this system, I have AdSense in place as a backup for those times when Federated Media isn't able to provide any ad campaigns for my site to run, therefore helping my blog get the best of both of these ad revenue worlds.

In the majority of cases, there is an approval process that your site must go through before you can join a network, some of which are by invitation only. The main criteria are always traffic and content quality. If you show up with a brand-new site and little traffic, relatively few ad networks will take you on. Build a following first.

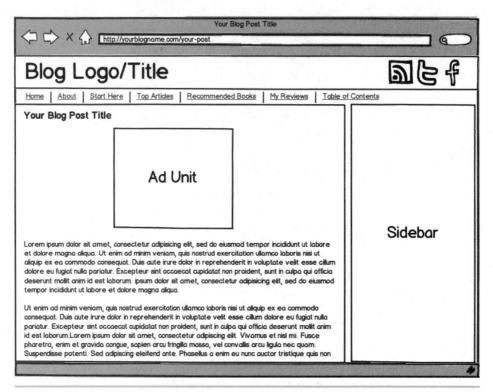

Figure 27—A high CTR ad unit

Ads and Technical Audiences

Placing ads on your blog is a straightforward monetization strategy, particularly if you stick with a network like AdSense, which won't make you jump through hoops in order to have your site accepted. Unfortunately it's not the most profitable way of monetizing your blog, and it comes with a series of negative implications. Let's review the most noteworthy shortcomings.

- Ads tend to put visitors off, particularly technical folks. Don't place too many ads or your blog will end up looking like a spam site and you'll be bouncing visitors like a pinball machine.

- Accept that many technical users will have ad-blocking browser extensions installed, such as AdBlock Plus.[5] Don't try to detect and block these users from viewing your content, as some sites do. It's your right to show ads with your content. It's your visitors' right to decide not to see them.

---

5.   adblockplus.org

- Search engines tend to dislike overly commercial sites that are filled with ads and other offers and may penalize your search result ranking if you go overboard.

- Technical audiences tend to ignore ads. This means that your click-through rate will be low, which in turn means that for every thousand impressions of your ad, you'll only get a few clicks and bring in very little revenue. The end result is that your average RPM (again, your revenue per thousand impressions of an ad unit) will not be worth boasting about. In most cases you're looking at the lower end of the $1–$5 USD range. In turn, this means that if you manage to attract 10,000 visitors in a given month, that ad unit will only bring you between $10 and $50, and the actual figure will probably be in the lower end of the range. This is why AdSense is sometimes humorously referred to as *blogging social welfare*.

- It can be argued that you are inviting the visitors you worked so hard to attract to leave by clicking ads at the rate of mere pennies per visitor lost.

- At times, people have been banned from ad networks like AdSense through no fault of their own, simply because foul play has been suspected. Many thousands of dollars have been lost by bloggers in such disputes, where there is little recourse for the innocent.

Should You Place Ads on Your Blog?

In the beginning, when you're just getting your site off the ground, don't place ads on your blog. Initially you'll have relatively little traffic, so the chances of earning anything substantial from ads are immensely slim. On the other hand, the chances of putting off your early visitors are substantial.

Tip 25

Content, not ads, should dominate the page.

As a general rule of thumb (and depending on the economic goals you've set for your blog, if any), don't place ad units until your site is established and receives at least 10,000 pageviews per month. However, I would think twice before placing ads in your feed even at that point, as they'd be going out to your most valuable readers, the people you want to maintain and not annoy (with ads) the most.

Also keep in mind how well defined a niche your blog is. A targeted audience will generally perform better ad-wise than the audience of a general blog. In the case of contextual advertising through programs like AdSense, the ads that are shown will be more relevant and interesting to your audience, who will then be more apt to click and, in turn, generate more revenue for you.

Use a tasteful number of ads (e.g., one or two per page) once you've managed to attract a decent following and have established yourself somewhat in your niche. Don't consider ads to be your main source of income for your blog, because they likely won't be. Instead, ads can be *one* source of revenue in a diversification strategy that includes multiple sources of income (as you'll see in Section 10.6, *Case Study: My Monthly Income*, on page 196).

Tip 26

Diversify your sources of blog income.

Finally, don't place ads on your company blog. Your main objective with a company blog shouldn't be to make an extra $100 a month by filling your blog with ads. Your primary product, whatever that is, has far more potential to earn you real money. Putting off readers or sending them away from your site when they click an ad doesn't make sense from a business perspective.

10.3 Make Money with Sponsors

Conceptually not far from ads, sponsorships are an excellent way to make money with your blog. The basic idea is that you find companies that are relevant to your niche and then contact them about sponsoring your blog. In exchange for a monthly fee, you'll provide them with high visibility to your blog's readership.

For example, the popular blog *Daring Fireball* makes a substantial income by offering RSS feed sponsorships.[6]

Before you approach potential sponsors, though, you should have detailed information about your audience, which is easily obtained from Google Analytics. Prepare a page on your blog or as a PDF that you'll send by email with the details of your demographic as well as with details about what you're

---

6. daringfireball.net/feeds/sponsors

offering. If you are good with graphic design, make your presentation appealing and be sure to include lots of attractive graphs. Eye candy sells.

Key information you should enclose in that page or document:

- *Site usage statistics:* The average number of unique visitors and pageviews per month, as well as your subscriber count. Include trends if your blog is growing rapidly.

- *Geographic information:* Where are your visitors from? Include the top ten countries and the percentage of traffic these locations provide.

- *Demographic information (optional):* If you've run surveys and know about the profession, age group, income, and other demographic information about your visitors, include these stats, too.

- *Relevant keywords (optional):* If the majority of your organic traffic comes from keywords that are relevant to the sponsor, consider including the top ones in the information package you send out so as to show that your blog has the right audience.

- *Your offer:* Detail exactly how much you'd like potential sponsors to pay for the sponsorship and what you are offering in exchange. Clarify whether you are offering sole sponsorship or cosponsorship of your blog.

Traffic stats aside, what really seals the deal is an appealing offer. You could offer any or all of the following perks to potential sponsors.

- A banner advertisement in a predefined format and position on your blog (a so-called *media buy*). Link to the sponsor, of course, but opt for a nofollow link (i.e., rel="nofollow"). This way Google won't think that you are selling links for PageRank purposes. In your offer, let the sponsor know that such links will be nofollow to comply with Google's policies. Specify if you are limiting the offer to the frontpage (unusual) or throughout the blog (more common).

- A thank-you note and backlink at the bottom of your posts. For example, "This post was sponsored by Acme, the best solution for all your cartoon explosion needs."

- A periodic thank-you post that includes a shout-out to your sponsors, links to them, and a brief explanation of what they offer your readers. If your sponsor turnover is not significant, this kind of post can become annoying for your readers, thus you'll want to keep them infrequent (e.g., once per quarter).

- Interviews, guest blogging, and other content-based arrangements that benefit both the sponsor and the readers. Always disclose your affiliation. Don't hide the fact that you have a sponsor from your readers.

- Trials, giveaways, and special offers that are useful to your reader and great marketing for your sponsor.

If you don't have any companies in mind, do some research to see if there are companies in your niche that are already sponsoring other blogs. It's far easier to convince them to also sponsor you than it is to approach a company that has never heard of blog sponsorship before.

Tip 27

Make it easy for your sponsors to say yes.

You can also have an Advertise page in your navigation bar as well as a Your Ad Here banner or button in a spot that you're offering to sponsors that links to that page. Making a post in which you explain that you're accepting sponsors is also an aggressive but legitimate way to go about it.

There are companies that facilitate the whole process so that it's virtually identical to selling ads through a network, but part of the benefit of sponsorships is that you deal with a handful of companies only, one on one, for months or even years at a time. So once your initial agreement is set up, there isn't much work to do on your part except for collecting payments. You may as well cut out the middleman, establish good professional relationships with companies, and keep all the revenue for yourself.

Should You Find Sponsors for Your Blog?

Without a doubt, sponsorships are a great way to generate recurring sources of extra cash as a technical blogger. I don't advocate you seek sponsors the same day you launch your blog, though. Establish yourself first, and then go after sponsors. If you're lucky, you may even be approached by companies who are interested in a media buy before you've started looking for them.

For the record, on my programming blog I currently offer a full banner ad (468 x 60 pixels) on top of each new post for $200 a month and two half-banners (234 x 60 pixels) at the top of my sidebar for $100 each. I also offer my sponsors the ability to be interviewed or reviewed (with full disclosure) when a new product of theirs, one that's relevant to my audience, comes out. That's $400 a month, or, if you prefer, $4,800 a year, right there. (I usually sell sponsorship placements for three or six months at a time.)

You can set your own price by basing it on a honest RPM/CPM. If you require a sensible $3 CPM for a given sponsorship offer, you can divide your average monthly pageviews by 1000 and then multiply that by $3. So if your blog were to attract 100,000 pageviews per month on average, you can request $300/mo. from your sponsor. Generally speaking, the more prominent your banner and overall sponsorship offer and the narrower the scope of your blog, the higher you can go with your CPM rate.

Tip 28

Aim for high-quality sponsors only.

As usual, respect your readers. Opt for tasteful ads and banners. Don't permit Flash ads that include sounds, and limit the animation level of your banners to a minimum. Likewise, don't feed your readers low-quality, spam-like sponsors just to make a quick buck. I constantly receive offers for sponsorship and link purchases from companies I do not trust. I always turn them down, and so should you.

For startup or company blogs, just like ads, sponsorships don't make much business sense.

10.4 Make Money with Affiliate Offers

When I was a kid I created an arrangement with my local computer store in which I would refer friends and acquaintances to them, and the store would then give me a small percentage commission based on what those people bought. I didn't know it at the time, but the service I was providing to that store was a form of affiliate marketing.

This type of arrangement can be extremely beneficial for both the company and the affiliate. The company receives new business from customers it may not have reached otherwise, and the affiliate gets a commission for each sale that can be directly traced back to the affiliate's site (online, usually through a cookie or coupon).

Typically, online affiliate offers work like this:

1. The affiliate links to an offer with a tracking ID embedded in the link.

2. A visitor visits the link and is redirected to the landing page on the company's site.

3. A browser cookie is stored with a certain expiration date on the computer of the visitor. This cookie associates the visitor with the affiliate that referred them.

4. If the visitor makes a purchase at any time while the cookie is still valid, a commission is provided to the affiliate by the company.

Depending on the type of goods and the company's approach to affiliate marketing, the commission can be anything between a few percentage points to 100 percent. Yes, you read that right. Some companies will go so far as to give away the entire sale price for a promotional period in order to attract more affiliates and perhaps recurring customers.

More commonly for digital goods such as ebooks and courses, margins are exceedingly high, which means that content producers routinely offer affiliates a 50 percent commission rate for all sales made within a large period of time after the initial referral (e.g., sixty or ninety days, which, again, is often tracked via cookies).

As you can imagine, you can generate a substantial amount of money from affiliate marketing if you have a large enough audience that you're offering relevant services and products to.

As a blogger you already have the audience, and as we'll see in a moment, you can find relevant affiliate offers to present to your readers. Affiliate marketing really is the one monetization strategy you can't afford to ignore.

Before jumping into key affiliate programs for technical bloggers, I want to provide you with a little background about the stigma associated with affiliates (and affiliate marketing) in general.

The reason affiliate marketing has gained such a bad reputation is that the economic incentives to promote a company's products are very high. Here we're not playing around with a dime a click. Depending on the product and the commission, we could be talking as little as a few dollars or as much as hundreds—if not thousands—of dollars (on the higher end of the scale) per referred customer.

Affiliate marketers have gone to great lengths to grab such generous commissions, including spamming, misleading, and downright scamming users.

I really encourage you to look past the negative connotations that are associated with affiliate marketing. In this section we'll take a very ethical approach to this subject, which can reward you handsomely without the need to mislead, spam, or promote crappy offers or products to anyone.

Amazon Associates: A Blogger's Best Friend

Note: Unfortunately, due to sales tax disputes with several states, the Amazon Associates program for Amazon.com is currently unavailable to residents of Arkansas, Colorado, Illinois, North Carolina, Rhode Island, and Connecticut. Check the complete, up-to-date list in the operating agreement, which you may want to read in its entirety.[7]

Amazon Associates was one of the earliest and most popular affiliate programs on the Web.[8] Every time you refer a customer to a given Amazon site (e.g., Amazon.com) with your tracking ID, you'll receive a small percentage of the total cost of whatever that person purchases during the next twenty-four hours.

Some affiliate marketers and bloggers greatly underestimate the earning potential of Amazon Associates on the basis of the tiny cookie duration (only twenty-four hours, instead of, say, sixty days) and the small commissions (usually between 4 and 8.50 percent, depending on your monthly sales volume, instead of the 30 to 75 percent commissions that are common for digital goods elsewhere).

While both counts are true, there are many benefits to Amazon that make it a very worthwhile program for reputable bloggers.

- Virtually everyone knows and trusts Amazon as a store. You don't have to convince your visitors that their credit card number won't be stolen when they shop there.

- Amazon's inventory of physical products is fantastic. They carry so many items that you can always find something of quality to promote, almost regardless of your particular blogging niche.

- Amazon spends millions of dollars studying ways to increase the percentage of visitors who end up buying products (i.e., optimizing the conversion

---

7. affiliate-program.amazon.com/gp/associates/agreement
8. affiliate-program.amazon.com

rate of their pages). Your main goal is really to send traffic to Amazon by way of your affiliate links, after which Amazon will take care of converting many of these visitors into customers, thus earning you a commission on all of those sales.

- Unlike other referral programs, you get a cut for every sale that's made within a twenty-four-hour period, not just for sales of the product you promoted. My technical blogs have received commissions for goods that I never promoted, including watches, swimming pools, and adult toys. That is because you may send visitors to check out a book, but once on Amazon they may purchase other books or other products (either instead of or in combination with the original item) within the twenty-four-hour period for which your tracking ID is valid. Those unexpected, additional sales add up quickly.

- Unlike some other affiliate programs, it is considered normal for bloggers to routinely link to Amazon in their posts. This means that your archives will contain many posts including Amazon affiliate links, generating you commissions long after you initially posted them.

Earn Money with the Amazon Associates Program

Head over to affiliate-program.amazon.com and apply for the program. You can sign up even if you're not a US resident. You'll be asked about a series of things, including payment information and details about your blog. The overwhelming majority of people who apply are accepted.

Note that once you are approved, you'll be able to use Amazon affiliate links on a variety of sites you may own and not just the one you applied for. Remember to use disclaimers everywhere you use affiliate offers, as previously discussed in Chapter 4, *Customizing and Fine-Tuning Your Blog*, on page 55.

Amazon has several associates programs, depending on the locale of the store you are targeting. Currently, there is a program for the American store (Amazon.com) and one for each of the Canadian, British, German, French, Italian, Spanish, Chinese, and Japanese stores. Again, you don't have to reside in one of these countries to sign up for any of their respective affiliate programs.

Register for each of the programs according to the demographics of your traffic and your blog's language. For example, if most of your traffic arrives from the States, the UK, and Canada, then apply for each of those three Associates programs. (You'll be applying three times.) You can select the locale using the drop-down menu in the top right corner of the Amazon Associates login page.

Build Links with Your Associates ID

Your Amazon Associate account will be provided with an initial tracking ID (known as your *Associates ID*) that is specific to a given Amazon site (e.g., Amazon.com). Such an ID must be embedded in the links you build and place within your blog. For example, the main Associates ID for my US account is antoniocangia-20. So if I want to link to a product on Amazon.com, I need to enclose my tracking ID in the right portion of the URL. Here are some link examples:

www.amazon.com/exec/obidos/ASIN/1934356344/antoniocangia-20/ref=nosim/

Or:

www.amazon.com/exec/obidos/ASIN/1934356344?ie=UTF8&tag=antoniocangia-20.

Note that 1934356344 is the ASIN number of this particular book, an identifier that can always be found in the URL of a product you visit on Amazon. The ASIN and Associates ID alone will uniquely identify a product on a given Amazon site and track your commissions (via a cookie that is set when the end user visits the URL).

You can build such links manually, or you can use one of Amazon's link-building tools, which are available from the Links & Banners tab in the Amazon Associates administrative interface (provided you are logged in to the site). When opting to create a Product link, you have an opportunity to select Text and Image, Text Only, Image Only, or Add to Widget, if you are creating a widget to display more products. Text Only and Image Only are the ones you should use to create textual links and linked images, respectively. (Others won't perform as well.) The resulting URLs will be more verbose than the ones I outlined above but equally valid.

Alternatively you can create a *bookmarklet* and add it to your browser bookmark bar. A bookmarklet is like a regular bookmark, but instead of a regular web address, the URL field contains JavaScript code that is executed when you click the bookmark.

To obtain a link with your Associates ID from a given product on Amazon.com, you could use the following JavaScript code and place it in the URL field of a bookmark. For the name of the bookmark, you can use something like Amazify (USA) or use whatever you like.

```
javascript: (function () {
    var usid = 'antoniocangia-20';
    var asin = '';
    if (document.getElementById('ASIN')) {
        asin = document.getElementById('ASIN').value;
        document.location = 'http://www.amazon.com/exec/obidos/ASIN/' +
                            asin + '?ie=UTF8&tag=' + usid
    } else {
        alert('ASIN not found. Are you on a product page on Amazon?')
    }
}());
```

Find a desired product page on Amazon and then click the bookmark. The address bar of your browser will now show you the URL with your Associates ID in the right place. Copy the URL and you are settled. Just remember to replace the Associates ID with your own in the JavaScript code above if you intend to use this method.

You can always use the Link Checker, which is available in the left sidebar on the Links & Banners tab, to verify if a link you've built is correctly attributed to your Associates ID.

I sometime provide links to multiple Amazon locales next to the name of the product by linking the words USA, UK, and Canada with the correct URLs for each, as follows: "The Passionate Programmer (USA, UK, Canada)." This way I can maximize earnings from users who don't shop at Amazon.com while at the same time providing them with the ability to quickly shop in the Amazon store that is most convenient for them based on where they reside or prefer to shop from. (I used to have a script that chose the store and associate ID based on the geographic location of the visitor, but geo-redirects are rarely a great idea from a UX standpoint.)

If you like this approach and you opted for the bookmarklet route, you can create three bookmarks, one for each locale, and use them to generate the three links each time. You'll need to replace both the Associates ID and the TLD of the Amazon site (i.e., .com) to create the, say, Canadian and British bookmarks. (When you sign up with a given local Amazon Associates program, you are assigned a unique Associates ID that's different from those of other locales.)

If you're unfamiliar with bookmarklets and using them sounds complicated to you, feel free to ignore my trick and instead build your links through the Amazon Associates product link building tools. It's not as convenient, but it won't affect the end result.

Use Multiple Tracking IDs

Click your Account Settings link at the top of the Amazon Associates page and then "Manage your tracking IDs." On this page you'll be able to create more Associates IDs for your account. Why would you do that? Mainly for the following two reasons.

The most obvious reason is to keep track of different sites (if you in fact operate more than one). When you pull reports for your earnings (via the Reports tab), you'll want to have different tracking codes for different sites so that you know which site generated which revenue.

The more subtle use is to distinguish what worked and what didn't on a given site. You could, for example, use an Associates ID for your posts, another for a certain sticky page, and a third one for a product you link to in your sidebar.

Use IDs freely enough, though don't use a different tracking ID per post, as you'd quickly run out of them (the default is 100 IDs per account). You would need to request additional IDs directly from Amazon, and your reports would be way too messy.

Understand Amazon Associates Reports

When checking out your reports (available as sidebar links in the Reports tab), focus on the Tracking ID summary report. This will show you how many clicks each tracking code received, how many orders were placed, how many items were shipped, what the total sales value of the shipped items was, and what your commissions (known as *advertising fees*) on those sales were.

You can select the report period, including the current week, quarter, or month so far, but by default you'll be shown yesterday's reports. The previous day's stats are usually ready by some time the next morning (e.g., 8 a.m. EST for Amazon.com).

You only earn a commission once items have shipped, not when they are ordered. This means that a tracking code may show you $0 in fees for the day before, even though there were many sales (assuming none of the items have shipped yet). The Earning and Order reports will clarify which items were ordered and when and which items were shipped and on what days they went out.

With a few exceptions for products such as Amazon Instant Videos or most electronics, your commission will be performance-based. This means that when you ship between one and six items in a given month, you'll get 4 percent of the sale price. If the number ranges from seven to thirty items shipped, you'll jump to 6 percent. Then, slowly, you can work all the way up to 8.50

percent if you sell a huge number of items that month. The commission rate is reset with each new month.

My commission tends to be in the 8.0–8.25 percent range, because in a given month I usually sell somewhere between either 631–1570 or 1571–3130 items (shipped). When the commission percentage changes throughout the month as you sell more items, your existing earnings for that month will go up accordingly so that the new percentage rate applies for all the existing items you've already sold and shipped that month.

Given that the commission percentage for all the items you sell is affected by the number of sales you make, it's important not to ignore the promotion of small, inexpensive items, too. They won't bring much revenue on their own, but they may increase the percentage fee you get on big ticket items such as expensive textbooks or DIY tools, both of which visitors seem to be fond of.

Refunds, which you'll see from time to time, will appear as negative values. You won't be asked to pay anything back out of pocket; instead they'll be deducted from the current balance (i.e., your future checks).

You can verify that your payment plan is performance based through the "Change your fee structure" link in your Account Settings. It makes absolutely no sense to opt for the Classic fee structure, where you get the bottom-of-the-ladder rate (4%) no matter how much you sell.

Earnings at the end of the month will be paid out in two month's time. For Amazon.com, US residents can opt to be paid directly via bank deposit. If you're located outside of the US, you can be paid by Amazon gift card/certificate (so not actual money) or by international check. In Canada, such checks in USD tend to be withheld by the bank for fifteen business days (as is standard practice for US checks) unless you have a different arrangement in place with your local branch. It's likely that other countries will have similar policies.

Tip 29

Review technical and business books you read.

That is to say, you'll get your money, but it won't be immediate in the beginning. Thankfully, as you routinely earn enough commissions to go over the set threshold for payments (e.g., $100 USD), you'll automatically receive payments each month.

Get the Best Out of Amazon Associates

Here is a cheat sheet for getting the best out of Amazon.

- Be genuine and caring. Don't promote a product simply to make an extra buck. Only endorse the kinds of books and other items you would recommend to your best friends.

- Write reviews of technical books you've read and products you've tried. A recommendation from someone who's perceived as an expert in a given niche can convert to sales like crazy, and people will love reading your thoughts on a given item that's near and dear to their interests.

- Create lists of products (e.g., 5 Books Every Agile Developer Should Read). They can be cheesy or downright good advice. Opt for the latter.

- Announce new books. Let your readers know when an important new industry-related book has been released—even if you haven't read it yet and therefore can't write a full review at that point in time. One time I announced that a new edition of a book was out. I wasn't the first to announce it, so I didn't even promote the post (it was a heads-up for my regular readers); however, someone saw it and submitted it on Slashdot. My announcement made the frontpage of Slashdot, bringing me an unexpected few thousand dollars. Results like this are not typical, but it does happen from time to time. Beside, you are offering a very valuable service to your readers. (Feel free to use my service, anynewbooks.com, to discover new books in the first place.)

- Mention books and other products. Even if the point of your post is not to review a product, you can still mention it. At times, that innocent mention can lead to awesome rewards if your post ends up getting popular.

- Start linking to Amazon right away. Unlike other forms of monetization, affiliate links aren't as annoying, so you can start using them right off the bat.

- Ignore Amazon banners and other similar widgets, as they have really lousy conversion rates. Focus on product links in reviews, lists, and other posts instead. People click links to books and products you promote because they trust your recommendation or mention. Automatic widgets and automated product listings look just like ads to most people and are bad for SEO.

- As well, ignore embeddable stores like aStore, as they generally perform poorly for blogs.

- Use images from Amazon in your posts. You can obtain these from the Image Only tab in the product link building area of the Associates site or directly from the publisher's/company's website. If you are adventurous, take your own pictures of products you're blogging about if you happen to own or have access to said items; this will prove that you are promoting something you tried yourself. When you include book or product images in your posts and pages, link them to Amazon with your Associates ID. Such images will increase your CTR and convert well.

- Don't cloak your URLs (i.e., hide that they are Amazon links) unless the tool you use to generate and track these links does it for you. Even then, use disclaimers and disclose that your posts contain affiliate links. Honesty and transparency are important currencies as a blogger.

- Don't specify an exact price. Prices vary too much over time, plus doing so is against Amazon Associates's terms and conditions. If you wish, say something vague like "which sells for less than $XX at the time of writing." Generally speaking though, steer clear of discussing prices unless the fact that a particular item is on sale is the whole point of your mention.

- Create resource pages. For example, I have a list of recommended Ruby and Rails books on my programming blog. On my math blog, I keep a list of recommended mathematical books that are organized by category. Both have brought me thousands of dollars over the years. Stop and think about if such a page can be created for your own niche and, if so, get to work making it. It will be a useful resource for your readers and an easy moneymaker for you.

- Make your Amazon links nofollow. Google and other search engines will be less likely to penalize you for the presence of commercial links.

- Finally, a counterpoint—if you are a founder who runs a company blog, it's your call whether or not to include Amazon Associates links when linking to products on Amazon. If your main objective is to promote your own product or service, losing Amazon's commissions in exchange for coming across as more genuine and less motivated by money in your recommendations may be a worthwhile trade-off. If you are an indie developer or small startup, the revenue such links can generate may help supplement your income, so opting for them can be a good choice. If you are blogging for an established company or a well-funded startup, then don't; you are after far bigger fish.

Where to Find Other Reputable Offers

Keep your eyes peeled for other reputable affiliate offers and networks. For example, alternatives to Amazon Associates (at least for books) are the affiliate program from The Book Depository and Barnes & Noble.[9] While these programs won't make you as much money as Amazon can, they are good alternatives if you were rejected, unable to sign up, or are otherwise opting not to go with Amazon.

Likewise, don't ignore niche-specific programs. For instance, a photography blogger can sign up with stores who offer affiliate programs, such as B&H Photo Video and Adorama.[10] Depending on your niche, there may be other companies looking for affiliates to promote their products that would be a really good fit for your site.

Check out popular affiliate networks that have a huge variety of products and CPA offers (which stands for cost per action, because the affiliate is paid a fee when the referred visitor takes a desired action, so this applies not just to a product purchase but also to other determined actions such as signing up for a given newsletter, a trial offer, and so on). Common players here are Google Affiliate Network, Commission Junction, and ClickBank.[11] Particularly with the last, you'll have a majority of low-quality information products, with a few gems here and there. If you can find decent products, there is no shame in promoting them from such a site. So apply for all of these programs as a publisher/affiliate.

Tip 30

Promote only products you'd buy yourself.

With the emergence of self-publishing, you should also keep an eye on new releases of good digital titles within your field. I make decent money from self-published PDF and video releases that are created by esteemed colleagues in the Ruby and mathematical worlds.

Finally, continue looking for possible offers among products you use regularly. Affiliate programs for technical audiences can be found virtually everywhere

---

9.   bookdepository.com and BN.com, respectively.

10. bhphotovideo.com and adorama.com, respectively.

11. google.com/ads/affiliatenetwork, cj.com, and clickbank.com, respectively.

these days. You can promote hosting, premium blogging templates, domain registrations, email marketing providers, and other similar products simply by using them and then advertising that you do and why.

10.5 Make Money with Other Monetization Strategies

Affiliates offers, sponsorships, and ads (usually in that order) are going to bring in the majority of direct revenue for most bloggers. However, if you're creative about it, there are several other monetization strategies to be found. The most common ones are subscriptions, donations, and merchandise sales.

Subscriptions and Membership Sites

Users are not exactly fond of *paywalls* (sites that require a payment in order to access articles), but if you attract a loyal following you can offer monthly subscriptions in exchange for some form of exclusivity. You could offer extra features to pro users (such as your articles in PDF and audio format), access to exclusive content that's not available to your regular readers (e.g., a screencast section of your site), or exclusive access to a useful resource (e.g., a private forum where you personally help people).

WordPress users can look into plugins such as wp-Member and WishList Member to obtain membership site features for their blogs.[12] Users of other blogging systems may have to get creative to find similar features for their blogging platform or use third-party scripts or services. The risk of membership sites is alienating your user base and creating two classes of citizens among your readers (paying and non-paying).

Be careful if you decide to experiment with this monetization strategy. It has the potential either to generate plenty of income or to destroy your community, so tread lightly in terms of how you go about this approach. In particular, do not make your readers pay to read your blog posts. Doing so goes against the spirit of sharing your knowledge via blogging.

Donations

Receiving donations is much simpler than adding premium membership features to your site. You simply add a payment processor button (e.g., PayPal) and invite readers to donate. You can make it cuter and ask for a specific amount that would pay for a coffee, beer, or slice of pizza rather than having this approach come across as out-and-out panhandling. Add a nice coffee

---

12. member.wishlistproducts.com and wp-member.com, respectively.

cup icon next to your call to action, and you may get a few donations here and there.

In my experience, donations are not a particularly lucrative approach to monetizing your blog. To make them work and be sustainable for you, you'll need a particularly large audience of very loyal readers. Furthermore, you may have to motivate such users by recognizing them in a page on your blog.

Another problem with donations is that if you try to earn money from your blog with ads, sponsorships, and affiliate offers, very few readers will feel like donating to you. And if you get rid of those revenue channels, you generally won't be able to make up for them with donations alone.

I have tried a variety of donation-related approaches, including accepting Bitcoins and receiving micropayments via Flattr and Readability.[13] Earnings were abysmal when compared to other revenue sources. One donation approach that I have seen work many times is having infrequent fund-raising posts,[14] in which the blogger outlines the expenses and time commitment required to keep up the blog and requests (perhaps once a year) that readers to chip in to reach a specific amount of money.

Tip 31

Consider services such as Pledgie.com for fund raising.

For genuinely useful blogs with a loyal readership, such donation drives can quickly bring in a few thousand dollars in a matter of days or even hours. One such drive allowed Jason Kottke,[15] a pioneer blogger, to switch to full-time blogging back in 2005. But the model hasn't been sustainable and his blog is now ad-supported (via The Deck).

Keep this tool in your belt for when things are not going well economically. (Should you ever find yourself in extreme dire straits, remember also that your blog is essentially a virtual real estate asset and can, if worse comes to worst, even be sold on sites such as Flippa.[16])

---

13. readability.com
14. quirksmode.org/blog/archives/2011/06/donation_drive.html
15. kottke.org
16. flippa.com

Sell Merchandise

Merchandise sales can quickly add up and, unlike the early days of the Web, you don't have to ship products out of your garage. Using services such as CafePress, Spread Shirt, and Zazzle,[17] all you really need is a nice design.

If you did a good job in terms of branding and ensuring that your readers feel a part of a community, you may end up selling quite a few T-shirts and other types of merchandise with your logo on it. If you have a cute mascot like Reddit or Hipmunk both do,[18] selling will be even easier.

Keep in mind that you don't have to limit merchandise to your logo or mascot. With the help of a good designer, you can very easily create cute, fun, witty T-shirts and other gift shop-like items that are relevant to your niche and make some extra money via that route.

For example, I could add another source of revenue to my math blog by simply creating a series of math-related T-shirts designs that I sold for a markup over the base price I was charged by a third-party service. So far, I have not tested my hypothesis on *Math-Blog*, but I suspect it might work well.

Much of what you'll learn in the next chapter, when we discuss techniques to help sell your own products, can be applied to merchandise as well. Keep this monetization strategy as something worth exploring later in your life as a blogger, perhaps a year or two after having established your blog.

10.6 Case Study: My Monthly Income

If there is one lesson you need to take home from this chapter, it is that you should find a good balance between the need to earn dollars from your blog and the risk of irritating your users.

The second important lesson is that you can't put all your eggs in one basket. Diversifying is a good strategy when blogging. Trying out a variety of methods to make money over the course of several months that turn into years will let you verify what works for your blog and audience and what doesn't. Find multiple streams of income that have proven to be worthwhile for you, and keep them working in tandem.

Keep track of your earnings and where they're coming from by adding such information in your blogging dashboard or key performance spreadsheet (if you created one, as previously suggested in the chapter about statistics).

---

17. cafepress.com, spreadshirt.net, and zazzle.com, respectively.
18. hipmunk.com

My March 2011 Blogging Income

To give you a better idea of what the income of a blogger may look like, I'm going to share the earnings in USD of my three main technical blogs for a good month in early 2011. The example month was above average, but it was not the highest grossing month I have ever had.

Here are the earnings by revenue source: (Note that percentages may not add up to 100% due to rounding.)

Revenue Source	Revenue ($)	Percentage (%)
Amazon Associates	3,531.77	76.57
Other Affiliate Offers	636.58	13.80
Sponsorships	300.00	6.50
AdSense	143.90	3.12
Total	4,612.25	100.00

Here are the earnings by site:

Site	Revenue ($)	Percentage (%)	Pageviews
Programming Zen	3,297.92	71.50	80,099
Math Blog	650.00	14.10	47,462
Any New Books	637.78	13.83	8,272
Other	26.55	0.58	< 1000

Although AnyNewBooks.com is a blog, it mostly acts as a notification service via email, so there is a very loose correlation between pageviews and its earnings. In fact, it currently receives about ten times more web traffic than it did in March 2011, but the earnings have not gone up tenfold.

And finally, here's the breakdown for the Amazon Associates commissions:

Site	Amazon Fees ($)	Percentage (%)
ProgrammingZen.com	2,491.34	70.54
AnyNewBooks.com	637.78	18.06
Math-Blog.com	376.10	10.65
Other	26.55	0.75

You may think that these numbers are great and start to imagine what you could do with an extra $1,000–$6,000 a month. Before you do though, remember that you'll also have some expenses, including hosting, domain renewals, software licenses, and the opportunity cost of your time investment.

You'll also need to declare every last penny and legitimate expense you make and pay taxes on your online earnings. Depending on where you live, that may mean reducing your blog-generated income by anything from 15 to 50 percent.

The good news is that in most countries you won't have to register a company until you earn a substantial amount of money from your blogging activities (in some countries that number is in the tens of thousands). So that's something else you can worry about once your site has been very successful for a while.

For the time being, you can slowly build up to a nonnegligible extra income. Such a reward can truly help keep you motivated, and if you don't need any motivation, I hope you'll at least enjoy the extra cash.

10.7 What's Next

We covered a lot in this chapter. You should now have all the tools you need to start experimenting with proven methods that can benefit you financially, if that is one of your goals.

But this is just the beginning. The benefits blogging can provide go far beyond affiliate offers and ads, as we'll cover in depth in the next two chapters.

Next to doing the right thing, the most important thing is to let people know you are doing the right thing.

➤ *John D. Rockefeller*

CHAPTER 11

Promoting Your Own Business

This chapter is dedicated to the topic of promoting your own business through blogging. It is beneficial to two types of readers: people who are interested in promoting and growing their company (or their employer's business) and bloggers who'd like to increase their income by selling their own products.

The distinction between the two is not that important because the information I provide here serves both categories of business well. If you don't run or help promote a business or don't intend to sell your own products (books, videos, software, etc.), then feel free to skip this chapter.

A company blog is not very different from a regular technical blog. What this chapter does is build on top of the knowledge you've acquired so far to help you hone a blogging strategy that's specific to your company.

11.1 A Checklist for Company Blogs

Let's start by reviewing some of the startup/company-specific concepts that have been introduced so far. This list acts both as a checklist and a quick recap.

- Identify why you're blogging. Is it for customer acquisition and to increase sales? Providing support to existing customers? Finding moral support and sharing war stories with fellow entrepreneurs? Expanding your team by recruiting new hires? Get to the root of what you want to accomplish with your company blog.

- Identify who you're blogging for. Now that you know why you are blogging, try to understand who your target readers are. This will help you determine what to blog about, with what degree of detail, what kind of tone, and so forth.

- Keep your blog on the same domain as your company. Opt for yourcompany.com/blog or blog.yourcompany.com.

- Prominently link between your blog and your site. Anyone landing on your site should be able to check out your company blog with ease. Much more importantly though, someone landing on a random post should immediately be able to find out more about your company and products. Whether the two sections of your site share the same navigation bar or not, the main marketing purpose of your blog is to get readers to discover your products. Make it easy and obvious.

- Use the same logo and general look and feel for your blog, even if the layout and style is slightly different from that of your main site.

- Don't place ads and offers from third parties on your company blog. As a business, income from sales should overshadow any extra income ads can provide. You don't want your blog readers to leave the site. Instead, have buttons, banners, and other ads for your own products in multiple spots around your blog template.

- Host your blog on a different infrastructure from your company site. If your site were to become unavailable, you'd still be able to communicate with your customers through your blog. This isn't by any means necessary, but it's a good trick that can facilitate communication during outages.

- Make it a team effort. Unless you are a one-person startup or a micro-ISV, you should try to enlist the help of others in your team when it comes to keeping the blog going strong. Depending on your company's age and structure, you can turn to cofounders or fellow team members. Even if you plan on doing most of the blogging yourself, don't forget to enlist the help of other experts on your team so as to enrich your collective company blog.

- Determine if you need more than one blog. Some companies choose to have two blogs; one for announcements and news and another for their "From the Trenches" or "Behind the Scenes" posts. Try to determine if a second blog could help you better achieve your blogging goals.

This last point is one that we have discussed the least throughout the book, yet it's an important early decision. Let's take a moment to discuss it.

Do You Need More Than One Blog?

Maintaining one blog is a sizable effort. Of course, it's one of the best marketing tools at your disposal. There's no denying, though, that it still requires work, consistency, patience, and commitment. Marketing is hard work (contrary to what some believe). The moment you introduce a second blog, you have if not doubled then at least certainly increased the challenge and responsibility you face. You'll also need to clarify which blog is for what so as not to confuse your customers.

As a big believer in the power of simplicity, my default stance is that you should focus on one company blog only unless you have a good reason not to. An obvious advantage of going the one-blog route is that your announcements and news will be shown to subscribers who mainly follow your site for the subject matter expertise you share. Remember that such posts are another occasion to get your products in front of your prospective customers.

To help you decide on this issue, ask yourself the following questions:

- Do I have enough product announcements and news to justify a separate blog?

- Do I have the manpower and drive to manage two blogs?

- Is there a big disconnect between the content and audience of my main company blog and those of a blog about my products? Keep in mind that this gap between the two is only justifiable if the purpose of your non-product-related blog isn't to acquire new customers (e.g., hiring, finding business partnerships, etc.). If your main objective is to get new customers and increase sales, the content of your company blog should be crafted so as to interest your prospective customers as much as, or more than, a dedicated product blog would.

- Do I post so often in my company blog that I want to provide a second, less frequently updated blog for those who are solely interested in news and announcements from our company?

If you answered yes to one or more of these questions, then by all means consider the second blog option. Perhaps host it on news.yourcompany.com or yourcompany.com/news or something equally telling, so that its purpose is readily apparent.

Likewise, ensure that your non-product blog (which is usually aimed at expertly discussing topics related to your niche or activity) has a clear title and/or tagline to identify its purpose.

Some companies go as far as having a multitude of blogs (e.g., balsamiq.com/blogs), and it's not rare for large companies to have various blogs operating on a department or industry basis.

> ### Joe asks:
> # Do I Need a Company Site?
>
> When I refer to having a blog on your company site, I'm working under the assumption that your company already exists and you have a site that sells products or services.
>
> If you are a blogger who managed to attract a following and is now trying to earn more money by selling information products such as ebooks, you may not need a separate site. Simply prepare sale pages on your blog that include some form of e-cart functionality that will act as landing pages for your products. Then link to and advertise about those pages and products on your sidebar and throughout your blog.
>
> To begin selling digital products, if you are such a blogger, look into e-commerce providers that handle everything for you, including payments and download delivery. Two valid options are E-junkie (e-junkie.com) and FastSpring (fastspring.com). For subscription-based products and services, you can check out Chargify (chargify.com) or Recurly (recurly.com).
>
> WordPress users may also want to check out WooCommerce (woothemes.com/woocommerce).

11.2 Identify and Understand Your Readers

Now that your company blog is in place, you'll likely be wondering what you should blog about. As you probably know by now, the answer is that it depends on your goals. But let's narrow things down.

Most companies are after new customers, increased sales, retaining customers, increased loyalty, and other traditional marketing purposes. So your main goal is likely to be getting your products in front of as many prospective customers as possible.

With such a goal in mind, you should blog about topics that deeply interest your prospective customers. Answer their pressing questions, clarify their doubts, stimulate their curiosity, inspire them to achieve their full potential and succeed (particularly with your products). Become that comforting, expert voice in their industry that readers can rely on and trust.

Meet Laura

Before you tailor content to your customers and answer their needs with your expert voice, you must first understand who your prospective customers really are.

Most marketers will tell you to think in terms of demographics. Your customers are in such and such an age group, are of this gender, and earn within a given salary range. All that info may be useful to know, but it's not the way to penetrate the minds of your customers.

To really feel empathy and understand what your customers want, what confuses them, and what inspires them, you need to get personal. You can't put yourself into the shoes of a whole demographic, but is possible to imagine one typical prospective customer and get to know that person better.

Let's say that your company sells educational iPad applications that are designed for young children. Who is your prospective customer? Well, let's see. She is a mom; let's call her Laura. How old is she? Let's say 33. OK, how many children does Laura have? Probably two. What ages? Hmm, a three-year-old daughter and a five-year-old son. What's her profession? She used to be an accountant, but now she does bookkeeping for small businesses from home so that she can spend more time raising her kids.

You get the idea. You can use this thought process to create a detailed profile of a possible customer and ask yourself questions in your head to get to know your target users better. Now assume that Laura doesn't know about your iPad applications and you want to reach her through your blog.

Will Laura find you when researching Objective-C vs. JavaScript-based mobile apps? Well, based on Laura's profession, that's very unlikely. What does Laura, a concerned parent who wants the best for her children, care about? What worries Laura? What is Laura's main objective? What's her problem in relation to the solution that you have to offer?

It's easier now to understand your customer because you can imagine how this person would react to what you write. You can also better assess what kind of questions your customer has and answer them. If you are an iPad developer, you may take many of your customers' questions for granted. What is obvious to you may not be to Laura. When you think about Laura, you can come up with all sort of questions that your posts should answer:

- Are iPads safe for young children to use?
- Is the iPad a good educational tool for children ages three to six?
- Can you use a pen to write on the iPad screen?
- What are some clever ways to use mobile devices to encourage children to learn?
- Are there fun iPad games aimed at young children?
- Is an iPad or an Android tablet better for educational purposes?
- Should parents buy their children an iPad?
- What can children learn through the iPad?
- What are the best iPad apps for young kids to use?

- Should children spend their time on the iPad?
- How do I teach mathematics to preschool kids?
- What software can teach young children how to read?
- Is software beneficial for the development of your child's brain?
- How can you assess and improve your child's IQ?
- How can you prepare your children for elementary school?
- How can parents and children use the iPad together to learn and bond?
- What's the difference between the iPad Wi-Fi and the iPad Wi-Fi + 3G?

These are just a few random examples of questions your posts could answer. Notice that some of these questions aren't even iPad specific. Laura is interested in her kids' education first and the iPad is just a tool that can help her with that goal. Talk about the iPad by all means, but focus on what the customer really wants to know.

Though this exercise may appear silly, you really need to connect with your customers at this depth in order to help them find your blog and, in turn, your products. Put yourself into their shoes, and if you have access to early customers, listen to what they tell you so as to better gauge what you can do to address their questions.

Tip 32

Use Google Keyword Tool to better identify what answers customers are looking for.

11.3 Craft Your Content for Your Prospective Customers

You can and should talk about your products at length in your blog. Showcase how they work, what they are good for, what's possible to achieve with them, what announcements you'd like to make (unless you have a separate blog dedicated to covering announcements), and so on. However, if you focus on your products alone, the audience you'll end up attracting will be rather limited.

You need to reach a wider audience of prospective customers with your content and then gently introduce them to what you have to offer. The key here is to persuade customers to purchase by first offering value so as to win their trust and respect. Once a relationship is in place, you won't have to rely on *hard selling* by being obnoxious and pushy in your efforts to have them purchase what you're selling. Instead you'll be able to perform a so-called *soft sell* on your landing pages. Your sales copy (the text in which you explain your offer) will be able to focus on the benefits of your product, and the reader will have more reason to believe your claims. Your friendly and conversational tone won't look out of place or unfamiliar, because it's the same clear and expert voice that has been providing valuable advice and knowledge, without any strings attached. In other words, your sales message will be more effective and welcomed.

You could, for example, append a banner ad at the bottom of each of your posts detailing what your company does and how it can benefit your readers. You are definitively selling, but you are not coming across as imposing or annoying. All you're saying is, hey, by the way, here is an offer that may interest you if you have found this post interesting or useful.

Returning to the example of the educational applications for the iPad, you could conclude a post entitled "How to Use the iPad to Teach Your Children the Joy of Learning" with the following paragraph:

> Thank you for reading this post. I hope you and your child will have tons of fun playing with your iPad and learn a lot in the process. And if you are looking for an application to help your child learn basic numeracy, check out MyNumbers in the App Store. We built it specifically for children between the ages of two and five.

In this fictitious example, our small ad in the text of the post does not comes across as invasive or out of place. If that helpful and inspiring post were to be read by thousands of parents like Laura, you'd be guaranteed to receive a significant boost in sales.

Tip 33

Be a person, not a corporation, when you blog.

Case Study: Promoting DB2

To further back up the approach I just suggested, let me tell you what I do to promote downloads of DB2 Express-C, a free version of the commercial database produced by IBM (my current employer) on my personal programming blog. You'd think that the best approach would be for me to talk about DB2 every chance I get (on my blog)—maybe even go so far as to call the site "Programming with DB2" and grab a domain name along the same lines.

That approach enriches the DB2 ecosystem but tends to be suboptimal in terms of actually reaching new developers. Who searches for a DB2-related blog? For the most part, people who already use DB2.

Instead, I blog about all sort of interesting topics for programmers who may have never heard of DB2. This way I built a large, receptive audience composed of the exact people IBM would love to see adopt DB2 Express-C. Every time someone reads an article on programming in general or on, say, Ruby, they'll see a DB2 download button toward the top of the sidebar. Out of thousands of readers, quite a few end up clicking and investigating what it's all about.

Then when I occasionally post about DB2, I have a very sizable audience of subscribers reading about that very database. Those articles are also hosted on a popular blog now, which in turn helps obtain better search engine rankings. Guess what happens? Over the years, hundreds of thousands of people heard about DB2 through my blog, and many thousands have tried it or switched over. It would have been virtually impossible to achieve this with a blog focused solely on DB2.

In your company blog, you should do the same thing. Mix some posts about your products with content that is not about your products per se but is still highly interesting and valuable to people in the industry you are targeting. Check out the KISSmetrics's and MailChimp's blogs to see two companies that nail content marketing.[1]

From the Trenches Blogs

It's very tempting to use your company blog to share all the good things you are doing from a business or development standpoint. Your blog "From the Trenches" can motivate you, help you clarify your thoughts and vision, and psychologically help you cope with the challenges that entrepreneurship will inevitably throw your way.

Remember, however, that if you are blogging for customer acquisition, your focus has to be on blogging for prospective customers. Of course, if your customers are fellow entrepreneurs, then you have a match between your marketing goals and your desire to share your business experiences and lessons learned.

---

1. blog.kissmetrics.com and blog.mailchimp.com, respectively.

In fact, if your customers are entrepreneurs, typically because you have a B2B (business-to-business) product, you may even go so far as to share detailed statistics about your success. People are attracted to successful companies and their stories. By showcasing how well you are doing, you will inspire and attract a serious following from the very people you are trying to market to. In addition, your articles will be heavily shared by these potential customers.

Throughout this book I've mentioned Balsamiq and 37signals a few times. Both companies used this technique to earn a great deal of respect (and new customers). Balsamiq shared its figures publicly from the very beginning, documenting its own journey from day one. Its unconventional approach truly paid off; there was a time when you couldn't stop hearing about Balsamiq on Hacker News, Twitter, and the like. The figure-sharing approach worked.

A smaller-scale and less famous example is KreCi, a Polish developer who published a series of income reports after quitting his job to develop Android applications.[2] He was one of the first developers to publicly share earning figures from Android apps, so he received a good deal of attention (particularly on Hacker News). When he came out with his short ebook on making money on Android, many were eager to buy it.

It's not just the strong allure of wanting to emulate and listen to someone who is making money; it's that when you are sharing your figures, you are being specific. And readers trust and appreciate specifics far more than vague statements such as "We did X and it's working for us."

If there isn't a fit between what you'd like to share and what your audience wants, consider starting an additional company blog or launching your own separate blog on the topic of entrepreneurship and startups. The former approach has SEO advantages, while the latter may put a greater emphasis on you, thereby boosting your personal visibility in the industry.

11.4 Convert Readers into Customers

By now, you should have a clearer picture of what to blog about in order to promote your business. What's left to explore in-depth is how to convert the audience you are attracting into actual customers.

---

2. kreci.net

Your Company Blog Layout

Just like your content, your company blog should be laid out in agreement with what you are trying to accomplish.

Consider Figure 28, *A sample company blog layout*, on page 209. This layout has the following characteristics:

- The company logo or title will typically link to your company site. This helps increase the number of people who will end up on your actual product site. Just ensure that there is an easy way to access your blog's home page (in our case, the Blog link in the navigation bar does that).

- The blog shares the same navigation bar with the company site.

- The sidebar gives priority to the newsletter and to your own product ads without ignoring the promotion of other blog articles. Note how the RSS feed and the company's social presence are easily accessible as well.

- At the end of each post, regardless of whether the content promoted your products or not, the layout embeds a signup form.

This is the type of template that will help your readers discover your commercial offerings.

When in doubt, use a heatmap service like CrazyEgg to see where your readers' clicks are focusing. Ensure that the attention is on your brand, your call to action (e.g., newsletter subscription), and whatever else you are trying to highlight.

Get and Promote Your Newsletter

A newsletter is your most valuable asset as a marketer. To show this, let's compare the interactions of three visitors on our site.

- Visitor A checks out a blog post and leaves.

- Visitor B checks out a blog post and clicks on our product ad. B may buy or may not be ready to commit to purchasing our product or service, so B leaves.

- Visitor C checks out a blog post and signs up for the newsletter before leaving.

Visitor C is far more valuable than B. Only a tiny percentage (e.g., 2 percent) of B visitors will buy our product. The rest may never come back to the site, and thus we won't have a way of communicating with them again. C visitors, on the other hand, are *leads*. They will be reminded about us and our products

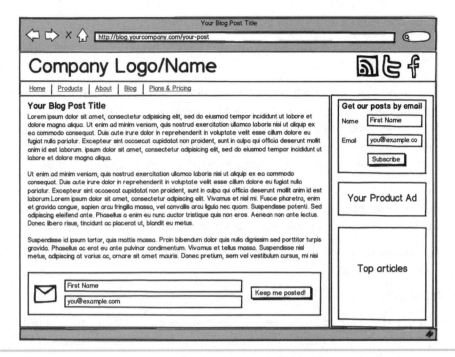

Figure 28—A sample company blog layout

every single time a new post is published, a new offer is sent out directly to subscribers, and so on.

This repeated exposure greatly increases your chances of making a sale. In fact, have you ever visited a site and in doing so seen ads for that particular site that suddenly pop up seemingly everywhere? This is called *retargeting* and it's very effective due to the repeated exposure, if albeit a bit spooky.[3]

So in your template, emphasize newsletter signups. If possible, create a freebie only available to subscribers to get more people to sign up. Make it a short guide, white paper, ebook, video, or anything else that your visitors will perceive as being valuable and useful.

How to Set Up a Newsletter

As a business you shouldn't rely on the email service provided by FeedBurner (use it for your RSS feed, though). Instead, get your own newsletter through a third-party provider such as MailChimp or Aweber. This way you'll have full ownership of the list and will be able to market it as you wish.

---

3.   adroll.com/retargeting

Here are the macro steps that you'll need to take:

1. Sign up for an account with your newsletter provider, and set up a new list.

2. Customize the signup forms and newsletter template. Require new users to only prove their first name and email. Requesting first names will decrease the number of signups slightly, but as mentioned before, doing so will help make email communication with your customers more personal, therefore increasing your newsletter's open and click rate.

3. Setup/customize a welcome message for your readers. This can be a special signup offer (e.g., 30 percent off for the first year), a list of selected articles for users to explore, or anything else you'd like to communicate.

4. Set up an RSS feed-to-email campaign so that new posts are automatically sent to subscribers.

5. Embed the signup form in your blog.

The newsletter can then be used for announcements that are not publicly made on your blog (if any), special offers (e.g., holiday discounts), and other promotions. You can get creative and do things like set up an autoresponder that sends out an offer for a discount on your product or service a week after new members sign up.

When you create a manual campaign (not one from your feed), ensure that you include the first name of the subscriber. There is usually a tag that you'll need to embed as you design the campaign (e.g., *|FNAME|*) that will allow for this. Placing the first name in the subject is a very powerful attention grabber that will increase your open rate, but don't abuse it.

One technique that I've found to be very effective is to create a campaign that relies on repetition. The basic idea is that you offer a great deal to customers for a limited time and email them two or more times about it.

For example, you could be offering your product for 50 percent off for three days only. You'd then send a persuasive email announcing this great offer on the first day, followed by a different email the second day, reminding subscribers that the offers ends tomorrow. And finally, a third email on the last day (e.g., "Antonio, last chance to buy at 50% off") to let them know the window of opportunity on this offer will be closed in a matter of hours.

Will this annoy a few of your subscribers? Almost certainly. You may receive a few extra unsubscribe requests and perhaps even a couple of "Enough with these emails already!" messages. But you'll also make a killing with your sales (particularly if your list has a few thousand subscribers). So it's up to you to decide if this is an approach that's worth doing or not.

This brings us to another important point with newsletters. You need to know which subscribers are customers and which ones are prospective buyers. You don't want to send an offer like this to those who have already bought the item or service you're offering at full price. Likewise, you don't want to send the second-day email to those who already purchased on the first day.

To solve this problem you can segment your list. Simply add a segment or extra hidden field that you can use to store details such as whether a subscriber bought your product already or what specific products the subscriber has purchased so far. Just ensure you update these fields when new orders are made.

Most e-carts allow you to invoke an API, such as the one provided by MailChimp, to update the list every time an order is placed. Consult the documentation of your newsletter provider to see how they handle segmentation and if they have an API. (In the past, I've made FastSpring and MailChimp work together quite nicely for this purpose.)

Track the Impact of Your Blog

OK, you are writing great content and promoting it as described earlier on in the book. You check your statistics and notice that your blog obtained forty thousand pageviews during the past month.

That's a so-called *vanity metric* for someone promoting a business. On its own it doesn't really tell you much. All you really can claim is that you attracted some traffic to your blog.

What did these people do when they landed on your blog? How many subscribed? How many ended up visiting your product pages? And how many went from being visitors to being customers? It's important to distinguish between vanity metrics and actionable metrics.

The first thing you need to do is to ensure that you understand which spots on your blog (or which email campaigns) are sending traffic to your product pages.

For newsletters, providers like MailChimp will automatically tag your URLs for you, provided you enabled statistics tracking for your links. Tagged URLs have a series of parameters that uniquely identify campaigns so you can understand where traffic is coming from when using Google Analytics and other analytics suites.

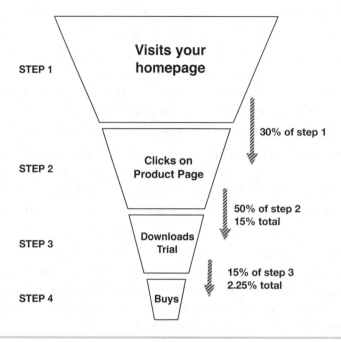

Figure 29—A sample sales funnel

For your blog you may want to manually craft a different URL for, say, your ad in the sidebar and another for the product ad at the bottom of your posts. You can do so by using the URL builder in Google Analytics.[4]

You can now track traffic that comes from your blog and newsletter to your product pages with a finer degree of control. There is still one other step, however, before you can fully make sense of that data and try to take action in response to the information you've collected.

Keep Track of Your Sales Funnel

You need to understand your sales funnel so as to determine and improve your conversion rates. You have a large group of people reading your blog, but how many of those visitors will actually end up clicking your product page? And of this smaller group, what percentage will actually buy your product? (See Figure 29, *A sample sales funnel*, on page 212.)

You can obtain these types of conversion rate metrics by defining your goals in Google Analytics or Clicky. Alternatively, you can use a dedicated conversion rate tracking tool like KISSmetrics.

---

4. google.com/support/analytics/bin/answer.py?answer=55578

Other Approaches to Selling More

It's out of the scope of this book to provide a detailed tutorial on marketing in general. That said, here are some promotional techniques that shouldn't be overlooked when it comes to marketing your product or company.

- Approach fellow bloggers and offer them the chance to receive your product for free in return for a review of that item, service, etc. Many people will take you up on this kind of offer, and you'll end up leveraging the existing audiences that those bloggers have already established. Guest blogging, extensively discussed before, is also a great tool for this purpose.

- Consider establishing an affiliate program. Good affiliates are formidable marketers who can help you connect with prospective customers that may otherwise be tricky (or even impossible) for you to reach.

- Consider a live chat widget for your site so as to support and engage your prospective customers. Olark and SnapEngage are two common choices (olark.com and snapengage.com, respectively).

- Don't ignore paid advertising, such as Google's AdWords program. Free traffic from SEO, blogging, and social media is probably the best tool you have in your marketing utility belt. It would be foolish, though, to put all your eggs in one basket. Always diversify your customer acquisition efforts, provided each channel continues to give you a positive ROI.

- Don't forget offline marketing efforts either. There are still companies out there doing extremely well through traditional advertising and publicity channels. Augment your online efforts by recruiting prospective customers in the offline world as well.

When you do so, you'll quickly discover what is and isn't working (and providing return on investment) for your company.

If you want to introduce changes and see how your conversion rate is affected, you should look into A/B testing tools or services, as these will allow you to test two different versions of a given page in parallel. Doing so will determine how a change affects the conversion rate in the next step of the funnel.

Small changes on your site can have a significant positive impact on your conversion rates within the funnel. Others won't, though, and some may even make your conversion rate worse. For example, adding social proof, such as showcasing a large number of Facebook fans, should theoretically increase your conversion rate. But there's always the risk that users will get distracted and end up on Facebook instead of completing the steps you want them to take.

How will you know for sure? Run an A/B test long enough to obtain statistically significant results. Every A/B testing tool worth its salt will automatically calculate this for you, so you don't really need a knowledge of statistics.

You can program KISSmetrics to do A/B testing for you, or you can use a dedicated, arguably easier tool. Visual Website Optimizer, Optimizely, and Website Optimizer by Google are popular choices.[5]

Always remember that your ultimate goals as a marketer are to attract a large targeted audience and to increase the efficiency of the sales funnel by improving your conversion rate at each step in the process of converting visitors to customers.

> ### Tip 34
>
> ## Bookmark all press and blog mentions of your company.

11.5 What's Next

This concludes our second and final chapter on direct strategies that will help you earn money from your blog. In the next chapter we'll focus on the nonmonetary benefits your blog can provide, like landing you a job or helping you find the perfect candidate (which will still end up making you money).

In the final chapters of this book, we'll delve further into the fascinating world of social media and step up our game.

---

5. visualwebsiteoptimizer.com, optimizely.com, and google.com/websiteoptimizer, respectively.

Diligence is the mother of good luck.
➤ *Benjamin Franklin*

CHAPTER 12

Taking Full Advantage of Your Blog

There are many non-monetary advantages that derive from having a popular blog. Some of these will inevitably benefit you economically, even if indirectly so. In this chapter we'll review the most common advantages and I'll provide you with some pointers for how to maximize your chances of obtaining these perks.

12.1 Improve Your Skills

As previously mentioned, blogging is not simply a pulpit but also a conversation starter. Your readers will generally be ruthless about inaccuracy and mistakes in your posts. Likewise, if your thoughts and ideas are flawed or can be stretched farther, chances are your visitors will point these things out.

This collaborative aspect of blogging has the huge benefit of helping you learn and grow, thanks to the power of constructive criticism and the discussions that will ensue from your posts.

The experience of blogging regularly will enhance your writing and technical skills, help you deal better with criticism, and possibly provide you with a thicker skin when it comes to handling harsh comments. It could be argued that, overall, you'll also become a better person and communicator because of your blog.

The benefits derived from blogging don't end here, though. When you are researching a topic for an article, you'll be doing focused learning for a specific and practical purpose (something that turns out to be very effective).

Teaching others requires a good mastery of the subject at hand. Personally, I find that teaching people something highlights the shortcomings in my own knowledge. If I can't explain a concept or subject simply and effectively to others, it means that I don't know that topic well enough.

Sometimes you'll have ideas or assumptions in your head that are nebulous because you haven't formalized them or fully thought them out. As soon as you start to make your case in an article about those ideas, you may find out that they were wrong, flawed, or weak. Or, on the flip side, it may turn out that it's a remarkable idea. Either way, blogging can help clarify, streamline, and spread your thoughts further, all with the help of your audience. So not only do you get to be a teacher who helps others, but you grow and learn much in the process as an individual.

Communication and well-defined ideas are at the heart of most professions. So if you are a programmer, blogging really stands to make you a better programmer. If you are a CEO, blogging can make you a better businessperson. Focus your writing on what you want to improve upon and not just on what you know best.

Finally, blogging can be a useful way to remember things you learned but have since forgotten, help you look up snippets of code from the past, and/or share technical information with a small group of friends or colleagues.

12.2 Advance Your Career

Blogging can advance your career in multiple ways. Improving your skills, as just discussed, is the first way. But there is much more to it, depending on your current position and ambitions.

As an Employee

Blogging can help you land a better job. There are two primary ways that such can be the case.

First, your blog advertises to the world that you exist. Prospective employers may come across a particular blog post and be impressed by your depth of knowledge and your personality (remember to have a distinct voice that shines through in your writing). A post on my programming blog helped me land my current job at IBM, and I constantly receive job offers from some of the most popular tech companies in the world as a result of my posts.

Second, your blog acts as an in-depth résumé/curriculum vitae. A blog can give you a much more detailed outlook on a person's interests, attitudes, and skills. If your blog is highly compelling and you come across as a friendly, approachable expert, your chances of getting hired when you apply for a job

Getting Political About Blogging

Some technical bloggers take a political approach to their blogging. They blog because they feel so strongly about their ideas that they want to convince others to believe in the same principles, with the ultimate goal of improving the field they work in.

Steve Yegge is one example of such a blogger (steve-yegge.blogspot.com). You'll find other examples if you search for blogs dedicated to methodologies, such as Agile development or Lean startups.

or when someone finds your blog are much higher. (Remember to include a link to your blog in your traditional résumé and also on LinkedIn.)

Tip 35

Blog for the position you want, not the one you have.

If your main goal is to find a better job, place a LinkedIn button/badge and a link to your printable résumé on your sidebar in a spot that's easy for visitors to quickly notice.[1] If you have other relevant or important presences online, such as on StackOverflow and GitHub, link to those or embed badges for them as well.[2]

In fact, if you are a student or are unemployed at the moment, don't be afraid of placing a call to action, such as "Hire me" or "Give me a job," within your navigation bar, sidebar, and so on. Then link to a sales page, where the thing that you're selling is effectively yourself.

Write a nice cover letter that details what you are looking for, and be sure to include links to your résumé, projects, open source contributions, etc. If prospective employers think you'd be a good match, they can use the contact form you provide on the page to get in touch and discuss interview and/or employment opportunities with you.

I would argue that a compelling, popular tech blog is one of the easiest way to obtain a job in today's rocky economy.

---

1. Sign in on LinkedIn, and then visit linkedin.com/profile?promoteProfile.
2. stackoverflow.com and github.com, respectively.

Promoting Your Open Source Projects

If you are trying to bring more visibility to your open source projects, or any kind of project really, you can adopt the same techniques described throughout this book (particularly in the previous chapter).

What may be different is the call to action. Since you are not presumably charging (though technically you could), your calls to action may be such actions as downloading your software, signing up for your web application, or contributing to a project rather than selling a product or service per se.

As usual, fine-tune your content, message, and calls to action so that they accurately convey what you're truly after.

As a Freelancer

Blogging can aid you as a freelancer by helping you find more clients and even command higher rates. The way you go about it is not all that different from the role of a job seeker.

You still need to blog on subjects you intend to write about as a freelancer while showing your expertise in the process. For example, if you are an Android OS freelancer, you'll want to focus on writing about developing Android applications in Java. Don't just talk about it, but show code and HOWTO material that clearly demonstrates your mastery of the subject.

If you can score a domain such as [TOPIC]freelancer.com, you'll position yourself ahead of the curve. Even if you can't, make sure that your blog does a good job of selling you and your expertise to both humans and search engines. Your theme keyword could be *Android freelancer*, for example. You'll want that same keyword throughout your blog, even if the site is actually located at firstlastname.com.

For example, your home page's title could be "John Smith's Blog—The Adventures of an Android Freelancer." And your tagline could be "The Adventures of an Android Freelancer."

As a freelancer, aside from making it obvious that you are indeed a freelancer, you need your "Hire me" call to action to be very prominent. In particular, the sale page for your services needs to be specific. Don't vaguely say that you'll do anything; instead, try to be specific about what you specialize in and what you're good at.

Above all, don't waste your and other people's time. Include your rates. You'll spare yourself the grief of dealing with low ballers, and you'll attract qualified prospects who are serious about hiring you for a given assignment. If you don't have a set hourly rate, provide a range or starting price point. For example, "Logo design starts at $2,000." Naturally, the higher your prices, the more impressive your portfolio and service need to be.

Your contact form should have a series of fields to collect information about a project, in case a prospective client wants to get the process started right away. Also include your information, such as your location, (business) phone number, and so on.

Another important point for freelancers to remember is to leverage guest blogging on other peoples' sites if your own blog isn't that well known. Guest blogging takes work, but taking advantage of large audiences on other blogs and online magazines could truly make the difference between a continuous stream of clients from the very beginning or a long dry spell as you gradually try to grow your own blog.

12.3 Obtain Freebies

A nice benefit of being a popular blogger is that you get contacted by publishers, publicists, and others who will try to give you freebies in the hope that you'll write about them or their products.

Publishers may offer to provide you with free copies of books that are relevant to your blog's subject matter. This is by far the most common type of freebie. There are other kinds of offers that may show up in your inbox, too, including mobile apps, desktop software, extended trials, free subscriptions to web applications or publications, and so on.

Such offers may look like subtle bribes to your average programmer, but that's the way the PR industry has operated for a long time. You can only review something ethically if you've used, tried, or read it first, and it wouldn't be fair for you to pay out of pocket for a product that a publisher wants you to consider. So the compromise is that you get a free review/media copy, without an obligation to review it if you don't like it.

Take advantage of this unique opportunity to obtain free books and other products that you're interested in. Sometimes you may even approach the publisher yourself and ask for a review copy, instead of having one come to you first. Over time you may develop relationships with publishers who will routinely send you books in an unsolicited fashion.

There are a few ground rules to keep things ethical and fair for everyone involved in these kinds of relationships. I suggest the following:

- Always use a disclaimer in your review, letting readers know when you've received a product for free. This isn't just ethical, it's actually the law (at least it is in the United States).

- Inform the publisher/publicist that you will only review the product if you find it to be worth recommending. It would be unfair to the publisher for you to bash a book that was given to you for free, and it would also be unfair to your readers to promote a book you found to be subpar.

- Only post reviews of books you've read (or products you have tested). Again, if a book or product isn't good, feel free to not review it at all and ideally inform the publisher about your decision not to post a review.

- If you requested the book, find the time to read it and write a review post in a timely manner. Then send the link to the publisher or publicist.

- Don't feel obliged to read books that are sent out by publishers to their list of media contacts if you haven't agreed to read a particular title and it just showed up at your door. Of course, if it's interesting to you, read it. If not, feel free to not review it and perhaps inform the publisher that the books being sent are not a good fit for you and your blog.

- There will be times when you may build up a backlog of freebies to review, which can become overwhelming. Time is your most valuable asset, so don't overcommit yourself to reviewing too many products during a given period of time.

- If a publisher is making you jump through hoops to get the freebie, consider giving up on the deal. Remember, you are the one doing the favor.

- Organize contests and sweepstakes in collaboration with publishers, as most publishers and readers alike will love this idea and be eager to go along with it.

If you follow these rules, you'll enjoy a wealth of great products for free, some of which can earn you money thanks to affiliate programs such as Amazon Associates.

Your readers will receive great product recommendations, and the publisher will get some much-wanted exposure for the new product. It's a win-win situation for all the parties involved.

12.4 Prepare for Success

As a successful blogger you'll be approached by a variety of people, not just by those inquiring whether you'd like to review their products. How you respond to these offers is up to you. In this section I'll cover some of the most common inquires and my personal philosophy about how to handle them.

- *Students asking for help with homework*: The response to this should be a no-brainer. Simply do not do other people's homework for them.

- *People asking for professional advice*: It's up to you to decide if you want to help such people. In general, I tend to—as long as doing so doesn't become a time sink.

- *People trying to connect with you personally*: You'll receive invites on LinkedIn, Facebook, and other social networks from people you've never heard of before. You don't know them, but they know you. Much like with celebrities, they may consider you a friend, even if you don't even know they exist. Ask yourself if you want to connect with everyone or if you're going to be selective. Does your take on this change based on the social network? For example, you could accept connections on LinkedIn but not on Facebook, or vice versa.

- *Outsourcing companies (or individuals looking for a job)*: If you are in a decent position at a well-known company, you'll be inundated by companies and individuals who are ready to work or consult for you. Depending on your position, you may not even be permitted to hire such people, though you still receive plenty of requests. Ignore or reply to them depending on your circumstances and available time.

- *Recruiters looking to hire you or asking you to help them find a candidate*: Do you burn bridges with these people by telling them not to bother you, or do you grow a relationship that could help you down the road if you ever need a job? I personally prefer to foster such relationships, freely referring jobs to friends who are looking for a position, as long as doing so doesn't require me to post job ads on my blog. That's where I draw the line, and it's been a compromise that's worked well for me so far.

- *Conference organizers inviting you to speak*: Being a speaker on stage is a fun, challenging experience unless you have stage fright. Unfortunately it often requires you to travel and spend copious amounts of time preparing a world-class presentation. Be very selective about this type of engagement. One remarkable presentation a year that gets everyone psyched about you and your message is far better for your career and blog than five unremarkable ones, in my opinion. (Always put your blog and main social media URLs on your first and last slide when giving a presentation.)

- *Bloggers and members of the media who want to interview you:* Interviews are another activity that can increase your blog's reach and your own visibility. Unlike conferences though, the amount of time required is usually way less substantial, so the trade-off between what you get and what you give is more in your favor. Don't miss out on worthwhile interview opportunities.

- *Publishers inviting you to write for them:* If you've always dreamed of writing a book, by all means take advantage of this opportunity. Just be warned from someone who has written more than one book—being an author takes time and it won't usually make you rich. However, it can be a career-altering move. As usual, figure out what you want, and then see if writing a book helps you reach that goal. Sometimes you may be asked to be a technical editor/reviewer rather than an author. The commitment and glory are both drastically lower than when you're writing the book, though this still requires hard work and an ongoing portion of your time.

- *SEO "experts" and link buyers:* People will contact you to tell you how your company (even if you don't have one) is not doing well with various search engines and propose all sorts of shady techniques to improve your Google rank. Save your money and ignore such emails. Reputable SEO experts don't usually spam people at random and propose their services to bloggers. Other times, such SEOs will want to buy links on your blog. It's not a good idea to do so, even if they are linking to a reputable source, due to Google's stance on purchased links. Ignore them, reply that you aren't interested, or propose a nofollow sponsorship if you want to see how legitimate they are.

- *People interested in getting an autograph:* OK, this one is much less common, but it can still happen to you. How would you react if someone at a conference were to ask you for an autograph? If you prepare mentally for this occurrence, things should go smoothly and you'll be able to enjoy this flattering kind of encounter. (Just remember, it's not an autograph if you're asked to sign a blank check.)

Think about how you want to approach these opportunities so that you can establish a consistent and fair policy before you're required to take action.

Usually such invitations end up benefitting you and your blog in some capacity. For example, an invitation to speak at a conference can further extend your blog's reach and get more people interested in your work. The downside is that it's easy to overcommit and either burn out or deliver poor results.

You must strive to avoid overcommitment, and being selective becomes key. You'll end up rejecting someone at some point, so you should also consider what kind of tone you intend to assume when replying to someone that you're not going to work with.

My suggestion is to avoid burning bridges or making people feel rejected. Instead, plainly explain why you are not interested. More often than not the case will be that you don't have enough time to commit to something new. Stating "I'm afraid I don't have the time X requires" is a sincere and gentle way of getting off the hook. If the person doesn't take the hint and insists, then feel free to reply in a firmer—but still polite—manner.

12.5 Other Benefits for Startups

Although customer acquisition is without a doubt the most common motivation behind why startup owners want to blog, there are other benefits for startups, too. Let's review the most typical ones.

- *Providing status updates during outages*: When the service you provide goes down, you may find yourself dealing with a mob of angry customers. As mentioned multiple times before, your blog can be an outlet to communicate with your users and broadcast status updates during crisis situations. If you wish, you could even have an availability status stream of updates at status.yourcompany.com.

- *Customer development*: If you write content that attracts your prospective customers from the very early days of your business, you'll be able to leverage this target audience by surveying them in regard to the urgent questions you have about their needs in relation to the way your business will attempt to meet those needs.

- *Attracting new hires and interns*: Talk about your wonderful offices, the great hardware and perks you provide developers, the state-of-the-art software engineering methodologies you employ, your team's bragging rights, and be sure to including lots of pictures. Paint an accurate picture of how cool it is to work for you and mention that you're hiring and/or looking for interns. You'll attract highly qualified candidates in little time, saving you many thousands of dollars in recruiting efforts. For an example of this approach at work, check out the "The Price of (Dev) Happiness" series of posts.[3]

- *Finding partners and investors*: This one is a little trickier, but business partners and investors can certainly be among your blog readers, too. If you blog about the cool things your company has been doing and the impressive metrics that show substantial growth, you may end up getting noticed by the right person. There is no magic wand that can make this happen; instead, it's all about increasing your "luck surface area."[4]

12.6 What's Next

Scaling your blog activities and enhancing your online presence via social media are the missing pieces of the puzzle. At this stage you're almost ready to take over the world.

This wraps up the three chapters dedicated to the benefits of blogging. The next and final part of the book is dedicated to growing your operation.

3.   blog.fogcreek.com/?s=The+Price+of+%28Dev%29+Happiness%3A

4.   codusoperandi.com/posts/increasing-your-luck-surface-area

Part V

Scale It

Ambition is the germ from which all growth of nobleness proceeds.

➤ *Oscar Wilde*

CHAPTER 13

Scaling Your Blogging Activities

By following the advice provided within this book so far, you should be able to create a fairly successful blog. This may be enough for you, or you may have even bigger aspirations.

For those readers, we'll now look briefly at the topic of scaling your blogging activities (both scaling vertically by stretching your blog's potential to the limit and scaling horizontally by creating further blogs).

13.1 Scale Your Blog Vertically

The growth of most people's blogs is not limited by the size of the niche they're part of. In fact, even successful bloggers rarely manage to reach the majority of their target online audience.

The real limit is often the amount of content that a single person can produce. Excluding a few bloggers who manage to obtain a celebrity-like status online despite publishing infrequently, there is a strong correlation between how much you publish and how popular your blog is.

By now, I'm operating under the assumption that your content is good, that you've presented it well, and that you've promoted your work through all the legitimate channels you can think of.

The easiest way to rapidly scale your blog at this point is to transform it into an online magazine or news site.

Online Magazine vs. News Site

Both choices are collective blogs that require the help of other writers. They mostly differ in their frequency and content type.

An online magazine like *Smashing Magazine* typically publishes one or two articles per day.[1] These articles tend to be HOWTOs about accomplishing certain web design–related tasks.

A news site like *The Next Web* publishes forty to fifty posts per day on tech-related events and announcements.[2] Smaller news sites, however, could get by with just a few stories per day.

Magazines tend to require a few writers who can publish in-depth, informative articles on the topic at hand. News sites will require many writers who are on the ball with what's happening in their niche and can quickly write a four-hundred-word piece before other news sites do (or at least create better content than their competitors while remaining timely).

Remember this important point when searching for bloggers/writers to hire. Before transforming your blog into a magazine or news outlet, consider what's made it successful so far. If it was the excellent writing, ensure that the writers you hire are on par with your own degree of writing talent. If you adopted a particular style or covered various topics in a certain manner, see if the same features that characterize your blog can be maintained as you expand it.

As usual, treat the process of expanding as an experiment. Make a gradual switch and see how your audience responds. Perhaps announce that a new writer is coming on board and then invite the community surrounding your site to welcome that person. If your audience is happy about it, slowly add more writers. Keep your readers in the loop and explain what benefits your decision to scale will bring their way.

13.2 Hire a Team of Bloggers

So you're getting serious about your blog and are now looking for new writers to help you produce a substantial amount of content every week. Here's how to go about it.

From Guest Bloggers and Your Community

The cheapest approach is to recruit guest bloggers, as discussed in Chapter 6, *Producing Content Regularly*, on page 103.

---

1. smashingmagazine.com
2. thenextweb.com

The main advantage is that you don't pay them. They are happy enough to do it for a backlink to their own site. The main disadvantage is that you don't pay them. How much can you really rely on someone you don't pay? I don't doubt you can get good articles from your most prolific guest bloggers, and you should certainly continue to promote your availability for guest posts.

Unfortunately, you can't expect these people to post on a regular basis and to (necessarily) respect your editorial schedule, nor can you request a specific number of articles per week from them. Unless you pay your guest bloggers, you should consider their efforts to be a helpful bonus. Every week you may have zero to N new posts coming from guest bloggers. These are certainly nice, but again, you can't rely on their presence or frequency.

If you introduce economic rewards, you can start to fish for writers from your existing pool of guest bloggers. You already know who did a great job and who didn't, so you can approach the right people with your proposition. Since you're paying them, if they accept, you can now rightfully request that they publish at least three articles per week or whatever schedule you agree upon.

Insightful commenters are another pool of prospective writers. Contact people that you feel fit this description and explain what you are trying to create and what you're offering, and then see what they think about this proposition. Keep in mind that people are not solely interested in money (particularly if you can't offer much). People yearn to belong to something important. Make your project that something important.

If you can't find the right amount (or type) of writers from among your guest bloggers and top commenters, consider asking your community directly. A simple "We are hiring" page and post announcement should attract a variety of candidates. The trick will be to select those who can write well and keep up with a regular schedule.

Specify how much you'll be paying up front so as to prevent wasting your and other people's time if economic expectations differ.

From Job Boards, Freelance Sites, and Outsourcing Services

In addition to paying guest bloggers and recruiting from your community, you should consider placing local ads, listing projects on freelance sites, using outsourcing services, and posting on niche job boards.

> **Joe asks:**
> # How Much Should I Pay Bloggers?
>
> The amount you pay your bloggers is a business decision you need to make. It is common to pay per article, per word, or per hour. I do not recommend paying per hour because your and your blogger's incentives are not aligned.
>
> Try to figure out how much additional income you receive on average per additional post. If you can't calculate that, guesstimate how much value you get out of it; then pay your writers less than that number, thereby leaving room for your profit.
>
> Your topic, requirements, the research level required to write an article, and the blogger's level of experience all affect the going rate. The range varies from five to several hundred dollars per article, though some publications offer more than $1000 per piece. More commonly though, you'll see mid-sized reputable blogs offering in the neighborhood of $20–$100 for an article of 500–1000 words.

Local Ads

The advantage of using ads on places such as Craigslist or Kijiji is that you may be able to find local talent that you can interview and meet in person and who can regularly contribute as a contractor to your blog.[3]

You could use this approach to assemble your own newsroom locally rather than virtually. In turn, this grants your team a better environment for communication and collaboration.

Of course, this also implies a more serious commitment to blogging as a business than your average virtual team of bloggers.

Freelance Sites

Freelance sites like Elance, Freelance.com, and oDesk are also decent venues to find people who are willing to write for truly reasonable fees (e.g., $20–$30 for a well-written article).[4] The main problem is that, in my experience, you'll have to be very selective and go through a series of low-quality writers before you find a person you can trust and rely on to deliver the kind of posts you're seeking.

Paying a little more and aiming to hire (actually) native English speakers is the way to go (assuming your blog is in English), if you want to keep the number of unsuccessful paid writer experiences to a minimum.

---

3. craigslist.com and en.wikipedia.org/wiki/Kijiji, respectively.
4. elance.com, freelance.com, and odesk.com, respectively.

Being clear and detailed about what you want is also a must. Some people even go as far as to include special requests in their job description in order to filter out those who apply without having carefully read the description. You could, for example, ask candidates to include an out-of-context word (e.g., peach) in their application so as to demonstrate that the candidate manually applied and carefully evaluated your position before applying.

It's also a good idea to check out the feedback and comments left by other employers, but view such comments with a grain of salt. In my early days of hiring paid writers, I had a few bad experiences with contractors who had fantastic feedback. Always remember that people who are desperate for work will go to great lengths to game the system.

Often contractors on freelance sites don't mind if you want them to act as ghostwriters whose name won't be attributed to the posts they write for you. This can have its advantages in some contexts, but I personally prefer not to publish other people's writing under my own name. Either way, specify in your requirements whether the article will be published in your name or in theirs.

Outsourcing Sites

Alternatively, you can consider outsourcing to services that provide articles on demand. The advantage of such sites over freelancing ones is that you don't have to go through the process of selecting writers, which will save you a considerable amount of time.

These types of services take care of assigning a prescreened writer to your article. If you order a set of posts in bulk, you may have several authors assigned to you who work in parallel, therefore reducing turnaround time and introducing a greater variety of writing styles.

On the lower end of the spectrum, you can get articles written for as little as $0.01 per word, which equates to a mere $5 for a five-hundred-word article. And such a piece will, generally speaking, be unusable garbage. This approach works for MFA (made for AdSense) sites and content farms that don't really care about the quality of the content, but it is absolutely useless for reputable technical or business blogs.

If you want to rely on these services for the convenience they offer, you need to aim for the higher end of the scale. For example, if you are using TextBro-ker,[5] a reputable outsourcing service, aim for their four- to five-star writers.

---

5.   textbroker.com

At their current rates, you can expect to spend $10–$15 and $30–$35, respectively, for a four- or five-star, five-hundred-word article.

The quality is still highly variable, but your odds of obtaining a well-written article increase. Start with four-star writers, and if you're not happy and your funds allow it, consider trying five-star ones. In my experience, five-star writers on TextBroker are better than four-star ones, but they're not three times better.

Once you find a writer you like, you can request that same person again the next time you place an order (if the person is available), hence introducing some consistency to the writing you've outsourced. This is equivalent to hiring them directly, with the added convenience of having the site handle payments and disputes.

Niche Job Boards

If you are looking for a longer-term relationship with a blogger who will produce content on a regular basis, you might also want to try job boards that are specifically targeted toward bloggers or at people in your niche. The Jobs board on ProBlogger is an example of the former,[6] while Careers by StackOverflow is one of the latter.[7]

For regular bloggers, you would typically establish requirements up front regarding the frequency, length, and types of posts you expect to see and offer a monthly payment. If you look around, you'll quickly notice that the going rate is not particularly high.

Of course, the more technical and specialized the content, the harder the time you'll have finding someone who's willing to work on the lower end of the scale. In other words, while some people may have lower income expectations when blogging for hire, you still get what you pay for.

More elaborate arrangements exist, such as offering 50 percent of the ad revenue, but such terms would generally not attract or convince many qualified writers to come work for you. (See *How Much Should I Pay Bloggers?*, on page 230, for further details on the going rates.)

Hiring bloggers can be a great business decision, but it's one that requires an investment of time and money, so it's the sort of option that's best left for when you have a clearer indication of the economic potential of the blog that you are trying to scale.

---

6. problogger.net
7. careers.stackoverflow.com

13.3 Build Your Blogging Empire

What do you do when you feel you have exhausted the economic opportunities your blog can provide? You can scale horizontally, rather than vertically. Instead of diminishing your returns by putting much more effort into a blog that is already providing as much as is reasonable to expect, you can start a second blog. The idea is that at times it may be easier to grab a second lemon than try to squeeze every last bit of juice out of the current one.

Blog Networks

It is not rare to see wildly successful blogs launch sister blogs. If a multitude of blogs are born over time, they'll progress into a network.[8] Each site promotes the network, typically at the top and the bottom of each site, in turn sending each other visitors, as shown in Figure 30, *A network bar*, on page 234.

One such example is the Cheezburger Network.[9] It all started with the popular LOLCAT blog *I Can Has Cheezburger?* and has expanded to now include dozens of blogs, including *FAIL Blog* and *Memebase.*[10]

Despite the humorous nature of these sites, networks like this can be very serious business. For instance, the aforementioned network received a $30 million investment.[11]

Another example of one of the oldest blog networks is Gawker Media,[12] which includes popular blogs such as *Lifehacker* and *Gizmodo.*[13]

Keep in mind that you don't always have to come up with new domain names. At times you may want to simply create new sections in your existing blog and dedicate the same kind of effort to them as if they were their own sites.

MobileCrunch used to be a site unto itself available at MobileCrunch.com; however, it has since become part of the new, larger *TechCrunch.*[14] In the case of *MobileCrunch*, it isn't even branded differently on the TechCrunch site. It's just a category.

---

8. Some blog networks allow third-party blogs to join under certain mutually beneficial conditions (sometimes economical). In this section, we are talking about a small network of blogs you own.
9. cheezburger.com
10. icanhascheezburger.com, failblog.org, and memebase.com, respectively.
11. blog.cheezburger.com/miscellaneous/omg-30-million1-thats-a-lot-of-cheezburgers
12. gawker.com
13. lifehacker.com and gizmodo.com, respectively.
14. techcrunch.com/mobile

Figure 30—A network bar

VentureBeat created ten or so brands; all kept on the same domain name.[15] Each section is branded as if it were a standalone site (e.g., MobileBeat) complete with its own logo.[16]

If the topics are not related enough, it is preferable to use new brands and domain names for sister blogs.

Launch a Second Blog

As you probably can imagine by now, it is possible to create a media empire online by running a series of successful sites that promote each other. Is it easy? Certainly not; but once you've established one blog and managed to make it very popular, launching a second one and making it successful, too, is not terribly hard.

Picture this: you are running a successful blog about cars, and you now want to launch a blog about motorbikes. Your second blog won't start from scratch. In fact, you've got the invaluable asset of firsthand experience under your belt now. Not only that, but you'll announce and talk about your new blog on your existing site so your feed readers can learn about it. And if you have a powerful presence on social networks like Twitter, your followers there will also learn about your new venture.

---

15. venturebeat.com
16. venturebeat.com/category/mobile

From an SEO standpoint it is beneficial to link to your new blog from such a popular preexisting site, even if both are on the same server. SEOs will give you all sort of tricks, such as hosting the sites on different class C IP addresses to convince Google that the two sites are not related and therefore the links from the popular one to the new one should be valued a lot. Ignore all that. It's not worth your time or money in a scenario where you are already so successful.

Remember to have links in your navigation bar, perhaps an ad in the sidebar, and to mention the new blog several times in your posts as your site is just beginning to get off the ground. Chances are, a percentage of your car enthusiast audience will also be into bikes and will therefore check out your new blog. Ta-da! Instant traffic for your second site.

Rinse and repeat the process of promoting new online properties from existing ones. Just be warned that if you are trying to create a network on your own, it can quickly become overwhelming. If you were posting ten times per week, now you need to post twenty, thirty, or more times, depending on how many sites you launch.

Networks are definitely not for everyone. They require multiple writers, ideally a few editors, and good management to ensure things run smoothly. You'll also need a good hosting solution to handle all the traffic that an entire series of successful blogs will attract.

On the plus side, networks have huge economic and influence potential. If you manage to attract a few million visitors a month with your network, you'll also have much more bargaining power when dealing with advertisers and sponsors, be able to command higher CPM rates, and also get larger deals.

13.4 What's Next

This chapter should have provided you with a picture of what it takes if you want to go about scaling your blogging activities. It was included for the most ambitious readers, but remember that it's perfectly fine to run a single successful blog that's never elevated to news site status or branched out into becoming a series of different blogs.

In the next chapter we'll go beyond blogging and enter the fascinating world of social media, dispelling some of the myths that surround this realm and establishing evergreen guidelines to help you succeed in creating a remarkable presence on such sites.

Interdependence is and ought to be as much the ideal of man as self-sufficiency. Man is a social being.

➤ *Mohandas Karamchand Gandhi*

CHAPTER 14

Beyond Blogging: Your Strategy for Social Media

Social media adoption has exploded over the past few years. It has become an integral component of any Internet marketing strategy, so it would be a disservice to you to leave it out, even if this book is really about blogging and not about social media per se.

Part of the reason why social media has become so prominent is due to the innate desire that humans have to get together, belong to something, and share what they know, what they think, and what they do with other people.

Social media is an incredibly fast-moving target, so I won't provide detailed signup instructions that will become obsolete before the ink even dries. (Case in point, Google+ didn't even exist when I started writing this book.)

We will focus instead on the essential notions you need to learn in order to establish yourself or your business on social networks like Twitter, Facebook, Google+, and whatever social media channel may become popular down the line.

14.1 Define a Social Media Strategy

Head over to *Gary's Social Media Count*,[1] and you'll almost certainly be impressed by how much user-generated content and interaction happens on sites like Facebook, Twitter, and YouTube in a matter of seconds.

We discussed social news sites like Reddit and Hacker News before, and in the rest of this chapter we'll chat about how to establish yourself on social

---

1. personalizemedia.com/garys-social-media-count

networks such as Twitter and Facebook. The actual steps may be slightly different, but the same principles will be applicable to other relevant virtual communities of your choice, present or future.

Plan and execute your social media strategy by following these steps:

1. Select the social networks you intend to target.
2. Create your social media profiles.
3. Cross promote your site and social properties.
4. Post frequently and interact with your followers.

Let's address each of these steps with a great degree of detail. You'll find common trends in the way you approach your social marketing strategy, regardless of the particular social network sites you're working with.

14.2 Select the Social Networks You Intend to Target

A large number of successful networks have been established over the past few years. The following list includes a few types of common social networking sites:

- General social networks (e.g., Facebook or Twitter)
- Professional networks (e.g., LinkedIn)
- Networks specific to a particular segment of the population (e.g., CafeMom or patientslikeme[2])
- Media-specific networks (e.g., Flickr or YouTube[3])
- Social networks around a particular interest (e.g., Geni or GoodReads[4])
- Industry-specific social networks (e.g., GovLoop or Channel DB2[5])
- Mobile and location-based social networks (e.g., foursquare[6])

There are thousands of social networks, with at least a few hundred well-known ones.[7]

The good news is that all these channels allow you to reach most of the online population without having to pay (although you can advertise on most social networks for a fee). The bad news is that there is a lot of noise. It's one of those situations where you're shouting in a very crowded, very noisy room,

---

2. cafemom.com or patientslikeme.com, respectively.
3. youtube.com
4. geni.com or goodreads.com, respectively.
5. govloop.com or channeldb2.com, respectively.
6. foursquare.com
7. en.wikipedia.org/wiki/List_of_social_networking_websites

and as a result it's not easy to be heard or communicate with the people you intend to.

The key here is to select the social media channels that best work for you or for your business. Then establish a remarkable presence that enables you to genuinely connect with a targeted subset of that audience, acquire new followers, and further promote your content, yourself, and/or your company. You can't go after every social network out there, nor after all of the users of said sites. Attempting to do so would be a colossal waste of time and effort. So you need to be selective.

My suggestion is to shoot for a presence on the largest ones, including Twitter, Facebook, Google+, LinkedIn, and YouTube. Then search for social networks that are specific to your niche or industry, if any exist. Your choice needs to be strategic and calculated, as each social network you add will generally require further promotion and attention on your part.

The choice you make will also depend on whether you're attempting to promote yourself or a business. There are perfectly acceptable communities to establish yourself personally in for which the creation of a company account would seem out of place or against the site's policy.

14.3 Create Your Social Media Profiles

Now that you have decided which social networks you intend to target, you should immediately try to secure your *social properties* (e.g., accounts on these sites with your desired user names). Depending on the network, you may be able to create a presence for your blog or business or you may have to settle for a personal presence only.

For example, the fictitious Acme Fireworks Inc. will want to register the Twitter account @acmefireworks, if available. If already taken, a variation using an underscore, prefix, postfix, or abbreviation may be necessary.

The same is true for YouTube, where you can create a video channel with the name of your choice, including your company or site name.

When it comes to Facebook, LinkedIn, and Google+, things are a little different. These sites, at least at this stage, require you to sign up as an individual and then allow you to add a company identity that you manage/represent.

For Facebook, once you have a personal account, you'll be able to define a fan page by clicking Create a Page.[8] On LinkedIn, you can click "Add a company."[9] Finally, visit plus.google.com/pages/create to do the same for Google+.

Personal Presence vs. Business Presence on Twitter

My Twitter handle is @acangiano (by the way, feel free to follow me there).[10] If I were to launch a consulting practice tomorrow, I would probably keep using my personal handle for that business. This is because the company would be focused around me, and its success would greatly depend on my personal online presence.

But what about a business that sells products as an online retailer or a SaaS? In such a case, I would absolutely need to create a dedicated account for the company. My prospective and existing customers would search for and refer to the company name on social networks, as very few people would even know who the founder of the company was. I could and would promote my company with my personal presence as well (e.g., @acangiano), but the business identity would be key.

OK, those two cases are straightforward enough. What about edge cases like a blog that's not a business per se? Ask yourself if the blog is mainly a single-person operation or whether it's collective. Collective blogs get their own account because they transcend your personal identity.

If it were to be a technical blog that I ran on my own on a domain different from my own name, I would probably go through the effort of securing a Twitter account for it if I was serious about the project. When I started on Twitter a few years ago, I didn't bother doing that for my sites *Programming Zen* and *Math-Blog*, but I did when I launched *Any New Books* (i.e., I used @anynewbooks).

Brand Your Social Properties

Your mindset for social properties shouldn't be intended to sell products outright like a used car salesman. Instead, you're trying to inject yourself into the active discussion going on within a community of prospective and existing customers (or readers, if it's for a blog). The objective here is to obtain

---

8. facebook.com/bookmarks/pages
9. linkedin.com/companies
10. twitter.com/acangiano

social currency, which is about affiliation, conversation, utility, advocacy, information, and identity.[11]

It's important to understand that these social properties represent you just as much, and often more than, your site does. This means that you should brand these properties within the limits of the platform.

For Twitter, you'll need to use a custom image (i.e., an avatar) representing your blog or business. Your icon will be shown along with each of your 140-character-or-less messages (known as tweets) to your followers. You want to be identifiable among the stream of messages shown to your followers, so make sure to pick a good avatar (such as the icon within your logo, if any).

Accounts with the default Twitter egg icon rarely attract followers. Likewise, you should commission a background design that includes your logo so that your profile page is better branded and able to convey a sense of profession-alism and care, as shown in Figure 31, *AnyNewBooks.com's Twitter back-ground*, on page 242.

Backgrounds on Twitter can also be used in clever ways. Some people opt to create a collage of tweets from customers and influential early adopters who have praised their company. Showing testimonials in this manner is a powerful social proof trick that increases one's conversion rate from profile visitors to followers.

Be sure to include an enticing description in your profile (as well as your URL in the appropriate field), as this will be shown at the top of your profile page and will help convince visitors to follow you. That's pretty much it when it comes to customizing your appearance on Twitter (it's really quite easy).

For Facebook, after you have created a fan page, you should provide a profile image, a URL, and a description that will appear in the sidebar and in the Info tab for the page. You'll also be offered the chance to choose a URL that will identify your Facebook fan page (e.g., facebook.com/anynewbooks).

In the case of both social networks, get your account/page name right the first time, as you won't be able to edit it at a later stage (technically you can on Facebook, but only if you have less than a certain amount of Likes).

Unlike Twitter, Facebook enables you to create custom tabs that you can use for newsletter signup forms, sweepstakes, and other activities that can rein-force your brand and help you interact with your followers.

---

11. en.wikipedia.org/wiki/Social_currency

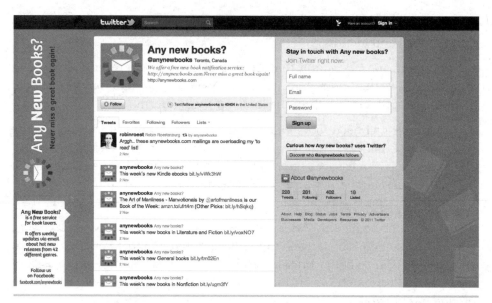

Figure 31—AnyNewBooks.com's Twitter background

To kick things off, you should post a welcome message that suggests you're open to the conversation. Being informal and relaxed is far better than portraying a corporate image. This is the microblogging equivalent to your welcome post on a blog.

Customize other social networks you are targeting in a similar fashion. Some are more liberal than others when it comes to branding your identity on the network, but you should strive for a professional look.

Social properties are an opportunity to reach new customers and readers as well as to strengthen your relationship with them. But if you use these sites incorrectly, they can do more damage than good. Starting out with a good branding effort is essential.

How to Get Your Initial Followers

All right, let's assume that by now you have your branded pages on a bunch of social networks that you intend to target. Everything is in order.

The problem is that you have zero followers/fans to start with. How do you go from zero to hundreds or thousands of followers? We'll discuss techniques to attract followers in an ethical way in a moment, but first it's worth clarifying that the viral nature of the beast requires an initial group of followers who can amplify your messages by rebroadcasting your updates to their followers.

On Facebook, as a page admin you'll be able to invite your existing Facebook friends to like the fan page. When I launched *AnyNewBooks*'s page, I selected about a hundred Facebook friends that I already knew were into books and technology. Many of these friends, colleagues, and acquaintances liked the page. Some did it because they were already existing users of the service, others because they were genuinely interested, and some, I'm sure, just to humor me.

Either way, it got my page more than fifty initial Likes. This means that new updates I posted on the page appeared in the News Feeds of these fans, who could then interact with the updates by liking them, commenting on them, or even sharing them with their friends. And hopefully their friends will do the same in turn, and so on. If your updates are engaging and your fans loyal enough, you can leverage a network effect and reach thousands of people's News Feeds very quickly.

For Twitter, I did something similar. I announced the new account from my personal Twitter account, leveraging my existing contacts in this case as well.

If you don't have the luxury of an existing account and network, fear not. We'll delve right into how to acquire fans/followers in the next few sections.

14.4 Cross Promote Your Site and Social Properties

You have a successful site and you've created various accounts on social networks. Cross promoting those accounts means promoting your social properties on your site and in turn, your site/blog on your social properties.

A successful blog has a constant stream of new visitors. Many of these readers will have accounts on major social networks. Your goal is to let them know about your presence there as well.

This will not only allow you to better connect with visitors in an environment that they're already familiar with, it will also help you grow your presence there. Furthermore, search engines are now considering social media signals more frequently when determining the ranking of your pages as well as when showing friends who recommended a page in the results.

Your network of followers and fans can quickly expand if your site or blog visitors engage with the social elements of your page.

For all these reasons, your blog should include widgets to +1 your business page on Google+, follow you on Twitter, and like your fan page on Facebook. You can find all sorts of widgets and snippets of codes to achieve these actions, including official resources from Google, Twitter, and Facebook.[12] In blogs, such widgets are typically located toward the top of the sidebar.

When a visitor decides to +1 your blog, your site ends up being listed and linked in the list of +1 for that user profile. When visitors follow you on Twitter, your follower count increases, which in turn shows social proof as well. Finally, when visitors like your fan page through your site, they'll increase your Facebook counter, automatically subscribe to your updates on Facebook, and broadcast that they just liked you to their friends.

A small percentage of their friends may decide to like you as well, and in turn, some of their followers will too, and so on. Again, a network effect can take place if enough people genuinely like your brand/site/blog.

For Facebook, opt to use the official Like button so as to show a random assortment of your followers. Faces add a powerful human element to what you're doing and may increase trust for your project or business as well as invite others to like the page also.

If you have Twitter embedded in your site, opt for either its compact Follow button or one of Twitter's widgets that showcase your latest tweets.

Your fan count should also be shown (both for Facebook and Twitter). As we discussed before when talking about FeedBurner counters, showing that you have a large following acts as social proof that what you are doing is worthwhile, interesting, and worth paying attention to.

If you are trying to attract a large following, you can make your social properties part of your call to action. At the bottom of your blog posts, for example, you could invite readers to like you, follow you on Twitter, etc. You could also place this call elsewhere, such as on the confirmation page for an order or a newsletter signup.

As of late, mentioning social properties has become increasingly popular in offline advertisement campaigns (e.g., fliers, billboards, and TV commercials and programs). Even software programs are beginning to integrate social features in an attempt to have users share with their friends the fact that they are using that particular software. It's all fair play as long as you don't trick or force your users into taking the social action you ideally hope they'll accomplish. Also remember not to go overboard. Your Facebook page may be

---

12. google.com/webmasters/+1/button, twitter.com/about/resources, and developers.facebook.com/docs/plugins, respectively.

Author Information in Search Results

It's becoming more and more common for Google to include social elements in its search results. By associating the content you produce with your Google profile, it's possible for your face to show up in the search results, thereby giving your entry that much more of a feature spot, as shown in Figure 32, *Author information in search results*, on page 246.

You can read about adding author information to search results at google.com/support/webmasters/bin/answer.py?answer=1408986.

important, but it shouldn't be included in lieu of your official site in any paid advertisements you may do.

After you're done setting up a way for your visitors to discover your social properties, you should ensure that the same is true the other way around, too. People may come to know you via social networks by way of their friends. You want them to immediately be aware of your site when they discover you this way.

This is why I recommended earlier that you include the URL of your blog (or site if you are representing a business) on sites like Twitter and Facebook. Include it in your background image as well (in the case of Twitter) and whenever possible in your status updates. Whatever you opt to do, don't be shy with your main URL on social properties (within the limits of each site's policy and the netiquette for that particular community).

14.5 Post Frequently and Interact with Your Followers

By far the easiest way to grow a following is to be interesting and approachable (which really isn't that different from regular blogging).

Post Frequently

If your blog is about JavaScript programming, your social properties should be used as microblogs that focus on JavaScript and related technologies. By all means rebroadcast your own blog posts by linking to them through these channels, as mentioned before, but don't limit yourself to just doing that. In order to attract more followers, your account needs to be seen as one from a subject matter expert who offers quick quotes, insight, comments, and shares links to interesting stories (from other sites) related to your niche. These stories will be, for the most part, published elsewhere by other people, not by you

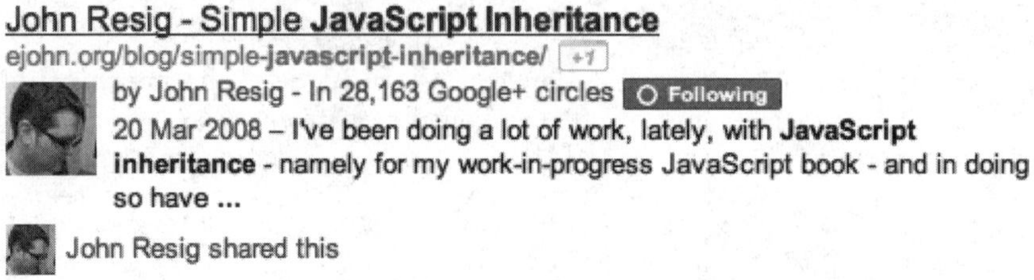

John Resig - Simple **JavaScript Inheritance**

ejohn.org/blog/simple-javascript-inheritance/ +1

 by John Resig - In 28,163 Google+ circles ○ Following

20 Mar 2008 – I've been doing a lot of work, lately, with **JavaScript inheritance** - namely for my work-in-progress JavaScript book - and in doing so have ...

 John Resig shared this

Figure 32—Author information in search results

on your own blog. You can also post announcements and status updates, share what you are working on, and give examples of praise you've received.

The same is true if you are promoting a business. Don't post a hundred updates per day, or people may begin to ignore the messages that are most important (and that you want them to care the most about). These are generally messages that announce something, sell something, or come directly from your blog.

Tip 36

Add #hashtag keywords in your tweets.

Why should people follow you? Because you post great links and comments about your industry. Again, it's not that different from what you aim for when blogging in its more extensive form.

The Twitter style you adopt should be similar to that of your blog but perhaps a little more relaxed. People expect to interact with a real person and not an emotionless corporate robot. Being witty and giving your audience a laugh here and there will do wonders for your brand, even if you're representing a Fortune 500.

Keep in mind that you can post on Twitter and then have the same message appear on Facebook. To do so, simply connect your Facebook account to your Twitter profile settings.

Creating Lists and Groups

To further promote your account on Twitter, you should also create lists of users who tweet about topics that are related to your main interests (a list of well-known Java-Script programmers, for example, if that's your niche). When people search for such a list, they'll find you and possibly end up following you.

For Facebook and Twitter, you can do the same by creating thematic groups or by interacting with existing ones and generally being helpful to others within these kinds of communities. In doing so, people will notice you and want to find out more about your blog or business. (Just don't spam such groups with your links.)

Tools for Twitter and Facebook

There are a few tools that you may find useful for managing your social media activities and keeping the posting frequency relatively high.

I like to use (or have successfully used in the past) the following:

- TweetDeck is my choice to monitor my accounts' streams, mentions, and a few target keywords (for example, technical blogging).[13] It can also be used to schedule tweets at specific times and is my default Twitter client (it supports other social networks, too). Another dashboard worth checking out is HootSuite.[14]

- SocialOomph is used to automatically send a direct welcome message text to followers (as well as to carry out other automated tasks).[15] An automatic welcome message can be particularly useful in opening up conversations and showing new followers that you are approachable. Just don't include your link within it or it will come across as aggressive at best and spammy at worst. In the past I've used automated direct messages to send out coupons after announcing a Twitter promotion so that those who followed me received a discount. It wasn't spam because the scope and context of the promotional message was clear to most followers.

- I use TwitterFeed to automatically broadcast every new post I publish on my blogs to Twitter (and optionally Facebook). To do so, all you have to do is provide a source (i.e., your RSS feed) and a destination (e.g., your Twitter account). TwitterFeed will do the rest for you. You can also define how the message will appear, what URL shortener (e.g., Bitly) should be used, and so on. I like to include a prefix such as "New blog post:" and

---

13. tweetdeck.com
14. hootsuite.com
15. socialoomph.com

then only include the title and shortened URL in the message to highlight that it's a post of mine and not just a link I'm sharing. You can customize virtually every aspect of the process, and TwitterFeed will even provide some basic statistics on the number of clicks each link receives.

• Buffer queues up tweets as I write them or as I find interesting links around the Web.[16] This app will automatically try to calculate the most beneficial times and schedule your tweets so as not to flood your readers with too many in a short period of time. The main aim is for your tweets to have the maximum impact and reach.

Tip 37

Post interesting stories directly from Google Reader.

Interact with Your Followers

What's the point of having a hundred thousand followers if they're not personally interested in your brand? If they are not involved? Along with being interesting, you need to be approachable and ready to converse with your audience.

When people ask you questions, try to reply to them whenever you can. When they praise you, thank them, and if the compliment is worth bragging about, rebroadcast it to your followers (on Twitter, this act is called a *retweet*). Doing so will give your followers further confirmation of their existing positive bias toward you and your brand and make the original commenter happy that you noticed him or her.

As a matter of fact, don't just retweet praise. Also retweet interesting people you follow when they post great messages or links. Doing so will make your participation valuable, and chances are they may do the same and reciprocate with you.

If you take the time to interact with your followers, you'll naturally grow your brand and, as a result, people will be more likely to share your important announcements, posts, and sale offers.

---

16. bufferapp.com

Remember that it's not just about being responsive there, you should be proactive in the way you interact with followers anywhere online. Engage them, both on Twitter and Facebook, by asking questions. If you're a company selling books, ask them what books they're currently reading, what's the latest book they bought, whether they give books as gifts for the holiday season, what their favorite book ever is, and so on.

So long as you don't constantly bombard your readers with questions, you'll see a great deal of participation from people who are eager to connect with you and share their knowledge or enthusiasm for the subject you're covering.

On Twitter you can also actively search for people who ask questions that you may be able to answer. In fact, you can even use the search function to find people who are interested in your specific topic. If you follow people that you find are genuinely interested, they'll take notice and some will start following and interacting with you as well.

Don't Try to Game Twitter

Resist the urge to game the system. The Twitter API has limits in place to prevent you from automatically following thousands of users at once, so if you had a bot that follows people in your niche in place, it would have to be a bit clever to bypass Twitter's detection. If you are caught doing such things, your account may be banned, so it's not worth the risk.

A lot of self-defined social media marketing experts will have thirty thousand or more followers on Twitter. When you take a closer look, you'll find that they often follow a roughly equivalent number of people as well. More often than not they used software that allows them to follow thousands of people over time and then automatically removed those who didn't follow them back.

Others will go so far as to use lists of people who automatically follow you back if you follow them in order to guarantee a larger number of followers— all for some form of social proof about their expertise. Twitter has become more aggressive in curbing this type of gaming. It's not worth getting banned just to obtain a large number of followers who will very rarely engage with you anyway.

Resist the temptation to spam users by messaging links to specific people by including their @name.[17] For example, the following message would be considered spam:

---

17. For a real life example of how this can backfire, check out the "Ragu Hates Dads" disaster at cc-chapman.com/2011/ragu-hates-dads.

Joe asks:

Should I Follow People Who Follow Me?

Scroll through the list of people who follow you on Twitter and only follow back those people you genuinely find interesting. Be selective or it will be really hard to inject yourself into conversations that matter.

If you follow people back almost indiscriminately, you may end up following spammers and other undesirables. And once you follow someone, you'll receive more notifications about their interactions with you via email (unless you change the relevant settings). They can even DM (direct message) you and spam you privately.

> @arrington check out my new book notification service at http://anynewbooks.com.

Alternatively, let's look at a different scenario, one where I am monitoring the keyword *new book* on Twitter, where someone has posted the following tweet:

> I loved Infinite Jest, can someone recommend a new book like it to me?

I could respond, even if the person is a perfect stranger, with a few book suggestions, and doing so would not be considered spam.

However, if I were to reply automatically through software or manually with the following tweet, it would be seen by many as spam.

> You can find out about new books on http://anynewbooks.com.

When you monitor keywords, be sure your reply adds value and doesn't just push your product or site. Your site can be mentioned if it's a good answer to a specific question though (just play things by ear in this regard). For example, check the following conversation on Twitter:

> Where can I find out about new book releases?

> @example You could try our free service at http://anynewbooks.com. Please let us know if it's what you are looking for.

This would not be classified as spam. But should you do it on a daily basis? Probably not, and not just because it's time consuming and may fail to bring a positive return on investment your way. The real reason is that overzealous people may mistakenly consider your message as spam and as a result flag you in the system. Furthermore, your profile page will look like a series of unsolicited "You can check us out"-type messages without the context of actual back and forth Twitter conversations.

You don't want your brand to be represented in that way.

Final Tips for Social Media

Here are a series of final tips that should help you live the social media experience in a positive way.

- Check your statistics to figure out how much return on investment you are actually receiving from your social media efforts. Remember, you are doing these things for social currency and for a lot of reasons that can't be easily quantified. Nevertheless, it doesn't hurt to figure out if there is a direct correlation between the links you share and the number of sales you receive.

- Monitor your influence over time by using services like Klout.[18] While these services are far from perfect, they should give you a general idea of where you're standing compared to others, as well as give you additional interesting stats (such as your true reach on Twitter).

- It's a numbers game. On average, only 5 percent of your Twitter followers will bother to read a random tweet you make, so keep tweeting and tweeting.

- At the same time though, don't obsess over numbers. Focus on adding value and building relationships with your customers or readers. Twenty early adopters who are raving fans of your brand are better than a thousand apathetic followers who casually followed you.

- Social networks are made up of people. Never forget to treat everyone with respect by making them feel welcome as part of your conversation. Also, cultivate your relationship with early adopters as much as you can; they'll provide invaluable feedback and help you increase your reach on social networks.

- Hecklers will criticize and attack you on social networks as much as commenters do on blogs. Follow the usual guidelines. Ignore trolls, but politely address valid criticism or misguided folks without belittling them.

- Don't waste money on pay-for-tweet services. Paying up to thousands of dollars to have someone popular plug your message is not the way to go about building a loyal following.

- Imposing a Like or a tweet before granting the download of a given product is not liked by many, but it can be very effective.[19] Likewise, sweepstakes,

---

18. klout.com
19. seomoz.org/blog/how-to-win-tweets-and-influence-search-engines-with-paywithatweet

giveaways, and contests wherein participants must take some social action are a great way to spread the word about your site or product.

- YouTube is the second largest search engine in the world. Grab a camera, get some screencasting software, and start rolling. If you create informative or witty videos, you'll quickly grow an impressive following. If it's funny or particularly impressive, your video may even go viral and become a meme. That's pure gold for your blog or business. (By the way, top YouTube vloggers (i.e., video bloggers) make a fortune from their clips.)

- If you are running a business, don't forget to try out paid advertisement on social networks that permit this. If the ROI is there, it's a fast way to earn new customers. On Facebook, you can even advertise your fan page and prompt people to like your page through your ad.

- What your friends buy affects what other friends buy too, and so on. Social media is a huge opportunity from this standpoint. If you have a business, you can greatly increase your revenue by crafting your site so as to encourage customers to share the fact that they are interested in an item, or that they just bought one, with their followers. (Don't forget social media when it comes to your thank-you e-cart page either.)

14.6 What's Next

This chapter should have provided you with some guidance on how to get started with your social media efforts. It's a very fast evolving world, but the principles and the human element are not going to change any time soon.

Get started as soon as possible, because building a solid presence on social media properties can take several months. Freely experiment and don't be afraid to veer away from the guidance provided within this chapter. You'll make mistakes, but the best way to learn is by practice and firsthand experience. Just remember to be genuine and honest. Readily admit to your mistakes and apologize; that way you shouldn't face any long-term consequences from errors you might make.

This chapter also concludes the instructional part of this book. Congratulations on reading this far. The remaining couple of pages are the conclusion, with a few final words of advice. Don't skip these pages, as they are where we'll say goodbye, and they include details on how to stay in touch.

The credit belongs to the man who is actually in the arena, whose face is marred by dust and sweat and blood, who strives valiantly, who errs, who comes short again and again, because there is no effort without error and shortcoming.

> ➤ *Theodore Roosevelt*

CHAPTER 15

Final Words of Advice

I started this book by telling you how blogging has the potential to change your life. I hope to have persuaded you about the actual possibility of that bold claim by this point. I also hope that the road map, or at least the principles I've outlined, will work for you, whatever your blogging goals may be.

15.1 Try It Out

It is my sincere wish that the preceding 250+ pages have managed to inspire and motivate you to take action and give blogging a try. If you don't take action, as discussed in the beginning, all of this information will have been only marginally useful.

Above all, be patient. Building a remarkable online presence takes years, not days. You may start to see benefits much sooner than that, but you are in this game for the long haul, not for short-term gain.

If you fail, change some aspects of what you are doing and see if things improve. As mentioned multiple times before, you need to treat all of this as a series of experiments. If you think that making a change will lead to a certain positive effect, you won't know until you test it. Use iteration, trial and error, feedback, and analytical measures to figure out what works for you as a blogger.

Also remember that blogging is mostly about spreading ideas. You want to do so with passion and professionalism. Put your heart into it, and chances are that blogging will give you what you are after, whether it's money, recognition, or something else altogether.

You know the classic adage that says "With great power comes great responsibility"? Keep that in mind; be genuine, respectful, and honest with the people you interact with online. Use your newly acquired influence to spread your ideas, to connect further, and to love, not to hate.

15.2 Blogs to Follow

If you want to read more about blogging and Internet marketing in general, I wholeheartedly recommend the following blogs. Consider adding these to your feed reader:

- ProBlogger: problogger.net
- Copyblogger: copyblogger.com/blog
- Webmaster Central blog: googlewebmastercentral.blogspot.com
- Google's blog: googleblog.blogspot.com
- Matt Cutts's blog: mattcutts.com/blog
- SEOmoz blog: seomoz.org/blog
- Seth Godin's blog: sethgodin.typepad.com/seths_blog
- KISSmetrics blog: blog.kissmetrics.com

At the time of this writing, I'm in the process of setting up and launching a blogging and Internet marketing-related blog myself, located at technicalblog-ging.com. You may want to subscribe to that one as well, as it complements this book.

15.3 Keep in Touch

You can further keep up with what I'm up to via Twitter (twitter.com/acangiano) or by adding me to your circles on Google+ (plus.google.com/104323476891214773710). I'm also on LinkedIn (ca.linkedin.com/in/antoniocangiano). Feel free to connect with me, and don't be afraid to say hi. You can even email me (info@technicalblog-ging.com) if you'd like to connect that way.

Finally, it has been an absolute pleasure writing this book and sharing my insight with you. Should you have any questions related to my book, you can ask them in the official forum of the Pragmatic Bookshelf.[1] I'll try to monitor discussions there and be active in my replies long after I've finished writing these words. If you want to showcase how this book has affected your blog, feel free to mention it there as well.

I wholeheartedly wish you the best in your career as a blogger, and I thank you deeply for reading my book.

---

1. forums.pragprog.com/forums/216

Bibliography

[Nö09]   Staffan Nöteberg. *Pomodoro Technique Illustrated: The Easy Way to Do More in Less Time*. The Pragmatic Bookshelf, Raleigh, NC and Dallas, TX, 2009.

Index

DIGITS

37signals, 5, 9, 207
99designs, 57

A

abandoned blogs, 6, 119
About page, 44
    links to, 64
abuse in comments, 169
ad hominem argument, 165
ad units, 173
    setup in Google, 177
AdBlock Plus, 178
adBrite, 176
AddThis, 67
Adorama, 193
AdSense Gadget, 175
advertisers, number bidding
    for keyword, 14
advertising, 173–180, 213
    for bloggers, 230
    company blog and, 200
    decision to include, 179
    feed and email subscrip-
        tion options, 74
    on sidebar, 63
    technical audiences and,
        178
Advertising.com, 176
affiliate marketing, 183–194
affiliate program, 213
aftermarket domains, 27
Akismet plugin, 48
alerts, 150
alexa.com, 155
Amazify (USA), 187

Amazon, TypePad use, 33
Amazon Associates, 185
    cheat sheet, 191
    commissions breakdown,
        197
    Reports, 189–190
Amazon AWS, 37
Amazon S3, 32
anchor text
    for backlinks, 127
    in links, 122
Android apps, 207
    Clicky apps, 62
animation, ads with, 183
anynewbooks.com, 191
    Twitter background, 242
Apache, 32
    for WordPress, 40
API key, 48
    for WordPress Stats, 60
Ars Technica, 4
article directories, 128–129
article marketing, 128
article spinners, 129
articles, promoting on social
    networks, 134–137
Articles Base, 128
Associates IDs for Amazon
    accounts, 187
    using multiple, 189
audience for article directo-
    ries, 129
audience for blog, xvi, 159
    brand names and, 25
    for company blog, 9
    reasons for subscribing,
        18

tracking, 57–63, 94
    tracking source, 149
audio interviews, 112
author name, for Blogger
    posts, 46
autoresponders, 72
avatar, 47, 241
average pageviews, 146, 148
Aweber, 71–72, 209

B

B&H Photo Video, 193
backgrounds on Twitter, 241
backlinks, 112
    anchor text for, 127
    characteristics to improve
        ranking, 123
    for sponsor, 181
backup of content, 100
BackupBuddy, 101
Backupify, 101
Balsamiq, 207
banner advertising, 182
    Amazon, 191
    for sponsor, 181
Barnes & Noble, 193
baseline traffic, vs. spike
    traffic, 145
benefits of blogging, xvii–xix
Best of page, 96
Bidvertiser, 176
biography, 124
Bitcoins, 195
black hats, 86
Blind Ferret, 176

blog authors, widget to create list, 54

blog networks, 233–234

blog types
abandoned, 6, 119
business blogs, 9–10
general vs. niche, 5–8
pundit vs. instructional, 8
solo vs. collective, 3–5
team blog, 5

Blogger, 32–35
AdSense Gadget, 175
backup, 101
customizing look and feel, 58
domain name use with, 39
labels, 64
settings, 46
social toolbars in, 68
steps not needed, 52

bloggers
paying, 230
sources for, 228–232

blogging
defensive, 165
political approach to, 217
potential impact, xiii
rumors of death, xiv–xvi
statistics, xvii
time requirements, 106–107
unpredictability in, 94

blogging benefits
career advancement, 216
obtaining freebies, 219
preparing for success, 221–223
skills improvement, 215–216

blogging clients, vs. web interface, 96

blogging services, 32–34
evaluating choices, 34

blogosphere, 130

blogpulse.com, xvii

blogrolls, 43

blogs
adding to planet sites, 131
of commenters, 161
foreign, 132–133
launching second, 234
recommended, 254

scaling horizontally, 233–235
scaling vertically, 227–228
tracking growth, 155
tracking impact, 211
from the trenches, 206

blogspam, 86

Bluehost, 37

bold text, 86

The Book Depository, 193

book reviews, 220

bookmarklet, 187–188

books, announcing new, 191

bounce rate, 147–148
Google vs. Clicky, 154

brand names, domain names and, 25

browser cache, 81

Buffer, 248

Burst Media, 176

business blogs, 9–10

buying links, 133

C

cache, performance and, 80

caching plugins, for Word-Press, 32

CafePress, 196

call to action, 160, 218, 244
in headline, 88
in resource box, 127
in sidebar, 63

Canada, 73

career advancement, xviii, 216

Careers by StackOverflow, 232

CC (Creative Commons) license, 98

ccTLD (country code top-level domain), 24

CDN (content delivery networks), 81

Chargify, 202

cheatsheets, 92

checklet counter, 74

Cheezburger Network, 233

Chitika, 176

Classic fee structure in Amazon, 190

Clean Archives Reloaded plugin, 96

ClickBank, 193

Clicky, 61–63, 149, 153–155
alerts, 150
dashboard, 154
on reader behavior, 156

Clicky Monitor extension, 61

client software, for blogging, 96

cloud computing, 36–37, 91

<code> HTML tag, 82

code highlighting, in posts, 82

Coding Horror, xiv

collective blogs, 3–5

colocation arrangement, 36

.com domain name, 23

commentary, 8

commenting system, Blogger and, 52

comments, xvi, 160
adding to blogs, 131
alternative systems, 48–50
moderating, 47, 168
response to, 161
settings on approval, 47

Commission Junction, 193

commissions, 183–184
from Amazon, 190

community, 159, 163
tools for building, 163–164

company blogs, 9
Amazon Associate links and, 192
checklist, 199–201
domain for, 200
identifying readers for, 202–204
layout, 208
need for multiple, 200–201
sidebar on, 65, 208
subdomain for, 22

company logo, 208

company website, need for, 202

compete.com, 155

competition, 7

Competition column, in Google Keyword Tool, 14

consistency in schedule, 105

constructive criticism, 164, 166, 215

Contact Form 7, 54

contact information, 44

content, xx, 160
  article translations, 114
  backup, 100
  book reviews, 220
  copyright, 96–100
  email interviews, 111–112
  finding ideas, 90
  getting readers to explore, 95–96
  Getting Started page, 95
  headlines, 87–88
  help from others, 111–114
  importance, 83
  linkbaiting, 86–87
  for prospective readers, 204–207
  quantity, 103
  resource pages, 192
  voice development, 89–90
  writer's block and, 109–111
  writing for web, 84–86

contests, 162

contextual advertising, 174

controversy, 89, 91

conversation, blogging as, xvi–xvii

conversion funnel, 150

conversion rate for subscribers, 72

cookies, for affiliate offer, 184

Copyblogger, 254

copyright, online content and, 96–100

Copyscape, 99

corporations, guidelines for employee blogging, 75

costs, of blogging services, 34

counter for subscribers, 74

country code top-level domain (ccTLD), 24

CPC (cost per click), 174

Crawlable Facebook Comments, 49

crazyegg.com, 65, 208

criticism
  forms of, 164–168
  handling, 169–170

CTR (click-through rate), 95

custom themes, 57

customers
  company blog for connecting with, 9
  converting readers to, 207–214
  finding new, xix
  status updates for, 33

customizing sidebar, 63–65

Cyberduck, 51

D

daringfireball.net, 8, 19, 180

DB2 Express-C, case study to promote downloads, 205

DCMA (Digital Millennium Copyright Act) takedown notice, 99

deadlines, 4

The Deck, 176

dedicated servers, 36–37

default theme in WordPress, disadvantages, 55

Defensio, 48

defensive blogging, 165

<del> HTML tag, 85

deleting, WordPress sample post, 43

Delicious, 135, 137

dig command, 38

Digg, 95

digital titles, 193

disagreement criticism, 165–166

disclaimers, 75–77, 220

Disqus, 49

diversifying, 196

DNS Made Easy, 38

DNS Simple, 38

DNS zone, 38

dofollow links, 128

domain
  for company blog, 200
  verifying setup, 38

domain names, 22–28
  aftermarket, 27
  configuring, 37–39
  guidelines, 23
  hyphens in, 26
  keyword-based, 24
  length of, 25
  registering, 26

subdomain for company blog, 22
  top-level, 23
  vs. blog name, 23

domainer, 24, 27

donations, 194–195

downloading freebies, 73

downvotes, 138

Dropbox folder, 91

dynadot.com, 27

DZone, 137, 141

E

E-junkie, 202

echo generator, xvi

editing, sidebar, 65

editor-in-chief, 4

Editorial Calendar plugin, 107

Elance, 230

Elegant Themes, 56

elevator pitch, 18

Emacs, 33

email
  exporting addresses from FeedBurner, 72
  following blog with, 71
  publishing posts directly by, 46
  replies to, 161

email interviews, 111–112

Email Subscriptions link, 71

employees, new, finding, xix

employer disclaimer, 75

engadget.com, 19

/etc/hosts file, 39

evaluation of readership, 21

Excel, 156

experts
  commenters as, 162
  email interview of, 111
  establishing self as, 7

expired domains, 27

eye candy, 55

Ezine Articles, 128

F

Facebook, xvii, 66, 135, 137, 239, 243
  creating groups, 247
  fan page, 241
  Like button, 67, 244
  tools for, 247

Facebook Comments, 49–50

FAIL Blog, 233

fair use doctrine, 98

fake blogs, 134

false negative results with Akismet, 48

false positive results with Akismet, 48

fan page, 240–241

Fantastico, WordPress from, 40

FastSpring, 202

Federal Trade Commission, 76

Federated Media, 176–177

feed, full vs. partial, 47

feed reader, 90

feedback, asking for, 161

FeedBurner, 209
    FeedSmith plugin, 70
    Publicize tab, 71
    setting up, 69–71

FeedBurner URL, 46

FeedFlare, 70

FileZilla, 51

first-month goals, 21

flame wars, 166
    comment moderation and, 47

Flash, 34

Flattr, 195

Flickr, 98

flowingdata.com, 19

followers on social networks
    getting initial, 242
    interacting with, 248

footer of blog, tracking code in, 58–59

foreign blogs, leveraging, 132–133

forums, 163

free themes, 55

freebies
    giving away, 73–74
    obtaining, 219

freelance sites, hiring bloggers from, 229–230

Freelance.com, 230

freelancer, career advancement as, 218

FTC disclaimer, 76–77

FTP program, 51

fund-raising posts, 195

Fusion Ads, 176

G

Gary's Social Media Count, 237

Gawker Media, 233

general blogs, 5–8
    identifying main theme, 12

Genesis framework, 56

Getting Started page, 95

Git, 33

GitHub, 217

GitHub Pages, 32

giveaways, 162

Gizmodo, xiv, 233

Global Monthly Searches, 14

goals for blog, 20–22

Google
    ad unit setup, 177
    duplicate content and, 78
    inclusion of social elements, 245
    post word count and, 104
    submitting blog directly, 122

Google +1, 67, 135

Google AdSense, 174
    alternatives, 176

Google AdWords, 13, 58, 213

Google Affiliate Network, 193

Google Alerts, 99

Google Analytics, 58–60, 92
    alert, 150, 157
    bounce rate, vs. Clicky, 154
    dashboard, 151–152
    statistics from, 151

Google blog, 254

Google bombing, 122

Google Docs, 91, 156
    Form, 91

Google Insights for Search, 15

Google Keyword Tool, 15
    for niche size analysis, 13

Google Page Speed, 81

Google Reader, 90

Google Syntax Highlighter for WordPress, 82

Google Translate, 133

Google Trends, 14–17

Google webmaster guidelines, 124

Google Webmaster Tools, 79

Google XML Sitemap, 53, 79

Google+, 135, 239
    author contact information, 254
    Hangouts, 164
    widgets to +1, 243

gray-hat marketing, 87

group chats, 164

groups, creating, 247

Gruber, John, 8

guest bloggers, 228

guest blogging, 112–114
    by commenters, 161
    marketing and, 124–128

H

Hacker News, xvii, 68, 88, 137, 140

hard selling, 205

header, of theme, 74

Headline Animator, 70

headlines, 84, 87–89
    in mathblog.com, 92–94
    for Reddit submission, 139

heatmaps, 65

home page, authority score, 43

HostGator, 37

hosting service, selecting, 35–37

hosts file, 39

hotlinks, 99

HOWTOs, 8

.htaccess file, updating, 51

HTML code editor, 45

Hub Pages, 128

hyphens, in domain name, 26

I

I Can Has Cheezburger?, 233

ICANN (Internet Corporation for Assigned Names and Numbers), 26

IconFinder, 98

ideas for posts, finding, 90

igvita.com, 8, 19

images
    from Amazon, 192

copyright on, 98
in posts, 85
inbound links, 86
inbound marketing, xix
income from blogging, xviii
with ads, 173–180
affiliate offers, 183–194
case study, 196–198
common strategies, 173
donations, 194–195
merchandise sales, 196
from niche blog, 17
sources of other rep-
utable offers, 193
sponsors, 180–183
subscriptions and mem-
bership sites, 194
infographics, 92
InfoQ, 4
Insights for Search, 91
installing
Clicky, 62
WordPress, 40–41
WordPress plugins, 51
instructional blogs, 8
IntenseDebate, 49
Internet Corporation for Assigned Names and Numbers
(ICANN), 26
Inverted Pyramid approach to
writing, 89
investors, finding, xix
iOS, Clicky apps for, 62
IRC (Internet Relay Chat), 164
italic text, 86

J

JavaScript, 34, 82
code for ad unit, 174
for link to Amazon prod-
uct, 187
for tracker, 57
tracking code, 58
Jekyll, 32
Jetpack plugin, 52, 60, 68
job boards
hiring bloggers from, 229
niche, 232
job offers, 216
Joel on Software, xiv

K

Keyword Tool, 91
keyword-based domain
names, 24
keywords
estimating search vol-
umes for, 13
number of advertisers
bidding for, 14
KISSmetrics, 206, 212
KISSmetrics blog, 254
Klout, 251
Kontera, 176
Kottke, Jason, 195
KPI (key performance indicator), dashboard, 155
KreCi, 207

L

labels in Blogger, 64
LAMP (Linux, Apache,
MySQL, PHP) stack, 40
landing page, 148
language and formatting settings in Blogger, 46
LaTeX, 52
LessWrong, 160
Lifehacker, 233
link blogs, 98
Link Checker, 188
link wheels, 134
linkbaiting, 86–87
LinkedIn, 239
author contact informa-
tion, 254
links
to About page, 64
building, 122–124
buying, 133
dark side of building,
133–134
dofollow, 128
nofollow, 127, 181, 192
to posts by others, 85
links list, xx
Linode, 37
LiquidWeb, 37
lists, creating, 247
LiveJournal, 32
loading time for page, 49
Local Monthly Searches, 14

login to WordPress admin
section, 42
loyalty, xix, 105
lurkers, 159

M

magazine, online, vs. news
site, 227
MailChimp, 71–73, 209, 211
blogs, 206
Markdown (markup lan-
guage), 32
Market Samurai, 14
marketing, xix, 66, 119
article, 128
blogosphere participa-
tion, 130
defining, 120
goal, 121
guest blogging and, 124–
128
leveraging foreign blogs,
132–133
mindset for, 120–121
offline, 213
other approaches, 213
on social networks, 134–
137
workflow, 135
MarsEdit, 46, 96
mathblog.com, headlines, 92
Matt Cutts's blog, 254
media buy, 181
membership sites, 194
Memebase, 233
merchandise sales, 196
meta criticism, 165, 167
meta tags for search engines,
79
metrics, key site usage, 146
microblogging, xv
micropayments, 195
mindset for marketing, 120–
121
misguided criticism, 165, 167
mobile and email settings in
Blogger, 46
mobile devices, blogging
clients for, 96
MobileCrunch, 233
moderating comments, 47,
168

motivation to write, 4
MySQL, 32

N

namecheap.com, 27
nameservers, setting to those of hosting company, 38
nearlyfreespeech.net, 38
.net domain name, 23
Netflix, Blogger use, 33
New Visits statistic, 147–148
news site, vs. online magazine, 227
newsletter management service, 71
newsletters, 71–72, 208–211
The Next Web, 228
nginx, 32, 80
    for WordPress, 40
niche blogs, 5–8
    identifying main topic, 11
    income from, 17
    restriction of, 6
niche job boards, 232
niche size analysis, 13–17
    Google Keyword tool for, 13
    Google Trends for, 14–17
nitpick criticism, 165–166
nofollow links, 127, 181, 192
noise, in social networks, 238

O

oDesk, 230
object cache, 81
Octopress, 32
office hours, 163
offline marketing, 213
Olark, 213
on-page SEO, 121
online magazine, vs. news site, 227
open source projects, promoting, 218
opt-in, single vs. double, 73
.org domain name, 23
outsourcing services, hiring bloggers from, 229, 231

P

page cache, 81
page loading time, 49

Page.ly, 37
PageRank, 122–123
    backlink distribution, 125
    Google algorithm, 43
pages, vs. posts, 44
pageviews, 21, 146–147
paragraphs, length of, 84
partners, finding, xix
paywalls, 194
permalinks
    in Blogger, 52
    in WordPress, 50
personal criticism, 165, 167
personal name, displaying publicly in WordPress, 45
photographs, on About page, 44
PHP, 32
ping services, 46
pingbacks, 48
Pingdom, 81
plagiarism, 99
plan for blog
    domain name choice and registration, 22–28
    goal setting, 20–22
    main topic definition, 11–12
    niche size analysis, 13–17
    reader retention and, 18
Planet Python, 131
planet sites, adding blog to, 131
Platinum SEO pack, 53, 77–79
plugins for WordPress, 51–54
    installing, 51
podcasts, 112
polls of readers, 161
Pomodoro technique, 107–110
pop-ups, 75
Posterous, 32
posts
    code highlighting, 82
    custom code at bottom, 74
    days best for adding, 105–106
    finding ideas, 90
    frequency of, 103–105

images in, 85
length of, 104
meta tags for search engines, 79
permalinks for, 50
schedule frequency, 105
translating, 114
TwitterFeed to broadcast, 247
updates, 85
vs. pages, 44
posts and comments settings in Blogger, 46
power tripping, 163
<pre> HTML tag, 82
premium themes, 55
press releases, for SEO, 129
Prettify GC Syntax Highlighter, 82
prices, in discussion, 192
priority, sidebar contents and, 63
privacy, WordPress settings, 50
privacy policy for blog, 175
pro users, extra features for, 194
ProBlogger, 232, 254
product blog, 10
products, disclosure of affiliation, 76
programmingzen.com, 6
    global statistics, 149
    referral traffic, 142
    sidebar, 64
Project Wonderful, 176
promoting, see also advertising
    open source projects, 218
    your business, 199
proofreading, 85
prweb.com, 130
pseudonym, writing under, 169
pundit blogs, 8
purchasing themes, advantages, 55
PuSHPress plugin, 53

Q

questions, replies to, 160

R

Rackspace, 37
rates, for freelance work, 218
Readability, 195
readers, *see also* audience for blog
    asking what they want, 91
    challenge to, 162
    Clicky on behavior, 154
    content for prospective, 204–207
    converting to customers, 207–214
    engaging, 159–163
    expectations, 6
    guiding to content, 95–96
    identifying for company blog, 202–204
    interaction with, xvi
    niche vs. general blog, 6
    polling, 161
    reasons for subscribing, 18
    targeting for company blogs, 199
    tracking, 57–63
readership, expectations for numbers, 21
real-time statistics, 61
rebroadcasting message, xvi
Received HTTP error, 70
reciprocity, 161
Recurly, 202
Reddit, xvii, 68, 137
    comments, 168
    submitting posts to, 139
reference material, 8
referral traffic, 94
registering domains, 26
RescueTime, 107
resource box, 124
    maximizing effectiveness, 127
resource pages, 192
retargeting, 209
Returning Visits, 148
retweet, 248
reviews, fake, 36
revision control, storing blog under, 33

RPM (revenue per mille), 175
RSS/Atom feed, 64
Ruby Row, 176
rubyinside.com, 19

S

sales copy, 205
sales funnel, 212
scaling blogs
    horizontally, 233–235
    vertically, 227–228
scammers, translated articles and, 133
schedule for publishing posts, 106
script library installer, 40
search box
    from Google AdSense, 175
    on sidebar, 64
search engines
    indicators for relevance and authority of pages, 50
    keyword-based domain names and, 24
    social indicators in strategy, 68
search results, author information in, 245
search trend, 14
sedo.com, 27
self-publishing, 193
self-sabotaging marketing, 120–121
SEO (search engine optimization), 7, 77–80, 121, 129
    content and, 83
    on-page optimization, 53
SEOmoz blog, 254
SERP (search engine result pages), 43
servers, for WordPress, 32
ServInt, 37
session, 146
Seth Godin's blog, 254
sethgodin.typepad.com, 19
setup for blog, software choice, 31–35
shared hosting, 35–36
    recommendations, 37
ShareThis, 67

sidebar
    code from Email Subscriptions, 74
    on company blog, 208
    customizing, 63–65
    editing, 65
    sample layout, 67
Signal vs. Noise, xiv, 5
signup, double opt-in, 73
single.php file, 74
single-author blogs, 3
skills improvement, 215–216
Slashdot, xvii, 137
slug, 50
SmartFeed, 70
smartphone devices, plugin for content presentation, 54
Smashing Magazine, xiv, 228
SnapEngage, 213
snippet-sharing service, 82
social currency, 241
social media
    creating profiles, 239–243
    final tips, 251
    sharing, 66–69
    strategy definition, 237
social networks
    buying votes, 133
    cross-promoting accounts, 243–245
    getting initial followers, 242
    impact on stats, 149
    promoting articles on, 134–137
    selecting for targeting, 238–239
    traffic expectations, 136
social properties, branding, 240
social toolbars in Blogger, 68
SocialOomph, 247
soft sell, 205
SoftLayer, 37
solo blogs, 3
sounds, ads with, 183
spam, 249
    Akismet plugin for dealing with, 48
    comment, 131
    comment moderation and, 47
    filtering in Blogger, 52
speed of blog, testing, 81

spell checker, 52
spike traffic, vs. baseline, 145
sponsors, 180–183
Spread Shirt, 196
Spy, 61
Squidoo, 128
StackOverflow, 217
Stacktrace, 4
static site generators, 32–33
statistics
  from Google Analytics, 58, 151
  on blogging, xvii
  real-time, 61
statistics analysis, 145
  baseline vs. spike traffic, 145
  key site usage metrics, 146
status updates, for customers, 33
storytelling, 90
straw man logical fallacy, 165
stream of consciousness writing, 110
strikethrough text for corrections, 85
StudioPress themes, 56
StumbleUpon, 135, 137
subdomain, for company blog, 22
subject of blog, controversial, 38
submission to directories, automated, 134
subreddits, 68, 139
subscribers, 69–71
  giving readers reasons to be, 18
  metrics for, 21
Subscription Form Code, from Feedburner, 71
subscription-based products, 202
subscriptions, 194
Subversion, 33
success, preparing for, 221–223
success stories, in company blog, 10
Sucuri, 54
SurveyGizmo, 91

SurveyMonkey, 91
surveys, running for free, 91
Syntax Highlighter MT, 82

T
Table of Contents page, 96–97
tablets, blogging clients for, 96
tags, on sidebar, 64
takedown notice, DCMA, 99
team blogs, 5
team of bloggers, 228–232
  for company blog, 200
  guest bloggers, 228–229
TechCrunch, xiv, 4, 19
technical blogging
  basics, xiv
  list of popular, 19
  sample, xv
technical instructions, 8
technical social news sites, 137–141
Template menu in Blogger, 58
terms of service, of blog host, 38
testimonials, in company blog, 10
testing, 253
  blog speed, 81
text editor, 33, 96
  for editing theme, 59
Text widget, 65
TextBroker, 232
Textile (markup language), 32
TextMate, 33
thank-you note for sponsor, 181
thedailywtf.com, 19
themes for blogs, 11
  ads in, 174
  general blogs, 12
  header, 74
  text editor for editing, 59
  in WordPress, 55–57, 70
time management, 107–109
time of day, best for posting, 106
time on site statistics, 147–148
time requirements for blogging, 106–107
time tracking software, 107

time zone, setting for WordPress blog, 45
top-level domains (TLDs), 23
Topsy, 66
trackbacks, 48
tracking
  audience, 57–63, 94
  blog growth, 155
Tracking ID summary report, 189
traffic
  expectations from social networks, 136
  reliability of comparison sites, 155
  social media impact, 149
  tracking source, 149
  visits quality and quantity, 147–149
traffic analysis tool, 57
translating posts, 114
Trash link, 43
trolling, 166, 168
trolls, comment moderation and, 47
Tumblr, xv, 32, 98
tutorials, 8, 91
TweetDeck, 247
Twitter, xv, xvii, 66–67, 135, 137, 239, 243
  author contact information, 254
  backgrounds, 241–242
  creating groups, 247
  custom image, 241
  gaming the system, 249–250
  personal vs. business presence, 240
  statistics, 251
  tools for, 247
Twitter widgets, 52
TwitterFeed, 247
TypePad, 32–33

U
underlined text, 86
unique visitors statistic, 146–147
Update Services, 46
updates, to posts, 85
UptimeRobot, 81
upvotes, 138
URL builder, 212

URLs, permanent for posts, 50

user account, for WordPress login, 44

V

Value Click Media, 176

vanity metric, 211

VaultPress, 101

VentureBeat, xiv, 234

verifying, WordPress install, 40

Vim, 33

visitors, metrics for, 21

Visits statistic, 146
  quantity and quality, 147–149

Visual Editor, 45

Visual.ly, 92

voice development, 89–90

VPS (virtual private server), 35
  recommendations, 37

W

W3 Total Cache, 80–81

web servers, for WordPress, 32

Webmaster Central blog, 254

white-hat marketing, 87

WHOIS database, 27

widgets, 65

wiki, 163

Wikipedia, on fair use, 98

Windows Live Writer, 46, 96

WishList Member, 194

WooCommerce, 202

WooThemes, 56

WordPress, 31–32, 34
  admin interface, 42
  ads in sidebar, 174
  Appearance menu, 65
  installing, 40–41
  membership site features, 194
  performance considerations, 80–81
  plugin for backup, 101
  plugins, 51
  restrictions, 34
  scheduling feature, 108
  setup wizard, 41
  widgets, 66

WordPress configuration, 42–51
  Links menu, 43
  Pages menu, 44
  Posts menu, 42
  Users menu, 44

WordPress settings, 45–48
  discussion, 47
  permalinks, 50
  privacy, 50
  reading, 46
  writing, 46

WordPress Stats plugin, 60–61

WP Authors plugin, 54

WP BTBuckets plugin, 74

WP Engine, 37

WP Greet Box plugin, 74

WP Security Scan, 54

WP Super Cache, 80

wp-Member, 194

WP-DBManager plugin, 101

WPtouch, 54

writer's block, 109–111

writing
  Inverted Pyramid approach, 89
  under pseudonym, 169

writing style, 89

Wufoo, 91

WYSIWYG editor, 45

X

XML Sitemap, 53

Y

Yegge, Steve, 217

Yet Another Related Posts Plugin, 95

YouTube, 239, 252

YSlow, 81

Z

Zazzle, 196

Zen and the Art of Ruby Programming, 6

ZippyKid, 37

New Programmer—or Renewed

Whether you're just starting out or starting to burn out, we'll share the experience to get you through.

It's your first day on the new job. You've got the programming chops, you're up on the latest tech, you're sitting at your workstation… now what? *New Programmer's Survival Manual* gives your career the jolt it needs to get going: essential industry skills to help you apply your raw programming talent and make a name for yourself. It's a no-holds-barred look at what *really* goes on in the office—and how to not only survive, but thrive in your first job and beyond.

Josh Carter
(250 pages) ISBN: 9781934356814. $29
http://pragprog.com/titles/jcdeg

You're already a great coder, but awesome coding chops aren't always enough to get you through your toughest projects. You need these 50+ nuggets of wisdom. Veteran programmers: reinvigorate your passion for developing web applications. New programmers: here's the guidance you need to get started. With this book, you'll think about your job in new and enlightened ways.

Ka Wai Cheung
(250 pages) ISBN: 9781934356791. $29
http://pragprog.com/titles/kcdc